The Art of Software Support

Design and Operation of Support Centers and Help Desks

Francoise Tourniaire
and
Richard Farrell

To join a Prentice Hall PTR internet mailing list,
point to: **http://www.prenhall.com/register**

Prentice Hall PTR
Upper Saddle River, New Jersey 07458
http://www.prenhall.com

Library of Congress Cataloging-in-Publication Data

Tourniaire, Francoise.
       The art of software support : design and operation of support
    centers and help desks / by Francoise Tourniaire and Richard
    Farrell.
       p. cm.
    Includes bibliographical references and index.
    ISBN 0-13-569450-7
       1. Software support.   2. Computer software industry—Customer
services. I. Farrell, Richard   II.Title
QA76.76.S66T68   1997
005.3'068'8—dc20   96-32907
                                                CIP

Editorial/production supervision: *Eileen Clark*
Cover design: *Design Source*
Manufacturing manager: *Alexis Heydt*
Acquisitions editor: *Mark Taub*
Cover director: *Jerry Votta*
Composition: *Thurn & Taxis*

© 1997 by Prentice Hall PTR
Prentice-Hall, Inc.
A Simon & Schuster Company
Upper Saddle River, New Jersey 07458

The publisher offers discounts on this book when ordered in bulk quantities.
For more information, contact:
       Corporate Sales Department
       Prentice Hall PTR
       One Lake Street
       Upper Saddle River, NJ 07458
       Phone: 800-382-3419 Fax: 201-236-7141
       E-mail: corpsales@prenhall.com

Printed in the United States of America
10 9 8 7 6 5 4 3 2 1

ISBN 0-13-569450-7

Prentice-Hall International (UK) Limited, *London*
Prentice-Hall of Australia Pty. Limited, *Sydney*
Prentice-Hall Canada Inc., *Toronto*
Prentice-Hall Hispanoamericana, S.A., *Mexico*
Prentice-Hall of India Private Limited, *New Delhi*
Prentice-Hall of Japan, Inc., *Tokyo*
Simon & Schuster Asia Pte. Ltd., *Singapore*
Editora Prentice-Hall do Brasil, Ltda., *Rio de Janeiro*

Pour Dominique

For Nell

ABOUT
THE AUTHORS

Francoise Tourniaire has over 12 years' experience in the software industry both in Software Support and in Training. She is the Director of Technical Support at Sybase, a major database and tool provider and has worked for ASK/Ingres (now Computer Associates) in a similar capacity. She has experience running large support centers serving customers with mission-critical applications. Her focus is on building customer-focused, people-oriented organizations that translate theoretical principles into practical work processes.

Richard Farrell has over 9 years' experience in Software Support. He is a Senior Technical Support Manager with Sybase, Inc. He has written and spoken on support management, particularly in the areas of productivity, profitability and morale. He owned and operated a retail business for 7 years and practiced law for 5 years before joining the software industry.

You can reach them by e-mail at info@supportline.com or from their website:
www.supportline.com

CONTENTS

PREFACE AND ACKNOWLEDGMENTS

This is a book about the design and operation of software support centers and help desks. It is a book primarily for managers, but also for executives and support engineers who are involved in the world of software support. In it we take you through the important areas of concern that every support operation must address. We cover the major principles of designing a customer-focused support operation to help you put your customers first as the cornerstone of your strategy for business success. Throughout the book we offer detailed, practical prescriptions and recommendations for structuring and operating a Support organization that can be used either to help you build one from scratch or to help you improve an already existing one.

As an executive, you will gain the background you need to make the solidly informed decisions on proposals brought to you by support managers. As a support engineer, you will gain a window on the larger world in which you work and see what lies in store if you choose to move into management as a career.

In writing this book we had help from many people. We are grateful to them beyond what our words can tell.

Our thinking on management has been greatly influenced by Fernando Flores of Business Design Associates. From Ken Williams at Intel and, later, Ingres we learned much about the art of people management. Barry Shamis contributed his expertise in that most important of management skills, recruiting. Sue Shields shared with us the fundamentals of world-class support as practiced by Hewlett-Packard. We benefited from many conversations on customer service with Ron Kaufman.

Our colleagues and associates at ASK and at Sybase provided much of our learning. They gamely accepted our experiments and questions and always generated more.

David Aune, Chris Davis, Chris Doell, Richard McIntosh, Roy Moore, and Darcy Van Vuren reviewed the manuscript, pointing out errors and contributing their experiences and insights where ours was lacking. Special thanks to Richard and Roy who went through the entire book and, especially, to David whose detailed suggestions contributed much to its final content. Sumi Sohari and Rafael Coto of Action Technologies, Inc. assisted us with the Basic Action

Workflow® Process Builder software used for the Basic Action Workflow mapping in Chapter 2.

Many thanks to Bill Rose, the ultimate and tireless advocate of software support as a profession, with whom we consulted when first starting out to redesign support at Ingres and from whom we first heard the richly descriptive phrase for the start of every day in the support business . . . *"It* begins."

We thank also Sandy Emerson of Sybase Press who encouraged us in this endeavor and helped us find our publisher.

Mark Taub, our editor at Prentice Hall, took a chance on two unproven authors. We are grateful for his trust and his straightforwardness in working with us.

Our warm thanks to Eileen Clark who patiently and thoroughly reviewed our manuscript and turned it into a book.

Oakland, California   FRANCOISE TOURNIAIRE
November 1996   RICHARD FARRELL
                                                                   www.supportline.com

CHAPTER 1
INTRODUCTION

1.1 DOES THIS SOUND FAMILIAR?

Tuesday, 8 a.m. You enter the building where you work as a Support Center Manager. Perhaps you work for an ISV, or perhaps you are responsible for the operation of your company's internal help desk. In either case, you have a plan of action for the day. You are going to write that report, coach that support engineer, work on a review, plan for a new product. Maybe you're finally going to convince your boss that you need those two extra support engineers so you can handle the call volume.

You sit at your desk with your cup of coffee. You're about to get started when . . . *It* begins.

The usual breakdowns and the odd emergency start to demand your attention, and you move from one of them to the next. The phone rings, the ACD light glows red, and you need to round up more support engineers to handle the phones; a support engineer drops by with a question, another with a customer escalation; your boss needs the response rate statistics *now*. Two of your people are out sick, and you have to juggle the schedule to cover for them while attending to outstanding commitments they have made to customers.

Soon it's 3 p.m. and you realize you haven't had lunch yet. You grab a snack from the vending machine, wishing you could eat more healthily. Then the flurry of activity begins again as the rest of the afternoon passes like the morning. By 6 p.m. you haven't accomplished any of the things you wanted to do when you came in. Having a bad day? No, it's like that every day; *It* ends when you walk out. Except *It* doesn't end, *It* just gets suspended until the next day, when *It* begins again disappearing all of your best intentions to plan, to implement, to complete.

Much like that of a hospital emergency room, a Support organization's day-to-day life is filled with routine problems and extreme emergencies. We work in a mode of constant reaction to the next situation, the next crisis that demands—indeed, grabs—our attention. This is not a life that allows for the careful design and regular, step-by-step implementation of a plan. Rather it is a life of coping with a swirl of requests constantly coming our way. But it doesn't have to be the chaos that it often feels like. When we are organized so we can respond effectively, it can be a coordinated coping, even a dance.

This is not to say that planning, or rather the structure and organization of processes that come from planning, is not necessary. Without organization the emergency room is chaos and patients die unnecessarily. In our world, customer problems don't get responded to or resolved in a timely fashion. If it is bad enough (and anything that does not result in high customer satisfaction is "bad enough"), customers will seek another provider at the first opportunity or remain in resentful bondage until they can escape in one way or another, taking out their frustration on us.

In addition to the interrupt-driven flow of events, there is an emotional aspect to the job, one that is compounded when chaos rather than coordination characterizes our work environment. In the best of times and with the best of organizations we are always dealing with customers whose emotions run from curiosity to panic and anger. Rarely does someone call with good news or a thank you. This, as is well known, can be a source of stress for us as well as the people who work for us. When our organizations are not designed well to handle the predictable unpredictability of support operations, we often encounter our own frustration and, even, panic and anger. These are predictable consequences when *It* begins in an organization not prepared to deal with *It* effectively.

Does this sound familiar? If you feel right now that you're totally overwhelmed and you can never get out of the hole, then this is a good time to invest in a some thinking and designing, because you *can* stop the overwhelm, you *can* get out of the hole.

You can get your organization into a state where coordinated coping is readily available, and what feels like chaos can feel like a dance—a fast one, yes, one that requires some improvisation, but, yes, one that can be learned and mastered and enjoyed.

Life in a support environment is never going to be like life in a marketing environment or an engineering environment, where there are regular periods of uninterrupted work, not to mention periods of calm and reflection. Technical support will always provide a certain amount of excitement and uncertainty, which is part of why many of us enjoy the work. That it's different each day is part of what attracts us. But in order to take care of our customers, take care of our staff, and take care of ourselves, we have to know how to deal effectively and efficiently with the *It* that begins each day when we walk in the door. This book will help you design your organization, your internal business processes, and your relationships with other groups in the company and your customers to help you do that as best you can.

So make time to read this book and use it to design your organization. We know you don't have "enough" time to do this. But we also know that if you don't invent the time to do it, the maelstrom will never cease. If you work in an open door environment, close the door. Better, don't come in for a day or two. Nobody will die if you're not there for a while. Sometimes we don't realize this. Work can go on without us. So declare time when you can get away and go someplace where you're not reminded of the day-to-day work and you're not readily accessible to people who are only too happy to add to the interruptions that make up your day.

1.2   IF YOU'RE DOING WELL . . .

If you have a handle on *It*, we are confident that we can help you improve your organization by giving you clear standards to assess it as well as ideas and practical techniques for making it better.

1.3   IF YOU'RE JUST STARTING OUT . . .

Don't let *It* manage you. You don't have to live in chaos if you start with the right processes. We will give you the practical tools you need to make a good start.

1.4   WHAT'S IN IT FOR YOU?

The outcome of investing the time and effort necessary to structure your organization is positive in two ways. One, you will save money (and improve profits if you have a Profit and Loss center). Two, you will increase job satisfaction for your people and for yourself as well. Much of the stress that characterizes Support organizations has its source in the very chaos that *It* is when we are not fully prepared to deal with the challenges that appear daily. Successfully dealing with these challenges means that we can help our customers more effectively. And, not to be maudlin, but the opportunity to help people is likely one of the reasons you (and we) chose support as a career.

1.5   SUPPORT AS A PROFESSION

One reason we have a sense of chaos in our work as support managers is that support is relatively new as a profession. Support has grown up historically as an adjunct to other business concerns. There has not really been much thinking or writing about shared experiences and practices among people doing support. So often we may feel we're out there on our own reinventing the wheel.

Over the last decade this has been changing. We are witnessing—indeed, we are participating in—the emergence of software support as a profession. We are now in the middle of the transition from support being something of an afterthought to the release of a software product to support being a profession whose practice is increasingly important for the company's continued success.

This is a general business trend, not just a software industry trend. Just think of the revolution in the shipping business. Once we sent a package from the post office and assumed, sometimes hoped, that it would arrive in a few days. Now carriers such as FedEx and UPS compete, not just on getting our packages to their destinations, not even on getting them there fast, but on how easy it is to track the package. Just connect to the appropriate World Wide Web site and point and click.

Another well-known example is the credit card business. At any time, day or night, we expect we can call a toll-free number to get a new card, find out our balance, increase our credit limit, and so on. Ask and you receive immediately. Transactions that once required our physical presence we can now conduct from remote locations virtually anywhere and at any time.

We usually think of the examples above as "service." But what, after all, is service in these cases but supporting the customer in resolving a problem the customer is having? The question "Where is my package?" does not differ in any essential way from the question "How can I do such and such with your software?"

1.6   SUPPORT AS A DIFFERENTIATOR

Just as good service (i.e., support) is a differentiator in the customer's buying decision in many businesses, more and more we see support becoming one in regard to software purchases. Good support—or, better, excellent support—is not a nice extra we provide customers but an essential part of what is required to have satisfied, loyal customers, which in turn helps to increase revenues and maximize profits.

1.7 SUPPORT AS A REVENUE GENERATOR

In many businesses that have set up their support operation as an adjunct to their main business, support doesn't generate its own revenue or at least does not generate profit. But the trend is toward charging for support and even treating support as a profit center, a source of transactions for which the customer is willing to pay that contribute to the company's profitability. The more this is the case, the more important it is that support be done in an effective, efficient manner.

The same is true in the world of the internal help desk, where there is a marked trend toward centralizing the help desk function and applying consistent practices to maximize efficiency and hence lower costs to increase the bottom line.

With the emergence of third-party providers, support becomes the business. Entire companies are now organized around providing support for software products that they did not create. The phenomenon of outsourcing has generated this new kind of support business, which, of course, has to stand on its own as a business.

The essential point here is that doing support well contributes to the bottom line of the company by developing and maintaining a loyal customer base.

1.8 INCREASING CUSTOMER DEMANDS

What is driving the increased importance of software support is what is driving many other aspects of business—the customers' demands for ever quicker completion times for their requests. They (we in our lives as customers) want what they want sooner and sooner, faster and faster. It's as if "as soon as possible" has become the standard and is moving closer and closer to "now."

In the world of support we can see this in the trend of callback models giving way to direct access to the person who can solve the problem. Rather than having a receptionist or a dispatcher be the customer's first contact in making a request for help and then having that request passed on to a support engineer, the request instead is routed by the phone system to the desk of a support engineer who can begin immediately to resolve the issue.

Another trend is customers' demand for one-stop shopping in our ever more complex support world. This is particularly evident in the world of client-server computing, where the problem could lie in the products of multiple hardware and software vendors—computer, disk drive, network hardware, operating system software, network software, applications software, and so on. Customers are less and less willing to place multiple support calls, but instead want the first vendor they call to manage the resolution, if this spans multiple products.

One-stop shopping is clearly a requirement for internal help desks because they are the sole providers to their customers already. The hardware and software infrastructure of companies is not homogenous but is increasingly heterogeneous. There can be several different kinds of software, different hardware environments, and different networking environments, all to be supported by one organization.

1.9   FROM PRODUCTS TO RELATIONSHIPS

Increasing customer demands for fast, one-stop shopping in turn may be seen as a part of the general shift in focus from product to relationship. Successful companies no longer sell "things" (both products and services) so much as they become partners in furthering their customers' business aims. This means that listening—truly listening—to customers, real and potential, becomes a crucial skill to learn and practice. Another such skill is the development of trust and creditability with our customers, who must necessarily rely on us for solutions to complex problems they often don't understand.

The crucial, indeed, indispensable role of "listening" in achieving business success may seem obvious, now that the phrase "customer satisfaction" is close to becoming a cliché. But not too long ago in our world, even making a list of known software bugs available to customers was considered heresy. Why, they might think that the product indeed had bugs! Perish the thought that we could admit what everyone knows: software has bugs. Now proactively announcing important bugs is becoming a regular practice with more and more software publishers. Why? Because if we are going to be partners with our customers, if we are listening to *their* concerns, we must warn them of potential problems in advance of their finding it out on their own, possibly to their great financial detriment.

As you will see, we have placed the support customer at the core of this book, basing all discussions of support models and implementation on what is desirable from a customer's point of view.

As the business shift from products to relationships pervades the world of software support, it is going to amplify the role of Support groups. This in turn is good for us in terms of increased visibility, respect, and autonomy inside the company and a lessened struggle to get resources needed to support customers well.

As we move from the world of the more or less isolated support managers into the world of a network of professional software support managers and executives, we see the development of newsletters, professional associations, and books, all pointing toward the development of generally agreed-upon practices that in turn provide the foundation for future innovation. Concomitant with this is increased respect inside companies, and, to the extent that support centers are true profit centers, increased power.

1.10 WHO SHOULD READ THIS BOOK?

While this is primarily a book for support managers and support supervisors, it addresses three other audiences as well:

- Executives who want to understand what it takes to provide high-quality support and what the ROI (return on investment) can be.
- Entrepreneurs who need to make the right decisions about how to provide support.
- Support engineers who want to understand the business they are in.

For support managers and supervisors, this is a book about running support centers and help desks. It is a manual for designing and creating the business processes that make a support center run well and a guide for implementing them day by day, month by month, quarter by quarter, year by year. It details how to be successful (or more successful) at software support, winning at the game of software support, and knowing that you are winning.

This book is not a list of "best practices" developed by interviewing people doing support. It is an integrated nuts-and-bolts, step-by-step guide to running a support center, written from our experience as support managers who have "been there and done that" and have shared ideas and tested techniques with colleagues in our emerging profession.

For executives, this book provides a useful background on the fundamentals of good support, so you can interface with support managers and evaluate the requests for resources that they will bring you.

For entrepreneurs inventing a new business, this book provides the basics to understand the world of support, so you can avoid pitfalls when creating your Support group and hiring its initial manager, who can then take over the support decisions.

Support engineers will find a larger context for what it is that they do everyday. The book also provides material for exploring support management as a career direction.

1.11 ARE HELP DESKS DIFFERENT?

A few words about help desks. Do they differ in terms of design or operation from support centers?

When we set out to write this book, we tried hard to find fundamental distinctions between the two. We failed. It is true that having internal customers and being internal to the company allow for handling some of the issues differently, and we point out where this applies; however, internal help desks have customers, and a customer is a customer is a customer. All support customers want timely response to their requests for help, timely solutions, and human and professional interactions with support personnel.

1.12 WHAT IS DIFFERENT?

The fundamental differences in the world of support that require design differences have to do with call volume and complexity. High vs. low call volume and simple vs. complex problems do affect the best way to do business, the best way to support our customers, whether they are internal or external. We highlight these differences in the book, where relevant.

1.13 WHAT DO WE COVER IN THIS BOOK?

Chapter 2: Call Management Models discusses call management or call flow models. We explore the general concept of customer satisfaction and how to achieve it within a support center context. We introduce call flow models for handling the life of a customer call from inception to resolution. We end with a discussion of escalations, the "difficult" calls. In doing this we make recommendations on what models are available and how to go about making decisions about models. If you are starting out, or have some doubts about the model you have in place, you will find this chapter essential for developing a successful support center. If your center is working well, this chapter will highlight the principles being applied in your center and will challenge your convictions about what could be done differently.

Chapter 3: Call Management Implementation moves from theoretical considerations about service models to more practical matters, such as how customers report problems, how problems are routed to the proper support engineer, and how escalations are handled. After reading this chapter and applying it to your specific situation, you should have a detailed view of how problems enter a Support organization and flow through it until they get resolved.

Chapter 4: Measuring Support Center Performance discusses what kinds of measurements are necessary or useful to run a support center. It describes what to do day-to-day to keep your support center healthy and successful, based on studying and acting on the measurements you choose. It also suggests analyses to conduct from time to time to determine whether large changes in your organization or processes are necessary.

Chapter 5: Packaging Support Programs describes in detail how to package various kinds of support programs for both internal and external customers. We detail when to make multiple support offers and how to differentiate them from each other. We also discuss whether and how to charge for support services.

Chapter 6: Support Organization Structure explores ways to organize the support center, both internally and within the larger organization it belongs to, in order to create maximum efficiency and customer satisfaction. We present the different possible alternatives, and we help you decide what to choose, based on your requirements and preferences. We address the issue of outsourcing, as it is an increasingly important aspect of Support organization.

Chapter 7: Managing Support People explores managing the people within the organization. Since there is much literature on people management, we concentrate on issues and concerns specific to the software support environment. We cover hiring, compensating, scheduling, and justifying people resources. We also discuss ways to manage the morale of your people and your organization.

Chapter 8: Managing Software Bugs and Code Fixes delves into the world of software bugs—specifically, how to track them, fix them, and deliver fixes to customers. Additionally, we cover the basics of bugs and code fixes to help you make support decisions and influence the code development and release maintenance process as needed.

Chapter 9: Tools for Software Support focuses on helping you define a checklist for what you need so you make the right choice of features, size, and cost for the various tools for software support. The tools highlighted include the phone system, including ACD, fax, call tracking, bug tracking, knowledge base, proactive customer communication, customer tracking, problem reproduction environments, call center management applications, and that largest of "tools," facilities.

Chapter 10: New Product Planning covers all aspects of planning for new products: training, beta programs, planning for hardware and software, and putting it all together.

The Appendices contain (A) a complete sample *Support User's Guide*, (B) a quick overview of the call resolution cycle, (C) a thorough method for determining staffing levels, and (D) a practical and effective approach to creating and, importantly, justifying your budget.

Throughout the book we have included checklists to facilitate review of, and, if you choose, implementation of our suggestions and recommendations. See the index under "checklists" for a listing.

1.14 HOW TO READ THIS BOOK

Your time is valuable, and we have written with this in mind. Unlike most books, there is little repetition, just enough to emphasize the most important points.

You may choose to read the book in order, from first page to last. Feel free, though, to start with whatever chapters or issues you find most pressing or interesting. If you do this, you'll encounter many cross-references and find yourself moving from chapter to chapter following them. This will be no hindrance to gleaning useful material as you go. Many complex discussions are summarized in checklists and flowcharts for quick reference. Also use the extensive index to help you find (and find again) relevant sections.

Having said this, we recommend that you start with Chapter 2, "Call Management Models," to get a sense of our approach as a whole before proceeding further. The discussions of the Basic Action Workflow and call flow models will provide useful background to orient yourself to the rest of the work.

For executives and entrepreneurs, we recommend you follow Chapter 2 with Chapter 6, "Support Organization Structure," which addresses the question of where support may fit in best with the overall business organization. "Tools for Technical Software Support," Chapter 9, will help you understand the justification for six- or even seven-figure purchase orders crossing your desk.

 Throughout the book, we have flagged interesting tips with a lightbulb symbol. Look for them for innovative ways to make your group even more effective.

1.15 WHO ARE WE?

Earlier we said we had "been there, done that" in regard to designing and running a software Support organization. Let us elaborate on this. In 1992 we found ourselves in the Technical Support department at the Ingres database division of the ASK Group. The company had already been struggling for a couple of years.

In 1992 the Technical Support department reported into the Sales organization. As ASK was fighting for survival, literally all executive attention was focused on selling. Francoise, as Director of Support, and her management team, which included Richard, were left functionally undirected, unmanaged by anyone, and presented with the unique (and certainly, for us, welcome) opportunity to exercise a free hand in structuring support as we thought best. In effect, a $60 million dollar a year support operation was self-contained with only three administrative levels: support engineers, managers, director. We support managers were in complete control of the business, a thought that must be the very stuff of nightmares for many corporate executives.

We made the most of it. Sixty percent of the support revenue went to the company's bottom line. Turnover went from 40% to 10%, response time was met at the 95% level and at 98% for emergencies, and overall customer satisfaction improved to an average of over 9 on a 0 to 10 scale.

During this experience we realized that support can be a straightforward business that can be readily learned. This book is the fruit of what we discovered during that time and what we have practiced since then. Every major problem in every Support organization that we have observed first-hand or through reports from colleagues has a straightforward solution, one of the straightforward solutions you will find in the chapters that follow. This may sound like a bold claim; we invite your evaluation of it after exploring the chapters below.

1.16 OUR PROMISE TO YOU

We close our introduction with a promise to you. After all, if you are reading this book, you are our customer, and as such, we owe you a promise in exchange for your time and your money.

Our promise is this: If you apply our recommendations, you will see noticeable, measurable improvements in the performance of your Support organization within three months at most. The extent of the improvement will depend, of course, on the current state of your support processes and personnel. But even the worst mess, we are sure, can be completely turned around in a year. So even in this "worst-case" scenario, in the second year you can enjoy performing in an organization that works in both business (including financial) and human terms.

We promise those of you who manage support centers that you will achieve faster response times and faster resolution times—two essentials that allow customer satisfaction to grow in your customers. High customer satisfaction (in survey terms, 9 to 10 on a scale of 10) generates customer loyalty of a kind that can result in repeat business and render customers willingness to stand as referrals for your sales force, leading, in turn to new sales. Additional benefits can include enhanced reputation and influence in your organization as well as the personal satisfaction that comes from playing a game well and winning.

Those of you who manage internal help desks, while having a different relationship to sales, will also see improvements in response and resolution time and growth in your customers' satisfaction with your support. Gains in reputation and influence can accrue to you as well.

In addition, your own bottom line will improve. To give you just a hint of the possible financial benefits: If, as in many Support organizations, your personnel turnover is high, just multiply the number of people you have to replace in a year by the cost of replacing them (use $50,000 as your figure, we give you a way to compute your number later). It adds up quickly. Other financial benefits will become apparent in the chapters that follow.

With this we conclude the introduction. Now comes the heart of the book on which we base our promise. We invite you to begin.

CHAPTER 2

CALL MANAGEMENT MODELS

The most important decision in setting up a successful Support organization is to start with a strong, clear model for managing customer problems to resolution. This design phase is just as important as when designing a software program. Weaknesses in the design will manifest themselves in the day-to-day running of the support center, and they will be difficult and expensive to correct, so spend some time thinking about how you want to set things up.

If you already have a process in place and you are not completely satisfied about how it's working, we encourage you to rethink your call management model. Despite what we just said about model changes being difficult, it's better to bite the bullet and change your model when necessary rather than to make window-dressing changes that do not attack the root cause, do not resolve the problem, and in their implementation simply consume a lot of time and resources.

If you are satisfied with your current process, this chapter will give you competitive information about what other Support groups are doing and will confirm the soundness of your model, or maybe give you some new insights into areas you may want to tinker with.

This chapter makes recommendations on what models are out there and how you should go about making decisions about models. If you are starting out, or have some doubts about the model you have in place, you will find it essential to your search for the successful support center. If your center is working well, this chapter will highlight the principles being applied in your center and will challenge your convictions about what could be done differently.

The concepts described in this chapter are completely general and apply just as well to help desks with internal customers and to support centers with external customers, to small and large organizations, and to support of simple or complex products. We give advice here and there when a particular idea applies better in one context than another, but again the principles are completely general and should be of interest to everyone in the business of software support.

You may find the descriptions in this chapter somewhat theoretical, and you may be eager to jump to implementing the models in your organization right away. Try to be patient and to spend enough time making and reviewing your choices. As in programming, a good design will save you a lot of rework and frustrations in the future.

The chapter is organized as follows. First we discuss the general concept of customer satisfaction and how to achieve it within a support center context. Then we introduce call flow models to handle the life of a customer call from inception to resolution. We end with a discussion of escalations—the "difficult" calls—giving some ideas for handling them within the context of good customer satisfaction.

2.1 ACHIEVING CUSTOMER SATISFACTION

The benchmark we will use throughout our discussion is customer satisfaction. That is, we believe a support process model is successful if it achieves high degrees of customer satisfaction. We must begin and end with the customer, because the customer defines and referees the competitive game.

This does not mean we are not concerned with other key factors such as costs, profits, or employee satisfaction. Indeed, you must achieve success on all those other factors as well, and we will consider them in our analysis, but we feel strongly that, unless a system can satisfy customers, no amount of cost savings or profits and no number of happy employees will save it in the long run.

2.1.1 Negotiating Service Commitments

So—what is customer satisfaction, and how does one achieve it? Clearly, customer satisfaction is defined by the customer. The ultimate "test," if we want a quantitative measurement, is whether the customer is willing to recommend the service to colleagues and acquaintances. In practice, customer satisfaction is expressed in thank-you letters, or, increasingly, in thank-you emails and phone calls. It also comes across in conversations with customers, which can be as formal as focus groups or surveys or as informal as the day-to-day conversations that occur each time a manager or a support engineer talks to a customer. Listen! You do not need a large survey budget to tell whether your customers are satisfied. Experience shows that surveys, when designed well, confirm the impressions of the support staff. This does not mean, by the way, that surveys are useless: they lend essential credibility to that impression and they can help to run your support center. We will cover customer satisfaction surveys in detail in Chapter 4, "Measuring Support Center Performance."

A common misconception is that customer satisfaction is the same as quality. That is not quite true. It's possible to achieve high customer satisfaction with moderate quality. Discount stores and fast-food restaurants such as

McDonald's are good examples of businesses that achieve high customer satisfaction with moderate quality in products and services. (We must admit it would be difficult to achieve good customer satisfaction with low quality.) Your quest for customer satisfaction is different from your quest for quality. You can and must manage customer satisfaction, and this requires you to know what it takes to satisfy the customer.

So how does a customer become satisfied? The standard definition is that the customer's expectations are met or exceeded. This is a good definition, except that it ignores the difficult topic of how expectations are formed in the first place. Customers come with all kinds of expectations from past experiences, including their upbringing, their cultural history, their interactions with their credit card's service hotline, as well as their last call to another software support provider. In other words, expectations of your support center are not created in isolation, but rather they are influenced by all kinds of other experiences. This creates very stringent service requirements for software support providers. For example, customers may expect no more than a minute of hold time if that's what they get from their credit card hotline; they may expect that most issues will be resolved within just one short call if that's what their bank provides. Since software support is more complex than the old art of banking, most of us will have to somehow reshape our customers' expectations before we are perceived as failing to fulfill them.

We will refer to this reshaping process as *negotiating service commitments*—that is, coming to an agreement with the customer in advance on what kind of service will be delivered (and at what price). This does not mean either that we impose our standards on the customer (who would be unlikely to agree to them anyway) or that we have to commit to delivering what the customer wants (which may well be impossible). What it means is that we have to be clear about what we can and will deliver. We must also ensure that the customer knows about it and agrees to the services as defined. Getting to a shared commitment does not imply that we change the customer's expectation. Even with a shared commitment accepted by both parties the customer may still have some expectation that is different from the commitment. You will, however, have achieved a basis of understanding for the service to be delivered.

Various levels of service commitments can coexist. In fact, most organizations would do well to define several levels of services with different price tags to satisfy customers with different requirements and different budgets. This is more apparent if you have outside customers. However, if you are running an internal help desk, the various departments you support may have different needs, and offering several service levels with assorted costs can be very helpful to you and them when it comes time to prepare a budget. We will discuss this topic in Chapter 5, "Packaging Support Programs."

It's important to communicate the service commitment through a service contract or agreement. This is usually required if the services are sold. Chapter 5 discusses service contracts and what they should cover. However, creating negotiated commitments requires much more than handing out what usually serves as a service agreement. Service agreements are often vague about exactly what will be delivered and how. They tend to stay at a high level and cannot possibly cover all situations. Part of the reason for the vagueness is the understandable desire for brevity. Also, and more importantly, the agreements are often negotiated by individuals other than the ones who will be using the service. For example, a buyer in the Purchasing department may negotiate an agreement for the IS group. So one must supplement the formal agreement with some other method of negotiating commitments.

A formal and effective way to create negotiated commitments is to create a *Support User's Guide*. For organizations with outside customers it may be a booklet, which is included in the software box or is mailed to each customer if, customers are expected to pay separately for support (see sample in Appendix A). For organizations with internal customers, a simple email message containing the same information may be sufficient.

The guide should cover:

- What kind of services are available, including any limitations on the support provided—for instance, what versions or configurations are supported. This is also the place to spell out, as much as possible, where technical support stops and consulting begins.

- The logistics of how to obtain support: phone number or alternate method, hours of operation.

- Who is authorized to call, and any restrictions on how often calls can be placed.

- How fast the request will be responded to, including a description of the various priorities, if appropriate.

- A description of the resolution cycle, with an emphasis on the collaborative nature of the process. Too often, customers think they will report a problem and the Support organization will solve it for them, when in fact they will often be asked to run tests, try things out, gather additional information, and, generally speaking, be engaged in the diagnostic process almost as fully as the support engineer. We will cover this often overlooked aspect of support below.

- Tips for obtaining the best service: information needed to place a call, basic troubleshooting information, test data to have handy, best times to call, and so on.

A Support User's Guide is only a one-way mechanism for communicating the support center's offer. However, spelling out your commitments makes it easier for the customer to agree or disagree with them and to request changes. Having a written description also helps to resolve disputes that may arise later. Defining what customers can expect from Technical Support is useful, whether or not customers are expected to pay separately for support. Actually, customers are often *less* satisfied with "free" support than with fee-based support, and one underlying reason may well be that free support is too often left completely undefined.

Having a clear definition of your services is essential if you are selling them. It's a good idea to distribute the Support User's Guide freely during the sales process to those individuals who will be using the support center (not just to the buyers or the decision makers), so they can be fully aware of what to expect. This is in addition to training and managing salespeople to properly set customer expectations. Finally, if there are several support packages to choose from, detailed descriptions in the User's Guide will help customers and salespeople choose the right level of support.

Whether or not you have a Support User's Guide, you will want to look at informal ways to communicate or reinforce expectations. One possibility is to add information to the "on-hold" message that customers get when they are waiting to get through. Also have the Support User's Guide available from your fax-back documentation system if you have one.

Regardless of the way you announce or negotiate service commitments with your customers, they must be confirmed at each interaction, and especially when a new issue is first reported. Support engineers must all be familiar with the details of how you set up your offerings. At the beginning of each interaction, they must explicitly articulate the commitment again as well as the understanding of the promise by drawing out the customer's understanding and either confirming or changing the promise. This is a delicate and poorly understood process, so we will devote some time and attention to analyzing it.

2.1.2 The Basic Action Workflow

Using work invented by Fernando Flores and his collaborators, we introduce the "Basic Action Workflow," that can be used to model and design interactions between customers and suppliers or performers, including support transactions.

The model includes four separate phases, each ending in a deliverable: preparation, negotiation, performance, and acceptance (see Figure 2–1). First, in the preparation phase, the customer makes a request. Then, in the negotiation phase, the support engineer and the customer negotiate an agreement. Part of the negotiation is to fully understand the request, including all the customer's background and goals around the request—that is, not just what the customer wants, but why and how he wants it. Possible responses to the initial request include:

- "I promise" (I agree to provide what you need, when you need it).
- "I decline" (there are clear boundaries around using that response in a support center setting, but the model provides for a negative response, essential if the request cannot be fulfilled).
- "I counter-offer," which includes alternatives as well as changes in timing, as in "I will do it tomorrow" when the initial request was for today.

Basic Action Workflow

Figure 2–1

If the customer and the support engineer agree, the request turns into a mutual agreement, which could be identical to the initial request or changed somewhat. If they do not agree, then the mutual agreement is "do nothing."

Once there is mutual agreement, the support engineer performs the promise and reports its completion back to the customer. That's the performance phase. In the acceptance phase, the customer evaluates the result against the mutual agreement. If the customer is satisfied, the action workflow is complete. If not, the customer reports that more work needs to be done, so the support engineer needs to go back to the performance phase.

When building an interaction model, most people would spontaneously think of a request and its execution, so the preparation and performance phases are easy to understand. However, the two other phases in the action workflow are very important to the successful conclusion of the cycle (that is, to creating a satisfied customer). Since they are often skipped in real life and in other business models, let us highlight them:

- The provider and the customer must come to a mutual agreement before performance can start. The negotiation period can be very short, all the more if the request is simple and the provider is a master of people skills. But it should not be skipped. Once the customer feels that the provider agrees to provide a certain service, he will then expect to get that service and will be dissatisfied if he is later turned down. Service providers must be well educated on the necessity to come to an explicit agreement on what is to be delivered, especially since only the most sophisticated customers will insist on a mutual agreement. Even when providers know they must come to an agreement, it's often difficult for them to express anything other than complete agreement to a request. Along with awareness of the step, training should also cover the boundaries of what can be done for customers, and how to elegantly decline or modify requests.

- The service interaction is not complete until the customer declares satisfaction. This is another key point (a nice counterpart to the first one, actually). Shipping a software patch to a customer is not a resolution. The support engineer must also check that the customer installed the patch and that the patch indeed fixed the problem as reported. Truncated transactions result in much unnecessary grief and must be avoided. Again, education is key. No transaction is complete until the customer declares satisfaction, either through a simple "Thank you" or a more elaborate "You solved my problem." Having a good definition of the mutual agreement can be very useful at this stage. The support engineer can remind the customer of what the agreement was and ask whether it has indeed been fulfilled.

The Basic Action Workflow is a very simple and robust structure that can be used to model many different interactions—it was not created to model the software support business. It can model the simplest of interactions ("May I have your contact ID number, please?") and it can be used to describe the interaction with the customer at a corporate level. If used in complex environments, it can be supplemented through "secondary workflows." For instance, if performing the request involves getting help from another department, that request can also be modeled through a workflow, which is grafted onto the performance component of the Basic Action Workflow (see Figure 2–2). Note that internal workflows also require all four phases: skipping the initial negotiation or the final customer's acceptance will lead to problems internally as well as externally.

Primary and Secondary Workflows

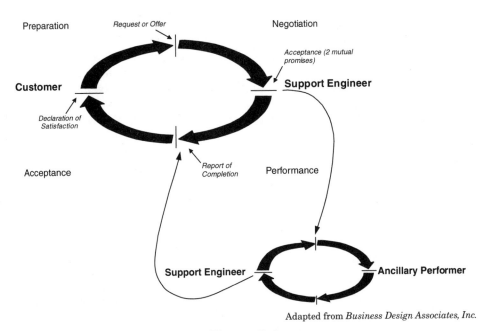

Adapted from *Business Design Associates, Inc.*

Figure 2–2

More details about the Basic Action Workflow and how it applies in the support world may be found in Appendix B. We will use the Basic Action Workflow as the basic building block of the support model we will explore later on.

2.1.3   The Spirit of Collaboration

Apart from the Basic Action Workflow, the other key ingredient for successful customer service is to create a spirit of collaboration between the service provider and the customer. Whereas the Basic Action Workflow is the business process side of the equation, creating a spirit of collaboration is the emotional side. This may seem uncomfortable to the more left-brained, more facts-inclined among us, but it is a key to successful customer service.

We have seen that customers' expectations are shaped by their prior experiences. They are also shaped by their emotional state. When customers call for support, they are unlikely to be in a neutral frame of mind: maybe they are angry that they are having a problem, maybe they are curious about why the software is behaving the way it is, maybe they are panicky that they will miss a deadline as a result of the problem. They are unlikely to be calm and purposeful.

The job of the support engineer is to bring the customer, as much as possible, to a spirit of collaboration, where he can see that a partnership with the support engineer is key to a swift resolution, and where focus on work and problem solving replaces the emotions of the beginning. The mood change must be managed during the acceptance (that is, negotiation) phase of the Basic Action Workflow and is an essential ingredient of setting the stage for what the service provider will need from the customer. The negotiation phase must include reading the current mood of the customer and moving from it to collaboration.

This can be a delicate enterprise for support engineers who are more interested in the technical side of things. We will see later how you can hire and train support engineers to understand that angry and emotional people in general do not behave cooperatively and must become calm and focused before "real work" can begin. Hiring and training must also consider the empathetic listening skills required to achieve the change of moods in the customer.

In summary, we see the goal of call management, and indeed the goal of the art and business of support, to be satisfied customers. Customer satisfaction stems from meeting or exceeding a customer's expectations. Expectations are shaped by all kinds of outside forces; therefore, the service provider must, formally and informally, negotiate service commitments before service is rendered. Even when there is a formal contract, the process must be reinforced at the start of each transaction.

The Basic Action Workflow (preparation–negotiation–performance–acceptance) embodies what must happen within each support transaction if it is to be concluded successfully, both from the customer's and performer's perspectives. Of particular importance are the often-neglected phases of acceptance, forming a mutual agreement, and satisfaction, when the customer confirms whether the goal was accomplished. We will use the action workflow as a benchmark of the call flow models we will explore next.

In addition to the process aspect of service transactions, attention must be given to creating a spirit of collaboration between the customer and the service provider. This is often tricky, as the customer may be in a highly emotional state at the start of the transaction, and requires fine-tuned skills from the service provider.

2.2   CALL FLOW MODELS

Let us now move from the theoretical plane of customer satisfaction and negotiated service commitments to the practical level of organizing the flow of
work. If you skipped the previous section, you may be missing some of the
upcoming points. Consider flipping back a few pages. We will use the principles embodied in the Basic Action Workflow to describe the various call flow
models, and we will analyze and judge the models on their ability to deliver
and reinforce smooth customer transactions.

First, let's define what we mean by call flow. Call flow is the process through
which problems are received from the customer, solutions are found, and
answers are returned to the customer. The choice of a call flow model is *the*
central issue in setting up a support operation. Your call flow model defines
how you apply the Basic Action Workflow to your support center.

The traditional call flow model is the "Frontline/Backline" model, also called
the "Foreground/Background" model. In the Frontline/Backline model, calls
come into a group of less experienced support engineers, who solve what they
can and pass the rest on to a group of senior support engineers. Based on both
the theoretical considerations we shared earlier in this chapter, and on our
practical experience as customers and support managers, we are strong proponents of a newer, less familiar, model, which we call the "Touch and Hold"
model. We will describe the traditional model, point out its drawbacks, and
then discuss the newer model together with the reasons why we advocate it.

2.2.1   The Frontline/Backline Model

The Frontline/Backline (FL/BL) model is sometimes called the tiered model,
since it organizes the staff of the support center into two groups: (1) a larger
group of less experienced support engineers who take the incoming calls and
try to resolve them within some short period of time, and (2) a smaller group
of senior support engineers who take the calls that the Frontline engineers
cannot resolve within the allotted time period (see Figure 2–3).

Calls come into the Frontline group. The frontliners are responsible for connecting with the customer as quickly as possible [if there is an automatic call
distribution (ACD) telephone system, as we will discuss in the next chapter,
they take calls right off the ACD]. Using what they know, the product documentation, and ideally a knowledge base of past issues and their solutions,
they attempt to resolve the problem within a given time frame. If they are
unable to resolve the problem, the call then moves on to the Backline group.

The Frontline / Backline Model

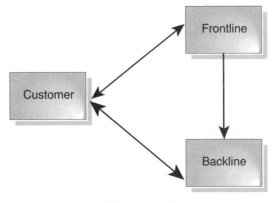

Figure 2–3

Backliners are more experienced than the Frontline engineers, so are better equipped to resolve problems. They are also organized and scheduled so they can spend long periods of time working on a particular issue without having to handle the incoming call load like frontliners. When a call is passed on to Backline, the customer is also passed on to the Backline engineer, who takes ownership of the call (in other words, this switch in ownership is visible to the customer).

The tricky part of the FL/BL model is the transition between Frontline and Backline. To avoid confusion, duplicated efforts, waste of backliners' work on easy tasks, and customer and staff frustration in general, it is essential to have a very clear definition of when and how calls are transferred from one level to the next. Typical criteria are time elapsed since the call started (a few minutes to a few days, depending on the average call complexity), and time spent working the call, which is also dependent on call complexity. Usually calls may also be transitioned to Backline as soon as they come in, if they are recognized from the start to be very complex.

Good implementations of the Frontline/Backline model provide for a call transition summary to be prepared by the frontliner before transitioning a call, so that all relevant information is gathered in one place, thereby minimizing the need to request the same information twice, requiring a minimal amount of rework by the backliner, and clearly defining the customer's expectations for the next step. The information is typically stored in the call tracking system.

The Frontline/Backline model is so popular and widespread that many customers and support professionals assume it's the only way to organize a Support group. It's not, as we will see later, but its popularity derives from its perceived advantages:

- It provides a rational staff utilization model by allowing the more senior support engineers to work on the more difficult questions.
- It provides a handy way of ramping up new staff.
- It gives a nice career path to the support engineers.
- It allows for a predictable model for customers: each call is handled in the same way, and customers are familiar with the model from past experience.

Since we are analyzing models from the point of view of the customer, it's interesting to note that the advantages come mostly from an internal perspective. And the last one, the only one that is from the point of view of the customer, may not be as positive as it first appears.

The consistency part of the argument (each call looks the same) sounds good, but is it such a good idea to treat all cases in the same way? If a call is more difficult, should it spend time with the frontliners, delaying resolution? What if the customer can tell right off the bat that the situation will require Backline assistance?

Familiarity also sounds like a good argument. Looking back, it's no surprise that the first cars looked like carriages, the first TV shows looked liked theater or filmed radio, and the first computer tutorials looked like books. But imitating an old medium does not exploit all the possibility of the new one, and familiarity eventually gives way to efficiency. Cars now look like . . . cars, and we think of the early cars as quaint and strange. A familiar model may not be the right model.

What about customer satisfaction? We believe that call management systems must be judged from the point of view of what the customer wants. The customer wants his problems to be solved properly and as quickly as possible. In addition, the customer wants to interact with as few people as possible, because more people mean more time, each additional person involved will require him to "start again," on some level, and because each person will require a new collaborative relationship be formed—that is, that a new Basic Action Workflow will be required.

The Frontline/Backline model does not fare well from the customer's perspective:

- All difficult questions require a hand-off from a frontliner to a backliner. Hand-offs take time, almost always result in information being lost and the customer having to furnish it again, and require customers to interact with several individuals. Typical organizations solve between 40% and 70% of the cases in Frontline, so conversely 30% to 60% of cases require a hand-off.
- Even if a customer knows that a problem is too difficult to be solved by the frontliners, Frontline cannot be bypassed
- There can be significant delays in getting a callback once a call goes to Backline, leading to more customer dissatisfaction.
- Customers, at least the more sophisticated ones, will pressure the organization to skip Frontline and go directly to "the people who know."

There are also internal drawbacks to the use of the FL/BL model, starting with its fundamental inefficiency: it violates a major principle of time management: "touch it once" (and resolve it). In addition, the FL/BL model has the following internal drawbacks:

- Frontliners are not able to come to closure on a large proportion of customer issues. This is frustrating to support professionals, who derive much of their job satisfaction from the customers' satisfaction.
- The compartmentalization between groups makes it difficult for frontliners to increase their technical knowledge and to move up.
- As a consequence of the issues above, frontliners' job satisfaction is low and their turnover is high.
- There is a tendency to "throw calls over the wall" to Backline without working them adequately, leading to frustration and overwork of the backliners.
- There is often an impression of a "caste system" between Frontline and Backline, leading to engineers' dissatisfaction.
- In an attempt to prove themselves, some frontliners hang on to issues for too long, delaying resolution.

At this point, you may be asking yourself: if the FL/BL model is so bad, why is it so pervasive, and why does it seem to work for most people?

First, we are not saying that the FL/BL does not work (it does, sort of). We are saying it has definite weaknesses when judged by customer satisfaction standards. We are also saying that we have been successful with a newer, challenger model, which has advantages for customers and for support professionals compared to the FL/BL model.

Second, what about the arguments in favor of the FL/BL model? It is true that the FL/BL model provides a way for engineers to ramp up, and a career path. However, the initial training is at the expense of the customer, and, as we have seen, customers will exert a lot of pressure to skip the untrained engineers they are likely to find in the Frontline group. For the latter, the career path is "obvious," from Frontline to Backline, but we have seen that it is difficult for frontliners to learn the technical skills they need to move up.

All models need to provide a way to train new support engineers and a way for engineers to become more skilled. The basic idea for all models is to recruit engineers who may be junior in their expertise, but who have the background and the skills to progress to a senior level. Engineers can be trained successfully in a variety of models. More experienced engineers come up to speed faster regardless of the model, and—again regardless of the model—it's difficult (and unnecessary) to predict who among the less experienced engineers will progress to become an expert. The way the FL/BL model implements initial training and career pathing is not the only way, and we will see how our challenger model deals with these issues.

Another argument in favor of the FL/BL model is that some support engineers genuinely like it and do not want to change. Part of that reaction is the universal love of familiarity and resistance to change. Part of it may be, for backliners, that they are afraid of the possible loss of status associated with a different model. It's a serious issue, since the backliners have the expertise you need to make the center run. The fact that backliners are attached to the model does not mean it's the only one that can work. Often, it's the only model they know. If you want to switch to a different model, you will need to enlist the backliners in the change process, since they are likely to be the informal leaders of the group.

Frontliners may be attached to the FL/BL model, because they may feel comfortable with the idea that difficult cases can be handed to the backliners. Our challenger model provides both for technical help on difficult cases and for call hand-offs when necessary, so no one needs to feel stuck with a problem that's simply too difficult. Also, if the frontliners' reaction is prompted by low skills and a low desire to improve, they may not be the kind of engineers you want serving your customers, anyway.

Finally, FL/BL is familiar and comfortable to the majority of support managers who have extensive experience and success with it, and they may be very unwilling to let go of the tried and true. The FL/BL model grew out of the hardware support business, where, if swapping boards would not resolve the problem, you really needed to bring in an expert. It was a good match for the need at that time. Times have changed, however; the technology is very different, and the software equivalent of swapping boards (reading the manual?) does not cut it anymore. We need a new way to manage calls, one that fully exploits our knowledge of customer requirements. Managers need to see that the change is necessary and embrace it.

The disadvantages of the FL/BL model have led us to experiment with another model, which has been extremely successful for us: we call it the Touch and Hold model.

2.2.2 The Touch and Hold Model

The ultimate goal behind the Touch and Hold (T&H) model is to get the right call to the right support engineer—that is, to maximize the chances that the support engineer who first takes the call is the one most capable of responding to the issue. The Touch and Hold model is still pretty rare, but we have had a great deal of success with it, and we believe it will be the next wave for software support. It is most clearly superior for complex support situations, but we believe it can be used successfully in all kinds of environments. At the end of this section we will give some guidelines for determining which model to choose.

At first glance, the Touch and Hold model may appear to be very similar to the FL/BL model in that it organizes the staff into two groups, one less experienced and one senior. The main difference is that calls do **not** move from one group to another. The "second-level" group, which we call the *Technical Advisors' Group* or *TAG* so as not to create confusion with the Backline label, functions as an advisory group to the "first-level" group rather than as another customer contact group. The advisory group in the Touch and Hold model allows the customer to complete almost all calls through one customer-initiated transaction cycle, a much better step toward customer satisfaction.

Another difference is that the proportion of technical advisors to support engineers is much lower than the proportion of backliners to frontliners (10% vs. 30%–50%.)

As calls come in, they are assigned through some algorithm (we talk about assignment algorithms in the next chapter) to a support engineer (see Figure 2–4). That support engineer is then responsible to take the call through resolution. To resolve the issue, the support engineer uses whatever means are at her disposal, including using her knowledge, the product documentation, the technical knowledge base if there is one, and in particular using the TAG team in an advisory capacity, all the while retaining ownership of the issue. There are no mandated customer call hand-offs. Hand-offs are rare and discretionary.

The Touch and Hold Model

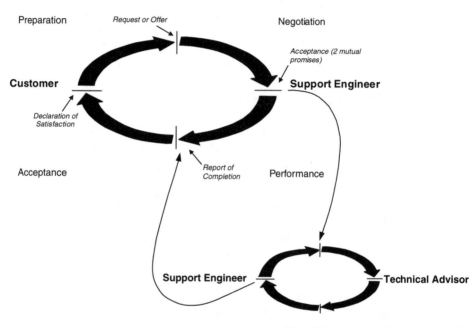

Adapted from *Business Design Associates, Inc.*

Figure 2–4

The technical advisors offer a help desk service to the support engineers, where they dispense advice, point to other sources of information, and work through difficult situations with the support engineers. The technical advisors are also responsible for creating a reference material infrastructure and for finding and repairing holes in the information available. Because they do not own customer problems of their own, they are available to help engineers freely. They are not completely cut off from customers, however. When they decide it is necessary, they participate in conference calls with the customer and the support engineer, either as leaders of the conversation to serve as a model for the support engineer or to speed up resolution. In special cases they may take ownership of a particular issue completely, including communication with the customer. This is extremely rare (it should not happen for more than 5% of the calls) in that it would defeat the idea of having them available to a wide range of support engineers.

The support engineers are the customers of the technical advisors and interact with them through the now familiar Basic Action Workflow. The main theoretical advantage of the model is that the second workflow is managed internally and its complexities and burdens are hidden from the external customer.

The advantages of T&H for the customer are as follows:

- There are few hand-offs, so the customer rarely has to start over. Note that some hand-offs are inevitable, since support engineers go on vacation, go to training, and sometimes plain don't know what to do with a call and must pass it on to someone more expert, even in this configuration; hand-offs are more common for complex support where issues take longer to resolve.

- In order for the T&H model to be viable, the support engineers need to have a medium to high technical expertise, whereas frontliners could make do with low expertise. Therefore, the first support engineer a customer talks to with T&H is much more knowledgeable than the average frontliner.

- As a consequence of the points above, resolution time is faster.

The advantages of T&H for the organization are as follows:

- All support engineers have a real opportunity to improve their technical skills.

- There is great satisfaction in resolving a problem for customers, and that can now happen close to 100% of the time for all support engineers.

- There is no artificial barrier between frontliners and backliners. (Granted, there could be a barrier between support engineers and technical advisors, but since engineers and advisors typically work together on the more difficult cases, it's easier to cultivate team spirit and the separation is easier to manage.)

- The work flow is smoother, since there is no forced hand-off after a given period of time.

- With many fewer hand-offs, throughput is higher. The effect is stronger when hand-offs are complex, as they are with complex support, and when hand-offs require callbacks to customers or otherwise increase resolution time significantly in a low-complexity environment.

With all its advantages to customers and the Support organization, the T&H model has some tricky implementation points that need to be made explicit, especially for centers moving from FL/BL to T&H:

- The T&H model requires a large pool of well-qualified support engineers. If you have a large pool of less experienced engineers, either because you have a brand-new organization or you have had to grow very fast, you will have a training challenge getting the engineers up to speed, especially if you support complex products. However, customer satisfaction will be higher if the initial contact is more qualified.

- Service can be more uneven than in FL/BL, since not all support engineers will be at the same level. In other words, with FL/BL the customer can pretty much expect a low level of expertise on the first conversations; with T&H, the expertise will vary from medium to high, which can be unsettling and perceived as unpleasant by the customers. The cure is to have a strong training program for new support engineers and to ensure from a management perspective that they are very zealous about getting help from other engineers and from the technical advisors. A strong collaboration between engineers and between them and the TAG group can correct this problem.

- Since the "automatic" check for aging calls between Frontline and Backline does not exist any more, you will need to provide for some call aging mechanism. (Note that, even under the FL/BL model, you need to think about call aging management, once the calls get to Backline.)

- The technical advisors must be carefully managed so they are sufficiently available, especially in difficult situations, without taking over the management of the calls and becoming unavailable for their help desk duties.

And what about cost? Could it be that the real reason for the popularity of the FL/BL model is cost efficiency, rather than familiarity? Working out exact costs is difficult, since there are lots of variables, including the percentages of easy and hard calls, which in turn drives the percentages of frontliners and backliners and also the compensation of support engineers, which varies according to the expertise required and the local market. We worked out costs for a small complex support operation as an example. Feel free to work out numbers for your organization, using the percentages that would work for you and the base compensation at the levels appropriate for your organization.

Say you need 10 engineers, with low-end compensation at 40K and high-end at 60K. With a FL/BL model, you will need 6 or 7 frontliners, the balance being backliners. Pegging frontliners' compensation at the low end and backliners' at the high end, your raw labor costs are at or above 40 * 6 + 60 * 4 = 480K.

With the T&H model, you will need 9 "regular" support engineers and 1 technical advisor. Support engineers will be paid in a range between the low and the high end, and the technical advisor will be paid at the high end. Your raw labor costs are 45 * 9 + 60 = 465K. Working the problem from the other end, you could pay your average frontliner up to 47K and still be competitive with the FL/BL model.

The figures would favor T&H even more with a high-volume, low-complexity operation, because support engineers' training requirements are lower. In any case, the T&H model does not cost more than the FL/BL model.

Finally, if we are so concerned about customer satisfaction, how can we advocate a model where the best support engineers—the technical advisors—are "hidden" from the customer? Actually, although it's true that technical advisors are not right there on the front line, they are available when needed. Preventing technical advisors from talking to customers is a cardinal sin of the implementation of T&H. At the same time, their expertise is leveraged across the organization and available indirectly to all customers through documentation, technical notes, newsletters, and so on. Their entire function is customer focused.

In summary, the T&H model leverages a small group of highly technical experts who function mostly in a help desk scenario supporting a large group of support engineers. Most customer questions can be handled within one Basic Action Workflow, simplifying the interaction for the customer and making the model satisfying to the support engineers.

2.2.3 Choosing the Right Model for Your Organization

So which model is better for you? Although we strongly recommend the Touch and Hold model, there may be exceptions. As we said before, support is an art rather than a science, so you will have to make your own decision. Here are some key decision points to help you (many overlap):

- *Call complexity:* do your calls tend to be quick and easy, or do they require individual investigation? For example, we would contrast low-complexity calls, which take an average of 10 minutes to resolve, with high-complexity calls, which take 2 hours. T&H works well with high-complexity because hand-offs are so difficult there. For low-complexity cases, see the next point.

- *Volume of relatively complex calls:* how many difficult calls (relative to your average complexity) do you get? If you get few "hard" calls (whatever hard means for your support operation), you may be better off with FL/BL, since you need few hand-offs. With a large number of "hard" calls, T&H should be your first choice. Think about the volume of calls as well as its proportion vis-à-vis the total call volume. Even with a low proportion of complex calls, you should consider using T&H if you have a high number of them.

- *Ease of determining call complexity:* how quickly can the support engineers determine whether a call will be difficult or easy? If it's going to take some time (and it usually does) before the engineer can be sure it's a difficult question, T&H is better, since the investigation time will not be invested in vain by a frontliner.

- *Existence and quality of a knowledge base:* if most problems are documented and require only a lookup in an information system, FL/BL may be quite comfortable for customers, since, again, there will be few hand-offs. Note, however, that a frontliner obviously reading a canned answer to a complex question may not engender a feeling of trust in the customer and may lead the customer to doubt the answer even if it is correct.

Although we believe that T&H is a superior model, there are some environments where it will be difficult to implement. If you are in one of the situations described below, do not automatically use FL/BL, however. Think of ways you can overcome the obstacles—if not right away, at least in the future—always keeping in mind what your customers would want.

- *Managers' expertise and risk taking ability:* most managers are comfortable with what they know, and what they know is the FL/BL model. They may feel it's easier to manage in a FL/BL environment with its clear delineation between groups, forgetting that morale issues are much more severe with FL/BL. It will take training and convincing to prepare managers for a change, but it will be worthwhile both for customers and also for the managers who will have increased their expertise and experience.

- *Customer profile:* less sophisticated customers are usually satisfied with FL/BL (not only because they may not know better, but also because they are subjected to few hand-offs). Remember that customer sophistication increases with time, so you may want to get ready for the time when your customers get more knowledgeable and more demanding.

- *Staff expertise level:* if your staff is mostly new, you may have to use FL/BL, because you just won't have the expertise needed to sustain T&H. Think about targeting some promising individuals as future technical advisors so you can transition to T&H in the future. At the same time, think about raising the technical level of the entire staff through training and mentoring.

- *Size of the organization:* T&H works best with a 1:10 ratio, so you will have to be inventive in a small organization. Can you partner with other related Support groups and create a "virtual" team of advisors? Can you use a vendor as your TAG team? Can you have one or several individuals perform TAG duties in some portion of their time? If your team is really small (fewer than 10 members), any model that requires creating separate groups is awkward anyway.

- *Staffing level:* if your group is seriously understaffed, switching from FL/BL to T&H will expose your customers to the full brunt of the problem. With a FL/BL system you can hide some of the pain in the Backline group, creating tremendous backlog for difficult calls, but allowing customers with short questions to continue to get acceptable service. With T&H all questions, even short ones, will be delayed. This is not, properly speaking, an issue with the T&H model, it is a staffing issue, which needs to be attacked with staffing numbers and justifications. See Chapter 7, "Managing Support People," and Appendix 3, "Determining Staffing Levels," for help in developing justifications to increase your staffing.

A special note to support managers who are using a FL/BL model and are happy with it: what would be the benefits to your customers of moving to the Touch and Hold model? We recommend you consider the move.

2.3   OTHER CALL MANAGEMENT CONSIDERATIONS

In this section we explore other areas of call management that you need to consider before setting up your support center. One key principle of Technical Support will be used over and over in this section and deserves a quick explanation.

In Technical Support, **Big is beautiful**. That is, critical mass is essential. Scheduling and coverage requirements are much easier to meet if you have a large group. If you have 30 support engineers capable of performing a particular task, you can afford to send a few to training and have one take a vacation at the same time.

If you happen to have a small support center, don't despair. With some ingenuity, many things are possible, and you can play up the advantages of small groups: more personal service and a more tightly integrated team. You will, however, need to devote much more attention to scheduling.

On the other hand, if you have a big support center, resist the temptation to slice and dice your group into a multitude of specialized subgroups. You will create all kinds of problems for yourself: scheduling conflicts, employee frustration, and poor customer satisfaction. We consider an ideal size for a team (focused on a product, or a set of customers, or a shift) to be between 6 and 12. Therefore, if a natural grouping for you, say around a product, yields a group of 25, you may consider subgroupings, although you don't have to. On the other hand, if you have a group of 12, be very cautious about subdividing it. If it's not absolutely required, your running afoul of the principle of critical mass will cost you dearly by decreasing customer satisfaction, decreasing employee satisfaction, and increasing your own operational headaches.

For a mathematical justification of the "Big is beautiful" principle, refer to Appendix C, "Determining Staffing Requirements."

2.3.1   Customer-based versus product-based groups

One of the key decisions you need to make is whether to organize your staff around customers or around products. The advantage of organizing around customers is that it creates a stronger ownership of the customer by the team, and that, over time, customers and support engineers will get to know each other very well. Going back to the Basic Action Workflow, aligning support engineers and customers allows you to create an ideal environment for smooth transactions. The drawback of organizing around customers is that it can prevent support engineers from acquiring sufficient expertise, especially if the products are complex or there are simply many of them.

A product-based organization allows support engineers to specialize and to become experts in their areas. This can be a significant factor for customer satisfaction, since questions can be answered faster. The drawbacks are reduced customer ownership and rapport.

Examples of product-based teams are teams based on a product or set of products—for instance: office productivity tools vs. networking vs. telecommunications, compilers vs. operating systems, UNIX vs. Windows vs. MVS, and so on.

Examples of customer-based teams are: East Coast customers vs. West Coast customers (this one can be useful to schedule shift work), the MIS department vs. the Engineering group vs. all other departments, your third-party partners (VARs—Value-Added Resellers, ISVs—Independent Software Vendors, and so on) vs. end-users.

So which model should you choose? Keeping in mind the principle of critical mass, you should avoid small groups, so first ask yourself whether specialization is really essential. If you must choose, we recommend organizing by products if you can meet both of the following principles of product-based differentiation:

- First principle: Big is beautiful. The product groups should be large enough to allow you to manage a schedule. Groups smaller than 5 create scheduling challenges. If you have a small group, you will have to live with it, but do not create small subgroups if you don't have to.

- Second principle: easy differentiation. It should be easy to determine what group each call is routed to. If you spend more than a small fraction (say 5%) of the call resolution time figuring out who should take the call, your product groups are not differentiated enough. A good test is that your customers should be able to determine where their calls should go by answering a few simple questions. If you are using an ACD, your customers should be able to self-direct their calls to the proper subgroup.

If you fail the criteria above, you need to redefine your product groups, usually by going to a wider grouping.

If the product knowledge requirements are not too high, you may want to organize your group around customer groups (or, again, keep one big beautiful group). Here are some situations where customer-based groups make sense:

- Most calls are easy and answers are clearly documented.
- Most calls are about general problems, such as setup and usage issues, that require only basic product and troubleshooting skills, such as when working with high-volume consumer products.
- Customer needs are very different from one customer group to the other.
- Many customers have multiple requests and do not want to be bounced from one group to another.

If you decide to choose the customer-based model, remember the principle of critical mass. If one individual or a small group owns a particular set of customers, who will cover in case of vacation or illness or, even worse, resignation?

An extreme example of a customer-based organization is one where customers have just one contact, a "dedicated" support engineer who handles all their requests. The benefit to the customer is that the support engineer will become very familiar with the environment and requirements of the customer, which will speed up the resolution of problems. Dedicated support engineers contradict the spirit and the letter of the "Big is beautiful" principle; however, some customers may require dedicated engineers because of the value of such a relationship in terms of speed of resolution as well as the human side. With dedicated support engineers, you get the ultimate level of complexity in scheduling, coverage, and breadth of expertise. Therefore, you must ensure that you can get appropriate funding for them. If the customer is willing to fund the model, a successful pairing of a customer and a support engineer will bring you a very happy customer indeed.

Considering the challenges of maintaining dedicated engineers for particular customers, we recommend a middle ground: have a small group of dedicated engineers instead. This will allow you to handle schedule issues as well as product coverage issues if your product line is large, while still providing very personal support to customers (and also being able to convince customers they will get personal attention).

If you have a very large group, you can mix and match customer-based and product-based. For instance, two support centers could each "own" customers in their region, with product teams within each center. It would be a perfectly workable model if you could, once again, ensure that each subgroup (customer- and product-based team) contains at least 5 people. We talk about the rationale for and against multiple support centers at more length in Chapter 6, "Support Organization Structure."

2.3.2   Generalists and Product Specialists

We have already talked about product-based and customer-based organizations, so what is this section all about? First, it applies only to product-based organizations—so, if you do not specialize by product, you may skip ahead.

Assuming that you have chosen to have a product-based team, we want to confuse everything and suggest that you should also consider reducing the gap between your product groups. Why are we suggesting such a thing? One of the big dangers in a product-based organization is that it can transform itself pretty quickly into a set of isolated subgroups that do not necessarily communicate very well, and between which customers can be shuttled back and forth when their questions happen to fall into a "gray zone" between two groups.

If you never have that gray zone effect, you need not worry about generalists, although it could be a good strategy to implement career paths and to simplify scheduling. If your customers sometimes fall into the gray zone (you can tell by tracking reassignments of cases between teams, especially multiple reassignments, as well as by conversations with unhappy customers), then you must rethink the way you handle problems that are difficult to categorize.

One possibility is to have generalists. Generalists are individuals who are skilled in more than one area and who can be brought in as advisors for gray zone cases, or even take them over. Generalists have breadth of knowledge, whereas specialists have depth.

Developing generalists can be a long-term enterprise, especially if the products you support are complex. Target those support engineers who want and like to have a breadth of skills. Although having a few generalists is handy, we do not recommend that it be a goal for everyone. Other individuals will prefer and be better at developing a lot of depth in a few areas, and you do need to develop experts.

Another approach to working the gray zone is to encourage engineers to work in teams on gray zone calls. A product-based organization should allow and even encourage cooperation between teams to handle special situations.

A special note: if you find yourself with a large proportion of gray zone cases, say above 5%, then you have a group differentiation problem which you need to attack by going back to the way you defined your product groups and revising your strategy. You are violating the second principle of product-based organizations: easy differentiation between calls that go to different groups. The reason could be either that your groups are not well differentiated or that the differences are not clear to your customers and your support engineers.

In summary, even with careful product specialization some issues will fall between two groups. Think about developing some individuals with multiple specialties, and, barring that, having engineers work on cross-specialty teams.

2.3.3 Field- versus Center-Based Support

One basic decision you will need to make is whether to locate your support engineers close to your customers, in a geographically dispersed pattern, or whether to have them sit all together in one or a few support centers.

Our strong recommendation, following the principle of critical mass, is for center-based support. (We will discuss the benefits of having more than one support center in Chapter 6, "Support Organization Structure.") You may want to choose field-based support in a few special situations:

- *When your customers demand it:* some segment of your customer population may need and be willing to fund onsite support. This is similar to the situation described earlier, where a customer wants a dedicated support engineer. It works, but it's expensive, so make sure you get the funding.

- *For emergency use:* as will be discussed in the next section, some special situations may require special handling, including onsite help. As your organization grows, it will be wise and cost efficient to preposition a few people closer to customers than the support centers you have. Only experience with your particular situation will tell you how many field engineers you need, but a good rule of thumb to start would be 1 field engineer for 40 center engineers. You probably don't want to even think about field engineers if your group is small. If you have no field engineers, or if you don't have enough at a particular point in time, you can always fly a center engineer to a customer if needed.

- *If your product requires it:* we strongly believe that modern software should be serviceable from afar, using modems, but you may have specific requirements for onsite support.

If you determine that some or all of your support engineers will be in the field, you need to pay careful attention to how they can be productive without being physically close to others. In particular, you need to ensure that your tools are robust enough to give a geographically remote individual full access to them. This is true of your basic call tracking system, but also of your information tools, including the knowledge base, and also the problem replication equipment. This last requirement is often the most difficult one to meet and is the reason why customer site support, although appreciated and requested by customers, is usually insufficient for modern software support.

In addition, field engineers will need to be recruited, trained, and managed. It's not an easy task from afar. If you are using your field engineers for emergencies, what will they do outside emergencies? Again, if emergencies are few, you may want to choose to fly support engineers from the centers when needed rather than creating a separate organization. As an alternative, you may want to use a third-party organization with a good network of geographically dispersed staff, such as a hardware vendor, which can receive some basic training on your software products and which you can back up over the phone from your support centers.

To conclude, support engineers belong in a centralized location to satisfy the principle of critical mass. Large organizations may want to preposition field engineers for emergencies; others may wish to investigate using a third party. In addition, some customers may require and fund onsite support engineers.

Escalations
39

2.4 ESCALATIONS

The word escalation is used a great deal by support professionals and with a large variety of meanings. For example, one might say that a call is "escalated" from Frontline to Backline. For clarity, we will use the word escalation in a very precise way: for us, escalations are the "bad" calls, the ones where customers are not satisfied with the way their issues are being resolved and that normally require management intervention to resolve them. We will refer to the other situations as "transitions"—transitions from Frontline to Backline, or from Support to the bug fixing group.

Escalations vary greatly in their causes and their intensity, as shown in the following examples:

- The customer was given a response time of one hour . . . yesterday.
- The customer's CIO is threatening to throw out your product if the issue cannot be resolved.
- The customer has installed two fixes for the problem, but they have not helped. If anything, performance is worse now.
- The customer cannot understand the accent of the support engineer.
- The software behaves erratically on one networking protocol, properly on another; after two weeks of work, no one in the Support group can figure out why.
- The customer feels that the support engineer is talking down to him.
- The problem has been open for three weeks without visible progress.
- The operators are outraged because it takes a full minute to repaint screens.

Let's analyze the root causes of these problems.

2.4.1 Escalation Types

Generally speaking, escalations can be classified into the following categories, all related to some aspect of unfulfilled expectations:

- Service issue: the customer did not get what he expected or was promised out of the Support organization. This includes problems with response time, resolution time, and professionalism of the support engineer.

- Sales issue: the product is not performing as sold. This may be as blatant as that the product cannot be installed on the customer's machine, or it may be a more subtle problem such as incompatibility with other software programs at the customer site, or poor performance.

- Technical issue: the product has a defect that prevents its proper functioning in ways that are not acceptable to the customer. This is usually a serious defect, the fix of which is not immediately forthcoming.

As an exercise, try classifying the examples above into the three categories. You will find that many escalations come from a variety of causes, and that some just don't have enough details to allow categorization.

Situation 1 is a pure service issue. Situation 2 could be either a sales issue or a technical issue, or maybe even a service issue, not enough detail is available. Situation 3 is a technical issue. Situation 4 is a service issue (engineer specific). Situation 5 is a technical issue, which may also have undertones of service issues. Situation 6 is another engineer-specific service issue. Situation 7 is a service issue with perhaps a technical issue lurking behind it. Finally, situation 8 could be either a technical or a sales issue (or both).

Why bother to categorize escalations, especially if most have several root causes? We can think of two benefits. One, you need to define the problem before you can start resolving it. For example, if the customer has unrealistic expectations about what the software can do, no amount of work on the service side will resolve that concern. In this sense, categorizing the escalation is part of the diagnostic process.

Also, at a more general level, you want to determine root causes of escalations so that you can address process issues once the crisis (escalation) is over. For instance, if a support engineer repeatedly creates the impression of talking down to customers, you will want to get her some coaching. Similarly, if a lot of escalations come from customers thinking that a lot of support engineers talk down to them, you will need to change your training and maybe even your recruiting practices. If salespeople make unfounded performance claims, you will need to work with the sales manager to address that issue. If a particular area of the product is buggy, you will need to alert the engineering manager.

Although we used "sales issues" and "technical issues" as category names, you, the lucky support manager, are responsible for resolving all escalations. You may and will need to involve other groups into the effort, but you need to drive the escalation to resolution. You own the satisfaction of the customer and you cannot give up control of the situation. In particular, you need to create a way to involve other departments into the resolution of the problem while maintaining a united front vis-à-vis the customer.

Let's now discuss models that can support the resolution of escalations.

2.4.2 Escalation Handling Model

Escalations are a special category of customer requests, so at a theoretical level they need to be handled through the Basic Action Workflow (see Figure 2–5). Escalations are special in that the request tends to be more intense and more emotional, so the initial (acceptance) phase is very delicate to handle. You are starting from a negative situation where expectations have been missed, and usually the spirit of collaboration is not present, to say the least. You will need to spend much more time and energy managing emotions, creating trust, and building an acceptable agreement than you would for a normal call, but the principles are exactly the same.

Escalation Model

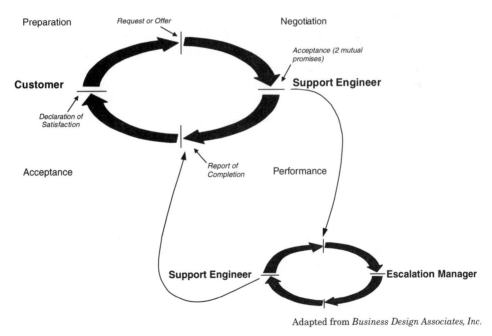

Adapted from *Business Design Associates, Inc.*

Figure 2–5

Similarly, the management of the end of an escalation workflow is more delicate than with a normal call, since ascertaining customer satisfaction is even more important than usual, and, again, customer satisfaction will be more difficult to attain. Achieving a successful conclusion will take more time, more attention, and more skill than with a regular call.

Another special feature of escalations is that they tend to come from various sources and through various vehicles, not neatly through the support hotline like calls. The first part of your model must include a way to properly funnel the escalations to you. Everyone in your group, your management chain, and anyone else who is in contact with customers should know to contact you (or an appropriate individual on your staff) when they receive a call from an irate customer. They are welcome to talk to the customer, get specifics on the issue, and promise to help, but they should stay away from making promises that cannot be kept (the customer has already suffered from that) and they should put you in the loop right away.

2.4.3   Do you need a dedicated escalation management function?

We have seen that product-based groups are often good, that customer-based groups are sometimes desirable, so what about dedicated escalation groups? First, let us hasten to say there are indeed individuals who are skilled at handling those difficult situations and are willing to work them. Having an escalation group is not a crazy idea. With proper processes and resources, it could be the perfect fit for the right individual.

What would be the arguments pro and against a dedicated function? From the principle of critical mass ("Big is beautiful"), we know that we should not create too many subgroups, or, to be precise, we should not create groups that are too small, so if your support center is small, you already know that you should not jump to a dedicated escalation group.

When deciding whether to have a dedicated escalation function, you must analyze the number and type of escalations you receive, since the handling of escalations depends on their type. Service issues need to go back to the support engineer or the Support group where they originated and to her or its manager so they can be addressed there. No amount of dedicated escalation management can fix performance or process issues: the manager of the group needs to be involved. Escalations from the second category, sales issues, go to the sales group and require only management coordination from the Support group, so, if you have many, you may want to create an escalation manager position (apart from having a good heart-to-heart with the sales manager, that is). Technical escalations are much like other calls, but they are much more intense emotionally, they last longer than a regular call, and they often involve a larger cast to resolve them. Support engineers should be able to handle escalations just like anything else. There is no requirement related to technical expertise to having a separate group to handle escalations; however, project management and cross-functional team skills are precious to success-fully resolve escalations.

There are two arguments in favor of creating a dedicated escalation function:

- Special skills are helpful to resolve escalations.
- More importantly, it allows for a smoother work flow.

Resolving escalations tends to require large amounts of time and energy from the support engineer working on it and from the manager driving it. If those individuals are also required to attend to a variety of other issues, they will either neglect the other customers (not good) or do a poor job of driving the escalation (very bad). Therefore, with a group of a sufficient size, say 30, and with enough escalations, it might be wise to have an escalation manager who specializes in driving escalations. With an even larger group, say 50, you may want to have an escalation team, adding one or more escalation support engi-neers. A dedicated escalation team is essential in large groups with substantial amounts of complex escalations. If you have a dedicated escalation team, you can recruit or develop individuals with specialized skills to be on the team.

In addition to the size issue mentioned above, we can see two drawbacks to having a dedicated escalation group.

- A dedicated escalation function may mask the real problems. Imagine that a large number of escalations revolve around long resolution times for bug fixes. Having a dedicated escalation team will make customers feel better because they are getting addi-tional attention, but it won't fix the root cause, and indeed it will create more and more work for the escalation function, as more customers and more support engineers realize that they will get expedited service by going through the escalation function. It's very important that the escalation function not take the place of properly functioning processes.
- A dedicated escalation function may weaken the ownership of cus-tomer satisfaction. If, as a support manager, I can simply throw over the fence to the escalation manager any problematic cus-tomer, my incentive to keep my customers happy is gone. To guard against this, we will see how you can put in place a qualification process that ensures that the escalation function is not used as a multipurpose disposal ground, but rather is used only in situa-tions where it can add value.

The model used to drive the escalation itself should be a "cradle-to-grave" model, where one individual drives the resolution and interfaces with the cus-tomer's management, and one or several support engineers work on the technical issues. Continuity is essential in escalations. Even more than with normal calls, you want to keep hand-offs at the absolute minimal level required to resolve the issue.

2.4.4 Post-Mortems

As noted above, the time during which you are working to resolve an escalation is not a good time to go back and analyze root cause. Speed is essential, and you want to concentrate your resources on resolving the issue. However, once the escalation is over and the customer is satisfied, you should go over the entire process, analyze what went well or not, and fix root causes so you don't have to go through the drill again for the same reasons. We refer to this process as a "post-mortem analysis," or post-mortem for short. The post-mortem should involve everyone connected to the escalation—that is, all internal players. The customer may be a part of a formal post-mortem discussion scheduled after the internal discussion. We have found that customers like to be invited into the process and that being open about internal failures and recovery plans strengthens the relationship.

Cover the following aspects during the internal post-mortem:

- What created the escalation.
- Summary of events.
- What went well in the resolution of the situation.
- What did not go well.
- What could have prevented the escalation.
- Recommendations for process change.

In order for the post-mortem to be successful it is essential to create a climate that allows all participants to be completely candid about their own and others' performance. An unwillingness to raise issues or strident attacks on other participants will not bring the desired results for the quality of the analysis.

You should formally record the results of post-mortems, at least at some summary level, so you can have that overall view of escalations we were alluding to earlier to allow process changes. The records need not be fancy.

Take action to implement the changes recommended in post-mortems, or your effort will be wasted.

By now, you should have a good idea of the model you want to use (Touch and Hold or Frontline/Backline), you should have some ideas of either product-based or customer-based groups you can use, and you should have started thinking about handling escalations, either through the existing management or through a dedicated function. It's time to move on to implementing your ideas and to practical considerations such as routing calls and responding to them.

CHAPTER 3
CALL MANAGEMENT IMPLEMENTATION

In this chapter we move from theoretical considerations about service models to more practical matters, such as how customers report problems, how problems are routed to the proper support engineer, and how escalations are handled. After reading this chapter and applying it to your specific situation, you should have a detailed view of how problems enter your organization and flow through it until they get resolved. The next step will be to discuss the actual organization of the group and how to run it from day to day. We will approach that in upcoming chapters.

To get full benefit from this chapter, you should already know what call flow model you want to use, or at least, you should have thought about the pros and cons of each alternative in your environment. In other words, you should have read Chapter 2 and thought about its application to your own situation.

The topics in this chapter apply to all kinds of support situations, although as we get closer to the details of how a support center runs we have to consider more and more specifics, such as size, customer requirements, and product requirements. Generally speaking, however, the topics in this chapter apply to large and small organizations, organizations with internal and external customers, and more or less complex products.

We will start by discussing how problems are reported to the support center, and we will concentrate on the phone system, since it's likely to be the mainstay. Electronic means of requesting support are discussed in section 3.5.

3.1 HOTLINE SUPPORT BASICS

In this section we will devote considerable attention to the incoming phone system to the support center. This is not to mean that the phone is the only interface customers can use, and indeed we will cover electronic means of communication in more detail later, but the phone is and will remain, despite technological changes and advances, the mainstay of support centers, and so deserves the prominence and detailed treatment we will give to it.

3.1.1   Hours of Operation

A key implementation question is when you will be available for your customers. You should base your decision on customer requirements as well as cost efficiency.

If you run an internal help desk, you need to follow the company's business hours, which may be different from standard hours. For instance, if you support a software development group, you may notice that the software engineers straggle in late and stay late too, and you may want or be required to be available during their late hours. On the other hand, if you support a manufacturing operation, the day shift may start early, and you may need to support several shifts. If you support operations in several time zones, you will need to design your work hours so that employees in remote offices get service similar to the ones at headquarters.

With external customers, too, you need to think about when they will need help. If you have commercial customers, you need to find out their business hours. As with internal customers, you will need to consider time zones as well. In some home software markets, evenings and weekends may be busier than normal business hours. You will also need to consider the competition. If everyone's offering round-the-clock support, you may need to provide it, too.

Opening your center longer than the standard business day means that you will need to stagger your staff's schedules and often pay shift differentials (more about compensation in Chapter 7). Therefore, you need to target your hours carefully. If your center is already in operation, you should chart the volume of incoming calls throughout the day to determine whether you should consider expanding or reducing your hours.

Although your general objective should be to restrict the hours during which the center is open, don't be excessive. If you have a West Coast center that serves customers on the East Coast and you decide to open at 8 a.m., you will find that pent-up demand from the East Coast, including having to respond to voicemail messages left overnight, can overwhelm your first few hours, so open at 6 a.m. instead (with a small staff) and enjoy a more relaxed schedule, not to mention happier customers. Keep in mind typical load patterns for West Coast and East Coast support centers, which suggest that centers be open between 6 a.m. and 5 p.m., Pacific Time (see Figures 3–1 and 3–2).

It is often appropriate to have several choices of hotline hours for different levels of support and to charge accordingly (see Chapter 5 for specific recommendations). Also think about positioning your support offerings that do not require personnel as alternatives for off-hours support. Faxback systems, Web sites, and bulletin boards can be accessible to customers around the clock without requiring round-the-clock staffing.

West Coast Support Center Call Volume

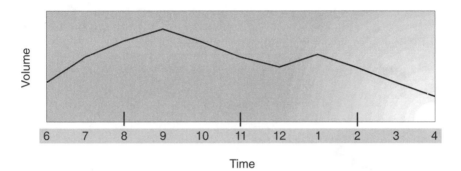

Time

Figure 3–1

East Coast Support Center Call Volume

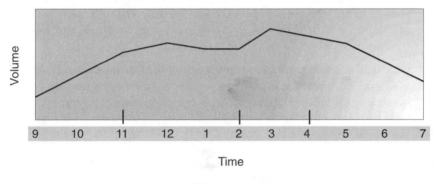

Time

Figure 3–2

In many cases, however, you will have customers who require personal support around the clock. Sometimes all your customers will need this level of service (say, if you support a software package used to run hospitals), and sometimes only some customers will require the service (say, the Accounting group at quarter-end and year-end). Since the principle of critical mass makes it difficult to staff off-hours shifts efficiently, let's discuss ways to provide off-hours support in a cost-efficient manner.

3.1.2   Off-hours Support

There are essentially four ways to provide off-hours support. The choice depends on the volume of calls you receive off-hours, how difficult the off-hours calls are likely to be, staffing considerations, and what kind of infra-structure you have in terms of support centers. Here are the four alternatives in order of increasing complexity, robustness, and cost:

- Pagers
- Answering service
- Off-hour shifts, either in-office or at home
- Follow-the-sun model

Under a pager system, customers page the staff member on duty, who then returns the call and handles the issue. This is a good system for low call vol-ume, since the infrastructure is very light (and cheap): essentially a pager subscription, which can be had for $10 or so per month, some compensation for the pager-carrying staff, and dial-in equipment for the staff on duty, such as a portable phone, a modem, and a laptop. If your ACD supports outward paging, you can program it to page a support engineer off-hours while allowing cus-tomers to call the same number day or night. The ACD may be programmed to automatically retry the page if there is no answer and can keep statistics on how many calls came in and at what time.

One drawback of the pager method is that pagers can be unreliable, both because of technical problems (e.g., the battery runs out) and also because of human error (the pager is left in a car or in another room). You may want to look into a backup solution, such as having two people carrying pagers with the same number, with instructions to the backup to respond only to repeated pages, or having two separate pager numbers for customers to use. If you are using your ACD, you can build the backup solution into the programming.

In addition, if you are supporting unsophisticated customers, it may be too dif-ficult for them to place a page, although the technique is being used so much that the problem is fading. Many doctors now use a pager system rather than have an answering service.

The pager system is the cheapest and simplest system and is ideal if you get a handful of calls a week. If customers expect to speak to a real person right away, if the support engineer carrying the pager is paged often, or is some-times paged while working on another customer's problem, you need to step up your call answering method.

The next level of complexity is to use an answering service. Under this model, customers call the answering service after hours (either by calling a special phone number or by calling the regular hotline number, which has been transferred to the answering service). The answering service is then responsible for contacting the people on duty, usually by calling their pager. The answering service is a safer way to go than pagers, since customers get to talk to a real person rather than paging a number and hoping for a return call. The answering service is instructed to call a backup if they do not hear back from the support engineer on duty within a given time interval. The answering service also allows you to handle the situation when multiple calls come in at once, either by dispatching them to different individuals or by juggling them with the same support engineer, freeing her to concentrate on helping one customer at a time.

The cost of using an answering service is slightly higher compared to using pagers only, since you need to pay the answering service fee, which can be a few hundred dollars a month depending on volume and the complexity of instructions to the answering service staff. Also, you need to pay particular attention to the training of the answering service staff. Answering services are excellent at answering the phone. Paging the support engineers, monitoring return phone calls, and especially juggling several individuals on pagers have been shown to be more problematic.

Using an answering service is more foolproof than relying on pagers alone, and it works well for small to medium call volumes. Sometimes, however, even an answering service won't be enough—either because the call volume is too high, or because it's necessary (or much easier) for the support engineer to be physically in the office to resolve the problem. In concrete terms, if you get one off-hour call a week or the support engineer has to go to the office once a month to resolve an off-hours problem, you're just fine with a pager or answering service solution. On the other hand, if you get four or five calls a night, or if the support engineer has to go to the office every other night, you need to move up to the next level of off-hours model. Customer complaints about the pager or answering service system can also be a reason to consider an alternative.

Because of the cost and complexity of implementing off-hours shifts, be very cautious before deciding to add one. You want to collect data on your experience for a few months and to analyze it carefully. For instance, you may find that Saturdays are really busy, but Sundays and nights are quiet, so you would need Saturday shifts, but you can get away with a lighter system at other times. Or you may find that you only need off-hours shifts at quarter-end. In many instances, one product line may require off-hours shifts but others generate very few off-hours calls and require only a pager. Most of the time, off-hours shifts will be worked in the office. However, if you have an ACD that supports routing calls to support engineers' homes, you may decide to route calls there. This is particularly handy if the volume of calls is not too high—for instance, to cover holidays—and it makes it much easier to recruit volunteers to work off-hours.

Finding, training, and retaining support engineers willing to work nights and weekends is difficult, so you will usually need to pay extra for those shifts (one exception that comes to mind is an academic environment where off-hours shifts may be just what graduate students ordered). If the staffing requirements for the shifts are small compared to your normal staffing level and the shift schedule is compatible with a normal schedule—for instance, if you need a couple of people to work Saturdays out of a pool of 50 support engineers—you should be able to solicit volunteers to take the additional shifts in exchange for appropriate compensation, typically 20%–25% over their normal daily compensation. Otherwise, you will need to hire staff dedicated to the odd shifts and to pay them a differential, typically 10%–15% for night or weekend shifts. You can get away with a lower differential for staff with a regular schedule as opposed to staff taking on additional shifts, although if you take benefits into account, the difference can go the other way. More details about structuring shift differentials can be found in Chapter 7, "Managing Support People."

If you are running off-hours shifts, you also need to think about your own support systems, including heat for the building if the support engineers work in the office, support for the phone system, the call tracking system, and other systems you use.

The advantage of using off-hours shifts is that it's a much more robust system than either pagers or answering services. Support engineers have full access to the tools they have during regular hours, phones do not have to be rerouted, and customers should experience little difference from normal-hours support.

The disadvantages of off-hours shifts are mostly the staffing challenges they create. It's difficult to find people willing to work off-hours, it's expensive to pay them, and it's difficult to keep them (they will usually move to a normal shift when the occasion presents itself, despite the shift differentials). On top of all that, if you are running small off-hour shifts, you need to ensure that people working those hours are not beginners, since they will not have the normal support system, including not having a full-time on-premise manager.

Because of the staffing issues, and if you can come up with the infrastructure required, you may want to look at a "follow-the-sun" model. In a complete follow-the-sun model, support centers in Europe, America, and Asia provide backup for each other during their daytime hours. For instance, a center on the East Coast of the United States handles daytime hours for North America. In the evenings, calls are routed to a center in Asia or Australia, since it's now daytime in those time zones. Finally, during nighttime in North America, calls go to a European center. In the morning, calls are routed again to North America, and the North American center provides support for the whole world during North America daytime hours while the rest of the world is off.

Table 3–1 shows corresponding times in various time zones. One can see how, as the United States goes into nighttime, Asia can take over, and then Europe.

Table 3–1.   Times in Various Time Zones

Area				
East Coast	8 a.m.	12 p.m.	8 p.m.	12 a.m.
West Coast	5 a.m.	9 a.m.	5 p.m.	9 p.m.
Australia (Sydney)	11 p.m.	3 a.m.	11 a.m.	3 p.m.
Europe (Amsterdam)	2 p.m.	6 p.m.	2 a.m.	6 a.m.

The advantages of a follow-the-sun model are that it frees local centers from having to staff at night (note that it doesn't help for daytime weekend work) and that it allows support engineers to function in an environment where they have full support from other people in the office. Once the initial jitters about talking to someone on the other side of the world are over, customers are usually very satisfied with follow-the-sun models, because they provide excellent support.

The disadvantages of the follow-the-sun model are numerous and take the form of very tough infrastructure requirements. To begin with, you can only implement a follow-the-sun model if you have support centers conveniently located in the different time zones and staffed with support engineers who speak a common language. Second, you need to organize automatic forwarding of the phone lines, since customers typically will not call an overseas number for support. Finally, you need to find a way to communicate between the centers on what happened at night (typically through a common call tracking system), and you also need a way to hand off problems once a shift is over.

Although the infrastructure requirements of the follow-the-sun model are large, it need not be an expensive model if the infrastructure is already in place. Essentially, the costs then are the additional phone costs to forward the phones to the appropriate center, and the coordination overhead for problem hand-offs and general management issues that arise when working between support centers. The costs are very competitive with (read: lower than) running off-hours shifts, and since the quality is improved and the staffing headaches are gone. The follow-the-sun model is a financially advantageous proposition once the infrastructure is in place.

Because of the infrastructure requirements, the follow-the-sun model is usually reserved for large worldwide organizations, but because of its advantages for staffing and customer satisfaction you can and should be inventive if your organization doesn't qualify as large or worldwide. For instance, say you don't have a center in Asia. You can still use the European center to cover for the North American night hours, do away with the North American night shift, and staff only an evening shift in North America. North America can cover European night hours, so that you have 24-hour support both in North America and in Europe without night shifts. Even if your centers are all in North America, say you have a West Coast center and an East Coast center, you can close the East Coast center at 5 p.m. and cover the evening hours from the West, and do the reverse for early morning hours so you can open the West Coast center at 8 a.m.

One last thought: although creating a support center specifically to accomplish a follow-the-sun model may be impossible to justify from a cost point of view, the combined requirements of local customers and of follow-the-sun customers may justify a new center in a convenient location (in terms of hours and language). Also, follow-the-sun requirements should be considered when locating a new support center. For instance, locating a European center in the U.K. or in the Netherlands satisfies the language requirements to do follow-the-sun with North America better than does locating a center in Germany or in France.

In conclusion, there are many ways to implement off-hours support. Your choice should depend on volume and customer and staff requirements. This is what we recommend:

- Use the simplest, cheapest system to meet your requirements.
- Don't hesitate to mix and match. Often, you will find that the ideal solution depends on the day and time.
- For low call volume and low requirements, use a pager system. It's cheap and sufficient for low requirements. Have your ACD do the paging if possible.
- For relatively low call volume and low requirements, especially if customers want a real person to answer the phone, use an answering service.
- For high call volume, use a follow-the-sun system if possible. Otherwise, schedule shifts at home if work can be done at home and if your ACD can handle outbound calls, or use in-office shifts. If you are lucky enough to have support centers in other areas, investigate follow-the-sun. It may seem daunting at first, but in the end it's much easier than hiring and keeping staff on the night shift.

Use the flowchart in Figure 3–3 for a structured approach to choosing the right off-hours support model for you.

Choosing an Off-hours Model

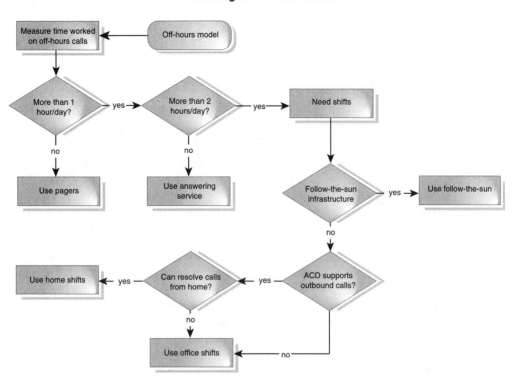

Figure 3–3

3.1.3 Scheduling Support Staff

This section covers issues related with scheduling staff and focuses on a big issue for support centers: matching staffing levels with call levels—that is, scheduling for peaks and valleys. Staffing models (which are discussed in Chapter 7, "Managing Support People"), can only predict staffing at the high level. In order to adapt your staffing to the actual needs of the customer, you need to dig deeper into when staff is needed. This is particularly important in high-volume environments. The variables to consider include:

- Time of day
- Day of the week
- Day of the month
- Quarter and year-end
- Holiday periods
- Right after a new release is shipped

Only experience can tell what the relevant variables are for you and how they affect call volume. Support centers that support business customers are usually busier during the day, with some slack at lunch time. However, if you support several time zones, their combination may fluctuate differently, as shown earlier in this chapter. If you support home users, you may be busier in the evening and on weekends. Business customers tend to call more heavily during the middle of the week. Financial applications tend to require heavier support at quarter and year-end.

You need to determine what your call load is for each hour of the day and to analyze whether the call volume and the patterns throughout the day vary with the day of the week and the other variables mentioned above. If your customer base remains stable, your load distribution over time should not change much either, although volume will vary. Use data from your ACD or your call tracking system. In very high-volume situations, you may want to track load by half-hour rather than by hour to get a finer level of analysis.

Once you define the load, define your staffing levels. You may want to use your experience, coupled with a high-level capacity model such as the one we discuss in Chapter 7, as a guide. For a more theoretical, robust, and mathematically-based approach, we invite you to discover and use the Erlang method in Appendix C. The method and the staffing software packages that use it may seem to be overkill for small support centers, but it's worth understanding the method. If you have a high-volume center, you may well want to use the method and even to purchase a staffing package based on it.

Once you determine, either with the Erlang method or based on your experience, what the staffing levels must be throughout the day, map out an actual schedule. Maintaining appropriate staffing levels is key in a support center. Even small deviations from the norm can create large breakdowns in the speed of response to customers (see our discussion on the Erlang method for examples). Share the models with your staff and make scheduling a group responsibility: everyone must understand the criticality of maintaining the necessary staffing level.

Your staff schedule should target the on-phone time, taking into account all variations, from breaks to sick days, and plan for them. If your call volume varies according to normal business norms, you will find that your scheduling is easy, since your staff's preferences will match the customer's preferences.

With a small center, you can draw up a schedule by hand. A simple spreadsheet should suit your needs in a medium-size center. For a large center, especially with a high volume of calls, you may want to invest in a scheduling package, perhaps an adjunct of a staffing software package.

Table 3–2 is a sample schedule for a West Coast support center. "P" stands for phone time, "V" for vacation. The staffing targets may be derived from past experience or the Erlang method. You can easily implement the table with your favorite spreadsheet, using one schedule for each queue.

Table 3–2.   Sample Schedule

Schedule for: Wednesday, May 15th

Time	6	7	8	9	10	11	12	1	2	3	4
Staffing	2	5	6	8	6	5	4	5	4	3	2
anna	P	P	P	P		P	P				
bridget	P	P	P	P		P	P				
chandra		P	P	P	P		P	P			
daniel		P	P	P	P		P	P			
eliza		P	P	P	P			P	P		
frances			P	P	P	P		P	P	P	
george				P	P	P		P	P	P	P
hugh	V	V	V	V	V	V	V	V	V	V	V
indro				P	P	P			P	P	P

Anna and bridget are on the 6 a.m. shift; chandra, daniel, and eliza start at 7. Note that if any of these people should be off one day, you would need to schedule someone to come in early to cover the 6–8 staffing requirement (assuming hugh works a regular shift). Frances and george are scheduled for 7 hours on the phone when everyone else is scheduled for 6, perhaps to compensate for hugh's being on vacation.

The schedule is built with blocks of two to four hours. If you have more flexibility, either because your calls are on the short side or because your team is larger, stick with two-hour blocks; it's more pleasant for the support engineers and it's easier to implement (can you answer the phone for four hours straight?).

In summary, study the patterns in your call load, review them continuously against the new data that's generated every day, and create a schedule based on the load. This should not be a difficult undertaking, although it is time-consuming and somewhat tedious. The consequences of not scheduling properly are very dire. If you have a large center, consider investing in a staffing and scheduling package.

3.1.4　Toll-free Numbers and 900 Numbers

If you are running an internal help desk, a regular phone extension is probably all you need (You may want to secure a number that is easy to remember, however.)

If you have external customers, then you should think about the necessity of providing a toll-free number. Toll-free numbers can be costly, since you pay the phone bill. On the other hand, your customers may expect one. Before you make a decision one way or another, think about the following points.

- Competitive requirement: if your competitors all provide a toll-free number, you may have to provide one, too.
- Competitive advantage: if your competitors do not provide a toll-free number, you may be able to differentiate your service by using one. Be sure it would indeed make a difference to your customers. For instance, toll-free numbers may not seem like a big benefit to corporate users, since they may not pay their phone bill directly.
- Differentiation for high-level offerings: an easy way to differentiate your support offerings is to offer a toll-free number for the higher levels.
- Cost: with a toll-free number, you pay the phone bill. You pay for time on hold, and you pay for talk time. It can add up. However, if you use a callback system, where customers leave a message and the support engineers call them back, it may not make much of a difference, since you originate most of the calls anyway (we do not recommend using a callback system, however). Also, if you support a complex product where many questions require calls back and forth, customer-initiated phone calls constitute but a small part of the phone cost.
- Rerouting flexibility: toll-free numbers can be rerouted easily either on a schedule (for follow-the-sun) or in an emergency (whether you or the phone company require it). It can make the difference in your choice.

If you are still unsure of what to choose, start without a toll-free number. It's always easy to add one later, since customers will perceive it as a benefit.

If you bill customers for their support calls, you may want to use a 900 number. With a 900 number, the phone company bills your customers by the call or by the minute in exchange for a percentage of the revenue. Note that some companies block 900 numbers, so you may want to check that your customers can indeed reach you. 900 numbers also have a limit on the amount that can be charged through them, so they may not meet your needs if your calls are expensive.

There are other ways to handle billing customers when they call, rather than using a 900 number. In particular, you can use a toll-free or a regular number and do your own billing. You are also free to mix and match approaches—for instance, have an 800 number for your contract customers and a 900 number for customers who pay per call.

So far, we have talked about when and how the calls come in. It's time to move on to how the calls are processed when they are received: the phone interface.

3.2 PHONE INTERFACE

There are essentially two ways to handle calls as they come in: handle the problem on the spot or call the customer back. Each method has variations, and your choice depends on logistics, customer requirements, financial investment, and the size of group. We will first describe three methods for handling incoming calls: through a receptionist, a dedicated Dispatch function, and directly to the support engineer, and then give some recommendations on what to choose.

3.2.1 Receptionist

Using a receptionist is a basic method, commonly found in small support centers that do not, because of their size, justify other mechanisms to handle calls. Calls come into a shared receptionist, although usually on their own (support) number. It's better to have a dedicated support number because it allows you to handle support calls differently, either right away or in the future, and also to account for them more easily. The receptionist greets the customer, confirms the problem, and either patches the customer to a support engineer (if one is available) or takes a message for a callback. Alternatively, the support engineers can take turns monitoring the support line, with the receptionist handling any overflow.

The obvious advantage of the receptionist model is its simplicity: it can be piggybacked on the existing administrative structure. In addition, customers always reach a real person who can help locate resources and give a good picture of any potential delay. Finally, support engineers usually like having someone else screen calls for them.

The disadvantages of the receptionist model are that the receptionist is likely to be busy with other tasks and unable to devote much time and energy to Technical Support calls. If receptionists change frequently, it may be a challenge to keep them trained even on the basics of support calls. Also, since receptionists will not be technically knowledgeable, the quality of messages or triaging they can do is often very low. Customers may feel that they are an unneeded obstacle in their quest to get a problem resolved and, from the efficiency point of view, it adds a step to the processing of the call without adding much value. Finally, and especially for low-complexity software support, working with callbacks is inherently inefficient.

A superior variation of the receptionist model is for the support engineers to take turns answering the support hotline and for the receptionist to handle overflow only.

In any case, any support center of a reasonable size (say, beyond 10 support engineers) will overwhelm the capacity of a shared receptionist, which brings us to the next level up: a dedicated dispatch function.

3.2.2   Dedicated Dispatch Function

The idea behind a dedicated Dispatch function is very simple: provide one or several administrative staff members whose mission it is to ensure that problems find an owner as quickly as possible. The word *Dispatch* comes from the old hardware support model under which an individual would be physically sent to the customer's site, so it's neither modern nor accurate. We would prefer to say *Customer Service* or even *Support Concierge*, but Dispatch is the most commonly used word.

Call dispatchers have the following responsibilities:

- Greet the customer.
- Confirm that the customer is a valid customer. This is particularly important if customers have to pay for support or if support is restricted in any other way. For an internal help desk, this step is a cursory request for a name and a phone number.
- Get a description of the problem and find an owner for it. If you have reached the stage where you can support a dedicated Dispatch function, you will also have an on-line call tracking system.

In this case the dispatcher will log the problem into the call tracking system (this requires basic technical knowledge to at least recognize the technical words being used). Based on the problem description and the call flow mechanism, the dispatcher will either transfer the call to an available support engineer or queue the problem for a callback.

If the Dispatch group is large, you will need an ACD (automatic call distribution) phone system to distribute calls to the dispatchers in an efficient way. The ACD will help you ensure that customers spend as little time on hold as possible. The accounting features of the ACD will also help you count and classify calls, a very useful feature for planning purposes.

The advantages of a dedicated Dispatch function over a shared receptionist are many. You now have a professional support administrator who is knowledgeable about how Support works, who will, over time, learn enough technical terms to converse with customers and engineers alike, who can validate customers, who can use the call tracking system, which a receptionist may not have the time or the skills to learn, and who can get the call to a support engineer with the specific product knowledge required.

The disadvantages of a dedicated Dispatch group are similar to those of the receptionist system: although some value is added to the transaction (the customer is validated, the call is logged), the first person customers talk to does very little to resolve their technical problem. Also, since you need a dispatcher for every 8 to 10 support engineers, the Dispatch group is likely to be small, creating the usual scheduling problems of small groups. Finally, as with a receptionist system, a Dispatch system that uses callbacks is inefficient, more so when calls take little time to resolve.

To remedy the issue of the first call going to someone who essentially adds no value to the transaction, you need to use technology—an ACD—to route the call directly to support engineers. Technological advances have made it much easier and cheaper to use ACD even for small groups, and the newer ACDs, properly programmed, alleviate most of the "phone ogre" feel of earlier ones. We strongly discourage using the receptionist or the dispatch and callback methods; they are not conducive to customer satisfaction and they are not efficient.

3.2.3   ACD to Support Engineer

The main difference of this method compared to the other two is that the support engineer is the first person the customer talks to. The phone system automatically routes the call to an available engineer, based on customer and product information if appropriate. From the customer's perspective, there is no time wasted discussing the problem with someone who cannot help them, and no frustration waiting for a callback at an unknown time. From your point of view, there is no time wasted trying to reach a customer who stepped away from the phone.

Modern ACDs can do much more than greet the customer and route the call to the first available support engineer. To start, they can and should handle necessary administrative functions. One is customer validation. Typically, the customer will be asked to enter an ID number and will be allowed through the phone tree if it is a valid number (see Figure 3–4). If not, the customer will be routed to an administrative function. (Therefore the Dispatch function does not disappear completely under this model, it just takes on more specialized, value-added functions.)

Once the customer has been validated, the call is routed to the next available support engineer. If the support center is organized by specialties, the call must be classified accordingly by giving the customer a menu of options to choose from. Menus must be short enough to be user-friendly, yet complete enough to make selection possible. Designing effective ACD trees (the entire selection set) and menus (the selection set at each level of the tree) is an art of which we can offer only glimpses. ACD vendors, who typically offer design services as part of their sales cycle, are a good source of help. Here are some general recommendations:

- Keep the number of levels in the phone tree as small as possible, if possible to less than three.

- Organize menus logically, and place the most popular items first whenever possible.

- In each menu include an option to request a repeat of the descriptions of the items on the menu and an option to back up to the last menu.

- Use mnemonic options if possible, and in any case be consistent. For instance, using "1" for "priority 1 call" is mnemonic, always using "9" as the option to go back to the last menu is consistent. This allows customers to enter strings of digits once they get used to the system without having to listen to the system prompts.

- At logical levels in the tree, include an "Operator" function (0, of course) to escape from the electronic ogre to a real person (this highlights another function of the Dispatch group under an ACD system: providing routing help to customers).

Sample ACD Tree

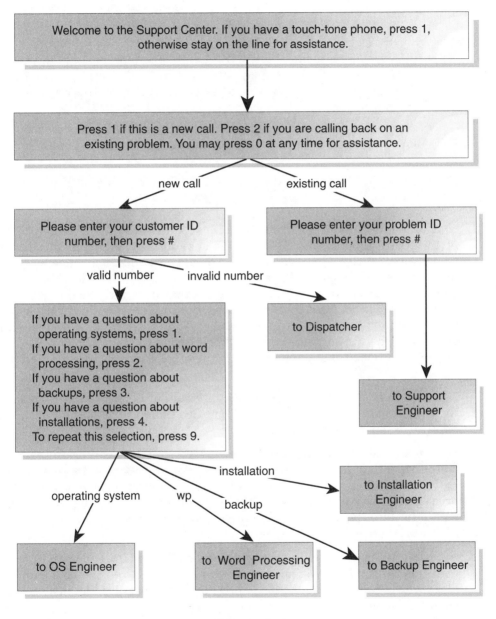

Figure 3–4

- Ask for only the absolute minimum information that is necessary to route the call. For instance, if your center is organized by geography and you ask customers to enter an ID number for validation purposes, have the ACD and its interface to your customer tracking system determine the geographical area from the ID number; do not ask customers to designate their location.

- Plan for off-hours menu trees. If you have a minimum staff during certain times, you will need a different tree for each configuration. Good ACDs allow you to store a variety of trees that are triggered at different times.

- Thoroughly test your ACD tree with real customers. Choices that sound obvious to you may be confusing to customers, especially in real time.

- Invest in a professional recording of the options. It's well worth the cost.

In addition to menu design, you should ensure you are taking full advantage of the many functions of modern ACDs to make the customer interface friendly and efficient. In particular, you should customize hold-time messages and options so customers have an idea of how long the hold time will be (whether in actual time, if you can predict that accurately, or in number of calls ahead of them), and they can choose their preferred option: wait, leave a voicemail message, or talk to a dispatcher. You can also allow customers to customize what (if anything) they will hear while they are waiting. We have already mentioned that support tips can be a good choice instead of on-hold music.

Some ACDs offer voice-recognition capabilities that allow customers to speak their choices rather than pushing buttons. See Chapter 9, "Tools for Technical Software Support," for more details.

You should also choose an ACD that allows you to juggle call priorities based on the urgency of the call and the customer type, rather than be locked into a strict first-in, first-out system. If you allow high-priority calls to override low-priority ones, be sure to model what happens to the low-ranking calls if many high-priority ones come in. Will they be on hold forever? You may want to limit wait time to a certain value.

ACDs can be used for return phone calls as well. If the ACD has an interface with the call tracking system, customers can be routed to the engineer handling it by punching in their problem ID number. Otherwise, the customer can enter the engineer's phone extension.

The key advantage of an ACD system is that customers get to talk to a support engineer right away. If you can set up a system where the wait time is acceptable, customers will prefer it to any other method.

The disadvantages of using an ACD are few, and most arise when switching away from a Dispatch system; if you implement an ACD right away, you will encounter very few problems. The drawbacks of ACDs are the high fixed cost (although that is offset over time by the smaller expense for the Dispatch group), the maintenance costs, both hardware and software, and the fact that many support engineers do not like direct call systems because they have no idea what the next call will bring. This last one is particularly an issue when switching from a Dispatch system to an ACD. In that situation, you will need to sell the system to the support engineers by emphasizing the efficiency (for them) of the ACD: no more phone tag, no more frustration trying to meet response time, and happier customers. Switching to an ACD may provoke some turnover of support engineers who lack the skill or interest to cope with incoming calls. This is a short-term loss, because you can hire individuals with this skill and interest. The people who depart will be happier and more successful in a different role.

What about customers? Sometimes the argument is made that people don't like to interact with machines and that a personal interface with a Dispatch group is preferable to a machine. This has not been our experience with software users, maybe because they are more predisposed toward technology than the general population. Generally speaking, the benefit of talking to a technical person right away outweighs the disadvantages of the ACD. As ACD usage spreads for other applications, acceptance of the technology should increase. Also, modern, well-programmed ACDs allow for much improved user interfaces, and in particular allow customers to request to talk to a live person when needed or desired.

One last point: if you are switching from a Dispatch system to an ACD and your staffing is inadequate, implementing the ACD will expose the staffing problem, which was (partly) masked by the old Dispatch system. Customers will end up spending a lot of time on hold. If they have an option of talking to a dispatcher, they will use it in large numbers, and your fancy ACD system will degenerate to the old Dispatch model. You will have wasted your hardware investment and have unhappy customers (and staff). The bottom line is that an ACD in itself will not resolve a situation where there are too few support engineers (although it will free up some dispatchers who may become support engineers with the right training). We will see later how to determine appropriate staffing levels.

3.2.4   What model should you implement?

We have discussed three phone interface models: the receptionist model, the dedicated Dispatch group model, and the ACD-to-support-engineer model. Here are some rules of thumb for choosing the phone interface that's right for you.

- If your Support group is very small (fewer than five or six support engineers) and you have the option of sharing an existing receptionist, take it. Set up a schedule for the support engineers to pick up the calls as a default with the receptionist handling the overflow. Avoid working with callbacks.

- As soon as your Support group grows to eight to ten people, investigate the option of an ACD, especially for an internal help desk. Basic ACDs, without validating or fancy routing options, are very affordable.

- If you have external customers and customer validation is a concern, find an ACD that can handle validation, at least in most cases. It is wasteful to have support engineers perform administrative functions, even when the validation can be done very quickly.

- Avoid the no-value-added Dispatch model. With an ACD, your administrative group can handle both the problematic customer validations and the nontechnical questions. Under this model, you shouldn't need more than one dispatcher for 10 to 15 support engineers.

In conclusion, we advocate an ACD system because it gives customers the most efficient and satisfying option. If you are currently running with a Dispatch system, consider switching. You should be able to make a financial case for buying an ACD over a one- to two-year period based on reduced personnel costs alone. The big obstacle is to sell the idea to the support engineers. If your staffing is adequate, there is no reason why you should not be able to do it.

We are now ready to turn to a key issue in call flow: routing the call to the right support engineer.

3.3 CALL ROUTING

The idea of call routing is to direct the call to the most appropriate support engineer so that the issue can be resolved as quickly and as well as possible. If you have a very small group where there are no specialties, your routing is simple: send the call to whomever is available. If your group is larger or if you have defined product or customer specialties, as discussed in the previous chapter, you need to spend some time establishing call routing procedures.

The tricky part of call routing is that speed is of the essence. You want to be able to route accurately, yet quickly, so you spend as little of the resolution time as possible routing the call. Testing the routing is a great test of your specialty definition: if an average customer cannot self-route, your categories need redefining.

This section applies regardless of what your phone interface you use. If you have an ACD, you will program the routing into the machine (that is, the phone tree is equivalent to the routing algorithm). If you have a Dispatch group, the dispatchers will execute the routing.

3.3.1 Handling Nontechnical Questions

Some of the problems coming to you will be of an administrative nature: incorrect media shipped, need to alter the support agreement in some way, need to order an upgrade or documentation, etc. It should be relatively easy to distinguish administrative issues from technical ones. Especially with external customers, the percentage of nontechnical questions could range from 10% to as high as 50% if you are responsible for handling upgrade requests.

Generally speaking, it's best to have nontechnical staff handle such questions. Our recommendation is to have the Dispatch group handle them. That is, avoid having both a Dispatch group who takes care of validation issues and phone overflow *and* a Customer Service group who handles nontechnical questions. For a small support center, critical mass requirements alone prohibit it. Even if your center is large enough to support separate groups, combining the functions makes for more interesting work and prevents having to bounce customers to several parties to resolve "small" issues.

Nontechnical questions should be tracked in the same way as technical questions, using an on-line call tracking system if you have one.

3.3.2 Routing

We will now discuss technical problems only, and only in contexts where you have set up product or customer specialties. Routing refers to the process by which calls find an owner. If you are using an ACD, queuing is done through the ACD. If not, routing is done by the Dispatch staff through the call tracking system.

First, you need to define the routing algorithm. It should follow the same rules mentioned in the ACD section (3.2.3). In particular, it should have as few decision points as possible and no more than three, and it should be very easy to use even for nonexperts, whether customers or dispatchers are doing the routing. Once you have defined an algorithm, ensure that each end point corresponds to a physical group in the support center. If you are having difficulty contriving a routing algorithm, it is a clue that you need to make major changes in the way you organize your specialty groups.

Once the routing algorithm is defined, it needs to be implemented in the call tracking system, and, if you have an ACD, in its call control tables, which define the phone tree. Modern call tracking systems enable you to define "queues"—that is, logical areas where calls of similar nature accumulate. You need one queue for each end point in the algorithm—for instance, a Word Processor queue and an Operating System queue, a Western Area queue and an Eastern Area queue, or whatever your algorithm is.

If you do not use an ACD but you have a dedicated Dispatch group instead, investigate whether the call tracking system can include a basic routing function that integrates the routing algorithm you defined so the task of the dispatcher is automated. This is not as daunting and artificial intelligence-like as it sounds. For instance, most call tracking systems record the type of software used and where the customer is calling from, so you should be able to implement most product and geography-based algorithms easily.

In a dedicated Dispatch system, the dispatcher places incoming calls in the appropriate queue based on the routing algorithm, then tells the customer that a callback will occur within a given amount of time. If the call volume is high, the support engineers assigned to the queue constantly monitor it (by looking at the call tracking system) and return the calls based on their urgency. We will discuss this further in the next section. Alternatively, the dispatcher pages or otherwise signals the support engineer that a call is waiting for them.

There are no absolute rules that govern how many queues you should have, beyond the critical mass principle. Queues are useful only for sorting incoming calls and managing the day-to-day business, so there should be as few as possible. Question any queue that corresponds to a group of fewer than five support engineers. Also question your queuing mechanism if any support engineer or manager must monitor more than a couple of queues (one is ideal).

Queues are sorting mechanisms only. Use another mechanism to run statistics on your calls. For instance, say you support several word processing packages and you want to know how many calls you get on each. If your routing algorithm is that all word processing calls go into the same group, you should have one word processing queue and count the kinds of calls in another way: by picking up the actual product name in the call, by using some kind of closure code, or even by placing calls in different queues when closing them.

Routing is only one aspect of getting calls to the right person quickly. You may need to have some kind of sorting mechanism to ensure that the most urgent requests are handled first. In other words, you need to have a priority scheme in place. We will look at that next.

3.3.3 Setting Priorities on Calls

Priorities define the severity of the problems and capture the impact to the customer. Priorities are useful to define what calls get handled first, and also what calls get more resources. Your support center may not benefit from setting priorities, however, in the following situations:

- Your customer problems are pretty much all the same with respect to severity.
- The overhead of setting priorities is prohibitive: typically, if your average call is short (say under 10 minutes), you are taking calls directly off an ACD, and most issues are resolved during the initial phone call, it's a waste to define priorities.

In many support centers, however, priorities allow a crude sorting (some would say triage) mechanism to allocate resources to the most important problems first. We strongly recommend you define a priority scheme if:

- You work with a callback mechanism.
- The problems you handle typically require several interactions and are likely to last beyond a business day.

The first step is to define priority levels. It does not really matter how many you have, as long as they can be easily distinguished by the average customer. A common setup is to have three priority levels.

- *Priority 1: emergency*: the software cannot be operated, with severe consequences to the user. For instance: all data entry is suspended, a manufacturing line is down, a critical company system is down, key data has been lost.
- *Priority 2: urgent*: there is some severe problem with the software, but the effects are not as devastating as for priority 1. For instance, only some, noncritical functions, maybe only one person is affected (so for them it's a P1, but in the big scheme of things it's a P2), or there is some kind of a workaround for the problem.
- *Priority 3: regular*: there is a slight problem with the software, or the user has a how-to question.

You should have a definition of the priorities in your formal support agreement as well as in your Support User's Guide, if you have one. In addition, each and every member of the support center should be very clear on how to classify problems. Spend time thinking through actual examples relevant to your user community. As much as possible, you want the priorities to be intuitive to everyone—customers and support engineers alike. Having clear priority definitions speeds up the negotiated expectations discussion which will take place at the beginning of each support conversation.

Priorities are important, because, all things being equal, high-priority calls will get more resources and faster than others. To start with, high-priority calls will be responded to faster than others. State of the art, at least for external customers, is immediate response for priority 1, no more than a business day for priority 3. This is another argument in favor of an ACD, since immediate response is difficult to achieve without an ACD technology. Internal help desk customers tend to be somewhat less demanding than external customers. Also, response times can be tuned according to the service level for a particular customer.

If you have an ACD, consider giving customers with high-priority issues the option to jump to the top of the line. Although there is a human tendency to want the best service, customers are surprisingly well behaved when they see that choosing a lower, more reasonable priority today will mean better service when they have an emergency tomorrow. If you choose to let high-ranking calls override low-ranking calls, make sure the low-ranking calls do get a turn and do not remain in the queue forever, being overtaken by high-ranking ones.

You may find, with or without an ACD, that the trend is for customers to set their own priorities. As mentioned above, most customers are respectful of the guidelines, but a few will abuse the system and inflate their priorities. First, make sure that the priorities are defined clearly to avoid confusion. If you have abusers, have a dialog with them to reaffirm the priorities and request that they not abuse the system. Refrain from taking priority setting privileges away from your customers for the sake of a few recalcitrant ones.

Priorities are usually set at the beginning of a call, but they should be dynamic. What is an emergency situation can be downgraded to urgent if a suitable workaround is found, and vice versa. Having proper priorities at all times will help you prioritize the work at any point in time, not just when the problem is reported. We will see how priorities can help you organize the work when we talk about running a support center in Chapter 4.

3.3.4   Response Time

Response time is the time between when a customer calls the support center with a question and when she gets to start exploring the problem with a support engineer. Response time is a key concept and metric for callback systems. If you are using an ACD, the time the customer spends on hold, although closely related to the notion of response time, is usually called "hold time," and you would be using response time to refer to those situations when the customer chooses to leave a message and be called back. Under an ACD scenario, you may also use the idea of response time to mean the time it takes for the customer to get help if the problem is not readily solvable within a few minutes of phone conversation. In other words, response time becomes the time between the first and the second conversation, although the perception by the customer is always more important than this theoretical definition.

The idea of response time is essential if you are operating on a callback system. You will want to define callback times based on the call priority (ideally, immediate transition for emergency calls, no more than 8 hours for nonurgent items). Once the targets are established, keep careful track of your performance in meeting them. If the performance is not where it should be, investigate why and take action to fix it.

Your on-line call tracking system should help you monitor and meet response time by calculating response time based on the priority and the customer type, and by displaying unanswered calls in the order in which they need to be handled. Once the queue is established, you can either have support engineers grab calls from the queue or assign the calls automatically. If support engineers grab calls, you can further have them grab the most urgent call first, or you can allow some latitude in grabbing calls based on expertise.

We recommend you use a random assignment mechanism, for two reasons: (1) It makes for much faster call assignment—and we have mentioned before that you should spend as little time as possible routing calls to an owner. (2) It makes for a more even distribution of calls, as everyone grabbing from the queue gets a mix of easy and difficult calls, thereby avoiding the "cherry-picking" phenomenon. If random assignment does not work well, it's a sign you should review your specialty groups: they are probably too wide to allow support engineers sufficient expertise in their domain. Random assignment models are tricky because they must consider whether people are available and what their load is. This is yet another reason to consider an ACD, since resolving availability issues is the logic embedded in ACD systems.

One last thought about switching from callbacks to ACDs: if you consistently beat your published target response times, your customers will start expecting shorter response times. It's a good time to reconsider your decision to work with a callback system. Talking directly to a support engineer on the first call is the wave of the future, indeed the wave of today for quality support.

In summary, response time is the initial time it takes to start working on the problem. Response time is a key concern in callback-based scenarios, less important in ACDs since hold time is usually more important. Meeting or beating response time is only the beginning, however. What really matters is how long it takes to resolve the problem. Let's explore that now.

3.3.5 Resolution Time

Resolution time is the time between when the problem is reported and when the solution is accepted by the customer. In other words, resolution time measures the time it takes to go through the Basic Action Workflow. Note that customers are always pushing for faster and faster resolution times as a general business trend, and support centers' customers are no exception.

Resolution time is sometimes called work time and, for support centers where questions are resolved within one phone call, is the length of that phone call including any wrap-up time.

By definition, resolution time exceeds response time, and it's much more difficult to predict and contain. Resolution time can be almost instantaneous for "easy" questions. On the other hand, if an issue requires a bug fix, it could take weeks or months! Therefore, although customers are always pushing for commitments on resolution time, it's a dangerous business to make one until you can be certain of the work that is necessary and can rely on the promises of any other departments who must contribute to the resolution.

Resolution time is tightly dependent on having a well-defined objective at the beginning of the support conversation (to use the terms from the last chapter, a well-defined mutual agreement). In particular, it's important to define what kind of solution is acceptable, and especially that the solution may be a workaround to a bug as opposed to an actual bug fix. Bug fix procedures, including what kinds of bugs will be fixed, what kinds of bugs will be worked around, and what time frames to expect for fixes should certainly be defined formally in the service-level agreement. More about bug fixes in Chapter 8.

Always let the customer determine when a problem is resolved. Again, if the mutual agreement was well understood at the beginning, it should be relatively easy to present the customer with a solution and obtain confirmation that the problem has indeed been resolved. It's often handy to give the customer a few days to test the solution rather than to press for a close. Occasionally, the customer will lose interest, or so it will seem, and will be unwilling to return phone calls. Put in place a policy of making reasonable attempts to contact the customer and closing the problem if you don't get a response. For instance, three unanswered calls over a two-week period could be a criteria you can use.

Keeping resolution time low is a key concern for support managers. We will explore techniques for monitoring resolution time in Chapter 4, "Measuring Support Center Performance."

3.3.6   Criteria for Call Transitions

Depending on the call management model you use, you will have from few to many call transitions (or call hand-offs). Call transitions are tricky because transitions are where information gets lost causing additional work and frustrations for customers and support engineers alike. In the previous chapter and this one, we discussed at length ways to minimize hand-offs, including appropriate queuing and routing strategies, and using a Touch and Hold model rather than the traditional Frontline/Backline model. You should periodically review your call hand-offs to ensure they are kept to a minimum.

Regardless of what you do, you will have some call hand-offs. If you are using a Frontline/Backline model, you will have the hand-offs from Frontline to Backline. If a group different from yours handles bug fixes (the usual setup), you will transition bug descriptions to that group (although usually not customers; we discuss bug fixing models and recommendations in Chapter 8, "Managing Software Bugs and Code Fixes"). With any model, you will have occasional call hand-offs when a support engineer goes on vacation or to training and needs someone to take care of the open problems.

To minimize issues associated with hand-offs, you should have some kind of a checklist, which the support engineer fills out before passing the call on. A senior support engineer should be able to come up with a checklist in a couple of days. The checklist should include basic information about the customer configuration, a crisp definition of the problem and the requested resolution, and a list of steps already taken.

The list should be kept on-line and be part of the call tracking system. Note that a well-organized support engineer will have all the elements of the checklist already defined and stored in the call tracking system. The checklist is just a method to get all the relevant information together in one place.

Checklists can also be used in other ways, most obviously as a problem solving checklist for each support engineer (they are lists of information that must be gathered to resolve problems). Checklists can be such a good tool that you may want to maintain different ones for each product or type of problems you encounter. You can also share the checklists with your customers, sometimes putting them right in your Support User's Guide and suggesting that customers gather that information before calling you.

At this point, we have covered the fundamentals of call routing, including how to route calls when they come in, concepts such as priorities, response time, and resolution time, and practical matters such as hand-offs. We now turn our attention to calls that are outside the norms: escalations.

3.4 ESCALATION MANAGEMENT

In this context, *escalation* refers to calls involving customers who are not satisfied with the way their issues are being resolved and that normally require management intervention to resolve. We covered a number of points about the escalation handling model in the last chapter, most notably:

- There are three types of escalations: service, sales, and technical.

- The support center must own the resolution of all escalations, even those requiring that other groups be involved in the resolution process, such as sales escalations or technical escalations

- Escalations are nothing more than a special category of customer requests, so they can always be handled through the same model: the Basic Action Workflow.

- You may want to have a dedicated escalation function, including dedicated escalation support engineers, rather than to have the regular support engineers work them, and you may want a support manager to drive them if you have many escalations, since escalations tend to require considerable amounts of time and do rely on special skills.

- Post-mortem analyses should be conducted once escalations are completed to spot process and personnel issues and resolve them before they create another escalation.

Next we discuss practical aspects of escalation handling: how to minimize escalations, how to funnel them into your organization, and how to organize the work during an escalation.

3.4.1   Minimizing Escalations

Escalations are a sign that something's not working properly, so rather than assigning more and more resources to handle them, you should invest in making sure the basics work. Are you meeting your response times? If not, why not, and what can you do to change it? Are customers unhappy with the professionalism of your people? What can you do about it? Is the problem with resolution time? Enlist your staff to work on a solution. The idea is to prevent rather than to cure.

To minimize escalations, start with an analysis of reasons why escalations occur. Be honest with yourself. If most escalations come from customers' negative perceptions of your staff and a few from product issues, attack the professionalism issue first. You may want to do the review on a regular basis. In addition, you may want to enlist customers (especially if they are internal) as well as members of other groups within the company to give you a broader, less biased perspective.

Remember that escalations are likely to increase cyclically: often on Fridays, when customers are ready to wrap up their week and get impatient that problems are not resolved; in many instances at month-end or quarter-end when problems have magnified consequences and systems are hitting peak loads and therefore are more likely to fail; and, if you have external customers, at the end of your company's fiscal year when the push for revenue is highest. Anticipate and accept the peaks and do not confuse them for genuine process issues.

3.4.2 Managing the Start of Escalations

Once you have done all you can to minimize escalations by strengthening your base model, the next steps are to define a process to route escalations from customers to the right person quickly, and to recognize and handle potential escalations and to handle them before they blow up.

Everyone in your group and your management chain should know to contact you (or an appropriate individual on your staff) when they receive a call from an irate customer. They are welcome to talk to the customer, get specifics on the issue, and promise to help, but they should stay away from making promises that cannot be kept. The customer has already likely suffered from that. Also, they should put you in the loop right away. This will require you to educate them in this regard.

You should also train your entire staff to recognize situations that are likely to turn into escalations. It's much easier to initiate contact with a customer (and, if possible, with the customer's management) and provide reassurance that you are working on a problem rather than waiting for the customer to call. If nothing else, initiating the call makes the customer feel that there is a process to spot problems and that someone cares. Consequently, you save a lot of effort trying to regain the spirit of collaboration down the line. The main obstacle is that support engineers sometimes take it as a matter of pride that their calls do not escalate, so you will need to do some convincing that proactive escalations are the "good" kind. We will see in Chapter 4 how you can put in place some monitoring to spot potential issues.

Finally, put in place an alert mechanism to notify senior management of escalations so they can demonstrate their knowledge of the situation should they get a direct call from the customer. The alert mechanism should also cover significant changes in the escalation situations. Customize your alerts depending on the size or importance of the customer.

3.4.3 Handling Escalations

At this point, you've done everything you can to prevent escalations, you've educated your staff and your management on routing escalations and proto-escalations to you, and now you have an escalation. What do you do? (See Figure 3–5.)

Escalation Workflow

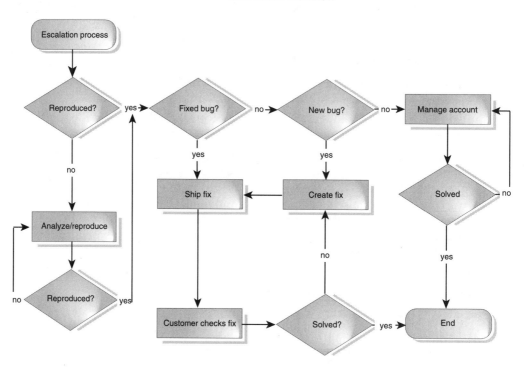

Figure 3–5

- Route it to the proper person as quickly as possible. This will typically be the manager of the support engineer who owns the call. If several managers are involved, pick one. Speed is important here.

- Decide whether a formal escalation process is warranted, using whatever criteria are relevant for your support center. Typical criteria include the severity of the impact of the problem to the customer, the technical complexity of the problem, the increased workload on the operations manager, and the strategic and financial importance of the customer to the support center or the company, as well as whether a formal process will indeed expedite resolution.

- If it is a "simple" issue, resolve it quickly by assigning the proper resource to it. Be particularly meticulous about expediting resolution and ensuring the customer is satisfied with the solution. Nontechnical escalations have only one step in the flowchart: "manage the account" (it's not always a quick step, however).

- If a formal process is warranted, start by taking stock of what is known so far. Many times, confusion is the main problem. By concentrating all the information available, patterns may emerge, and at least holes will become obvious. If you have checklists for your calls, complete one now. Determine who needs to be kept informed. In particular, define **one** path from the customer to the support center. (It's OK, and actually recommended, to have one management path and one technical path, but more than those two simply confuse the issues.) If you have an escalation function, it should take over at this point.

- Do what is needed from the technical point of view. It may be necessary to assign a new support engineer to the case because more expertise is required, or because your process requires it, or sometimes because the customer will no longer work with the support engineer who was handling the issue. Make sure the hand-off is smooth.

- Create a formal, written action plan to resolve the issue. The action plan is both a blueprint for action internally and an excellent tool. The action plan is revised throughout the life of the escalation. This is a key step, and, although there should be some kind of action plan to resolve each call, an escalation action plan needs to be both better defined and more formally communicated than that for an ordinary call. Store and maintain the plan within your call tracking system.

- Drive the plan to conclusion, updating it as new information is available. Keep in touch with the customer on an agreed-upon schedule. Depending on the particular circumstances, this could be as often as daily or, in extreme situations, even, hourly. Both parties should always be clear about when the next interaction will occur.

- As discussed in Chapter 2, prepare a post-mortem analysis of the escalation once it's over to pinpoint process failures and avoid them in the future.

If you depend on other organizations, internally or externally, to resolve issues—for instance, if bug fixes are generated outside your organization—you must work closely with those organizations both before and during escalations to ensure success. In particular:

- Set up escalation processes with those groups so escalations can be handled quickly and as painlessly as possible. Having a process will also help you manage the customers' expectations and emotions. Walking a customer through your internal processes is a powerful tool to define minimum fix times and give a sense of progress as milestones are reached. The customer is not left to expect the impossible and thus become more frustrated and dissatisfied when it does not occur. These conversations help to develop trust, as the customer sees you are open with the process that is being used to resolve the issue.

- Define a reporting process for escalations. This could be as simple as a "hot calls" meeting held daily with the Engineering group, or as complex as a formal report sent to various executives and reviewed at the executive level. Visibility is important.

- Negotiate clear, mutually understood commitments from the various groups on what is required for each escalation.

Escalations can be stressful and always require much additional work. By setting up a process to handle them, you can minimize the additional effort and trauma they cause. By adding post-mortem analyses you can decrease their occurrence and severity: that is a real benefit to you and to your customers. Escalations are a source of much waste in Support organizations. Reducing the number of escalations will, by itself, make your organization more productive.

Moving on to less stressful topics, we will now consider electronic support and proactive support in general.

3.5   NON-PHONE BASED SUPPORT

So far, we have discussed how to handle incoming phone requests. There are other ways to receive requests: letters, faxes, email, the World Wide Web, and other electronic applications. This section discusses all forms of non-phone based support. As we will see, most non-phone based support today is electronic. Also, electronic support goes beyond simply responding to requests, a reactive activity, but also includes proactive ways of delivering support by having information available to customers before they even encounter a problem, and also before they need to place a call.

3.5.1   Letters and Faxes

The speed required for efficient support pretty much rules out regular mail as a medium, but you may receive letters requesting support every once in a while, especially if you have international customers in remote countries.

Immediately enter the request in the call tracking system and attempt to transform the interaction into a phone conversation (it's exceedingly difficult and time consuming to resolve a software issue via mail).

Fax requests can also be used to request support, although we recommend that you discourage the method in favor of a direct phone call or some electronic method because of the overhead associated with handling fax requests, as well as the lack of feedback mechanism of faxes, which can create dissatisfaction where the requests are lost.

Faxes, however, are often an integral part of resolving problems for a number of reasons:

- Sharing complex information such as error logs, configurations, or a page from the documentation manual is easier and less error-prone in writing than over the phone.
- When the customer and the support engineers are in different time zones, asynchronous communication saves time.
- When communications are difficult because of language or other issues, the printed word is clearer than a live conversation.
- When a paper trail is desirable or necessary, faxes are the easiest way to create one.

Despite their usefulness, faxes have a big disadvantage: they are pieces of paper that can be lost and are difficult to share with others. At the minimum, you must have a system to log faxes in your call tracking system as any other piece of information about calls. That is, you should log the arrival and departure of both incoming and outgoing faxes. For those faxes which are necessary to exchange information, invest in an on-line fax storage system if you can. Finally, consider implementing an electronic call management system, so that most communications can be done electronically.

3.5.2   Electronic Call Management

Electronic call management makes selected parts of your call tracking system accessible to customers. Depending on the capabilities of your system, you may be able to let customers log new calls, check on the status of existing calls (their own, for security reasons), and even enter comments on existing calls.

The simplest piece to implement is call logging. This does not require much more than an electronic mail capability. Actually, you may simply allow customers to place requests via email. Email call logging can be an adequate system for a small customer base, but it still leaves you with the overhead of monitoring the email addresses, logging calls from email into the call tracking system, and getting back to the customer. This overhead may be greater than simply answering the phone.

Therefore, a better approach is to have an application accessible to customers that allows for automatic validation and logging of calls. This can be accomplished by either having customers log into your system through a bulletin board, by using the Web, or through a custom-designed application. Whatever the method, the customer enters a call in an on-line form and sends the request. The request is then automatically validated and logged as a call, and an acknowledgment is sent back to the user, including the call reference number. Once the call is logged, the interaction is mostly through the phone. In particular, the first contact with the customer is usually via phone, since it's the best way to provide clear proof that response time was met. However, especially with an internal help desk, the entire dialog may be conducted via email.

The advantages of this kind of electronic call logging are that it gives customers great flexibility in placing calls. Calls may be placed at any time during the day, including when the support center is closed or when the customer cannot have access to it. Furthermore, it allows customers to provide detailed information when logging calls, which will expedite the resolution of the call. Finally, it removes the overhead of validating and logging calls.

Call monitoring, however, can go much further than simple call logging. Call monitoring includes making the call tracking system available to customers on-line, so that customers can monitor calls throughout their lifespans. With internal customers, it's usually sufficient to make your application accessible in read-only mode, since call information is not confidential. With external customers, however, you will need to look at a security and authorization scheme so that customers can have access only to their own calls.

Full call monitoring allows customers to check the status of calls at any time, avoiding phone tag and the constraints of the hotline hours. If customers can also add comments to the call logs, the two-way communication may make phone calls back and forth unnecessary for some nonurgent matters.

We have shown that ECM has strong benefits for customer satisfaction, but is it cost effective? There are some very real costs associated with ECM. The main one is the upfront development cost. Although you are already paying for the brain of it, the call tracking system, you will need to add an interface that includes security checks if your customers are external. On an ongoing basis, you will need to maintain the system and the machines associated with it. If your customers are internal, the cost may be reduced to the overhead of the additional users, but you still have to consider that.

The financial benefits of ECM are the reduction in case logging expense, which can be very significant if you are using a dedicated Dispatch function, and the reduction in statusing overhead once a problem is open. The latter is more difficult to measure, but it is a fact that your support engineers will be more productive if they can communicate asynchronously and with a good level of technical detail with customers. Based on our experience, we believe the benefits are at least financially neutral. In any case, competitive requirements may force you to consider ECM.

3.5.3   Proactive Customer Communication

The idea behind proactive customer communication is unlike anything we have talked about. So far, we have discussed how to handle customer inquiries. Proactive customer communication brings information, especially technical information, to the customer before the customer needs to call for help. For that reason, proactive customer communication is sometimes called "call avoidance."

Proactive customer communication is a real advance in customer satisfaction. While there is no doubt that customers want their calls to be handled quickly and well, the bottom line is that they prefer not to have to call in the first place because they have the tools to fix the problem, and, going one step further, they have the tools to prevent the problem in the first place.

Implementing proactive customer communication does not require electronic means. A printed newsletter will do nicely. However, with modern technology an electronic medium is best, since it provides much greater flexibility for just-in-time delivery, and usually at a much lower cost. The key decision point is whether customers can be enticed to use it. If you are running an internal help desk, your job is easier in this respect, since your customers are already plugged in to a common system. If you have external customers, you will have some experimenting and convincing to do. The electronic systems must be easy to use, and easier than picking up the phone.

Common delivery methods for proactive information include the Internet or the World Wide Web, on-line services such as CompuServe, bulletin boards (BBS) maintained in-house and accessible via modem, fax-on-demand systems, and CD-ROMs shipped periodically to customers. Give preference to methods that allow you to communicate instantaneously to customers either new documents or new versions of documents. See Chapter 9 for more information about tools. Although customers like to have a variety of delivery mechanisms, you will probably need to stick to a handful to contain cost, so be sure to choose the one(s) that your customers prefer.

Populating the information database for customers is relatively easy if you have a good internal information database. The standard method is to extract those documents which are most relevant to customers (doing a survey of calls and identifying the top 10 topics is a great method), which you can share with them because they do not contain proprietary information, and to edit the materials to be legible and check-spelled. In other words, the customer information database is a subset of your internal database and is constantly augmented by refining internal documents.

The types of documents in the customer database are the same as in the internal database: white papers, troubleshooting guides, tips and tricks, programming samples, FAQs (Frequently Asked Questions), etc.

While it is clear that proactive customer satisfaction is something customers want and like, is call avoidance cost effective?

First, let's consider the costs of proactive communications. There is the cost of creating and maintaining the information, and there is the cost of delivering it. If you have a good system to create and maintain the information that piggybacks onto the system for creating and maintaining internal information, your costs there should be minimal. Essentially, you need to decide whether documents are customer viewable, and you need to edit them. Deciding whether a document should be viewable can be difficult, but most of the time you should be able to make it a simple step in the preparation and checking of a document. The editing step is trickier. You need to decide whether you need and can afford professional editing. The delivery costs are tightly linked to the mechanisms you use, and again you should strike a compromise between convenience and cost.

What is the financial benefit to you of a proactive communication system? The main measurement you will want to use is call volume. That is, your call volume per customer should be lower with a proactive system than without. (The customers who do not use the proactive communication should call you more than those who do.) Comparing the cost of resolving a call to the cost of proactive communication, you should find that it's much higher. In other words, you should be able to fund proactive communication out of the savings from not receiving the calls it will avoid. There are two caveats. The first one is that, in order to make a difference, proactive communications must be used by the customers, so you must have an information campaign and reminders. Use your marketing group or be creative on your own—for instance, remind customers of the proactive tools in your on-hold message or whenever they use your electronic call management system. The second caveat is that customers will give the proactive information a try, but they will keep using it only if they are likely to find the information they need. Therefore, to launch proactive communication you must have a system to create lots of interesting information. Your support engineers, or at least a portion of them, should be tasked and rewarded for creating information suitable for proactive communication to customers. We discuss some ideas for implementing such a system in

Chapter 7, "Managing Support People," and in Chapter 9, "Tools for Technical Software Support." Chapter 9 also provides tools for preparing a financial justification for customer communication tools.

We are strong proponents of proactive customer satisfaction systems, because they allow you to deliver better service with less money.

3.6 DISASTER RECOVERY PLANNING

All the plans and implementation details you have settled on so far come into question if your support center cannot operate at all—for instance, because of a power failure—or cannot be reached by your customers—for instance, because of a phone failure. Devoting some effort to planning for disaster recovery is a worthwhile exercise.

The basic issue is to determine the impact on your customers of a disaster. If your customers have noncritical needs and could easily make do without your support center for the time it would take for you to recover, you may be able to ignore disaster recovery entirely. If, on the other end, your customers depend on you for their mission-critical applications, you must plan for providing support during and after a disaster.

Most customers, even those with critical needs, may be able to tolerate a short down time (say, under one hour). A good rule of thumb is that you can afford to be down for the length of your shortest response time. In case of an extensive disaster, say an earthquake, customers will be understanding and may tolerate much reduced service for longer periods of time. However, your disaster is not theirs: a snow day on the East Coast will not be seen as an exceptional disaster on the West Coast.

Planning for disaster recovery makes the recovery process much easier, despite the necessary limitations on the scenarios that can be considered. It is pretty easy and extremely useful for the small problems that are likely to happen often, such as power failures and phone failures. On the other hand, recovery planning for an extensive disaster (say, a tornado destroys your building) can be overwhelming. Here are the three steps you should follow:

- One, make an inventory of possible disasters. Without worrying too much about being complete, and using the checklist below, make a list of disasters that could happen. Include big things (earthquakes, blizzards) and little things (power down for an hour). Again, don't feel you have to be exhaustive and don't bother to list events that are very unlikely to happen in your area (say, a hurricane in California).

- Two, make an assessment of the likelihood of each event and its impact. For instance, if you regularly have thunderstorms that cause power failures, but power comes back after a few minutes, make a note of that.

- Three, for each likely disaster, create a recovery plan for handling both the disaster and its aftermath. Since you may have quite a lengthy list of disasters, start with some likely events and work your way down.

Here are some planning ideas. Your inventory of disasters should contain, in no particular order:

- Call tracking system down.

- Phone system down.

- Machines down due to a network failure.

- Power failure: distinguish a general power failure from a local one if needed. Are your machines on another circuit or in another building? Will you have phone service if there is no power? If your customers are internal, will they need service during a power failure? What about right after the failure?

- Major local disasters such as hurricane or earthquake, depending on where your center is located. If your customers are internal, think about how they will be affected by the disaster. Maybe you don't need to do much during the disaster, but you might be particularly busy afterward.

- Minor local disasters such as snowstorm.

- Unusable building due to a gas leak or a bomb threat: this is probably a more unlikely event for you and can be considered later.

When you assess the frequency and impact of disasters, spend some time studying common occurrences. Is there any way you can decrease the likelihood of some disasters? It's awfully difficult to reduce the number of snowstorms (short of moving to another area), but you can and should do everything you can to reduce problems with the call tracking system and anything else you have control over. It can be much easier and cheaper to prevent disasters, especially minor ones, than to cope with them.

As you can see, some disasters are at the same time more minor and likely to happen more often. Depending on local circumstances, power failures may be quite frequent, and fortunately, they are quite easy to deal with if you are well prepared. Here are some ideas for you to consider when you are creating contingency plans:

- Have a paper system to back up the on-line call tracking system. It's actually quite easy to work without the call tracking system for short periods of time. If you use a callback system, figure out how call information will go from the Dispatch group to the support engineers (paper runners? fax?). A key point to plan for is whether and how you will enter events recorded on paper into the call tracking system when it comes back up.

- If you have several physical locations, route calls to another center if you have phone problems, or if one center is temporarily unavailable. This is very easy if you have an 800 number; however, you should have a contingency plan filed with the phone company. Note that the rerouting cannot be sustained very long, since you won't have the capacity of one of your centers.

- Barring the ability to reroute calls entirely, plan for a phone message that can be activated quickly as needed, indicating to customers that the support center is down. You may want to give special instructions to place emergency calls—using pagers, for instance.

- Use UPS (Uninterruptable Power Supplies) for key machines and phone system. Size the UPS based on experience. If you have lots of lengthy power failures, buy one that provides longer service. Be sure to test the UPS before you need to use them.

- Consider what you could do if your people had to work from another location. Can they work from home? from alternate offices? If you have a situation where an unusable office is likely, you may want to contract with disaster recovery specialists who provide alternate locations and equipment for a fee. Also, if the support engineers cannot work in the office, does it mean other services are likely to be impacted as well? Will you have machines? phone systems?

Work out very detailed plans for events that happen more often, such as the call tracking system being down. Create overall plans for very major, extended disasters. Everything else you may be able to muddle through using the principles you worked out for the other disasters. Don't spend much time mapping out what to do with really unlikely and unprecedented problems.

Store your plans where they can be accessed in a disaster. A great plan for recovering from machine failure that is stored on-line and nowhere else is useless. Make sure that everyone who needs to activate and work the plan knows what to do ahead of time. Plan for backups in case someone is on vacation. Pay particular attention to communications. Most disasters affect the basic ways we communicate with each other. If you have a sizable support center, communications during a disaster may be the hardest area to handle. Ensure each plan has a determination for when the disaster is over.

Rehearsing disaster plans is difficult, since disturbing the support center artificially is painful. If you choose not to rehearse, use every real disaster as an opportunity to practice your plan. Analyze your performance afterward and modify the plan.

Disaster recovery planning may not be an appealing topic, but it pays off. Plan before a disaster strikes. In this, as in day-to-day operations, it is much easier to follow a routine than to improvise.

CHAPTER **4**

MEASURING SUPPORT CENTER PERFORMANCE

This chapter discusses what kinds of measurements are necessary or useful to run a support center. It describes what to do day-to-day to keep your support center healthy and successful, based on studying and acting on the measurements you choose. It also suggests analyses you will want to run from time to time to determine whether large changes are necessary.

As we have seen, a lot of decisions on organizing a center are best made once you have some basic information such as call length, so maintaining a portfolio of measurements helps you make important and mundane decisions alike. Putting in place a set of metrics also enables you to benchmark new ideas against old ones. If modifications in the model result in tangible improvements, they may be worth adopting on a permanent basis. Even if you are not planning or implementing major changes, keeping a baseline of your performance allows you to ensure that you are maintaining or improving your support center's performance and gives you coherent, credible information you can use to obtain recognition, to justify resources, and to assess the performance of your people.

Statistics can lie, especially when poorly designed or poorly interpreted. The goal of this chapter is to help you design a coherent metrics program that allows you to make decisions with reasonable confidence, while avoiding an overabundance of data, which can deter from analysis and which can confuse rather than guide decisions.

We will discuss what to measure in some detail and give general guidelines about how to measure it, since your particular circumstances and tools will dictate the exact methods. With modern tools now being accessible to even small support centers, gathering statistics has become very easy, so that the key is choosing the right data rather than finding a way to obtain it.

We make a distinction between metrics you use on a routine basis to monitor the performance and health of the support center and metrics you may want to run on an ad-hoc basis to analyze the workings of the support center. For the routine metrics you will want to develop both so-called process metrics and customer satisfaction metrics. By process metrics, we mean all the internal metrics that refer to the mechanics of the support work such as how quickly phone calls are processed, how productive the support engineers are, and so on. Because they are internal metrics, they can be measured through internal systems.

Customer satisfaction data, on the other hand, must be gathered by going to the customer. You need both kinds of data, and we are considering them separately only because the gathering methods are different.

Analysis metrics, on the other hand, are not usually run on a set schedule, and they may vary from one run to another as you turn your attention to various issues. They tend to be more speculative and less well defined than the process metrics.

The ideas presented in this chapter apply equally well to all sorts of support centers. The kinds of measurements to make are pretty much universal across support environments, whether the software being supported is complex or not, and whether customers are internal or not. The main differences lie in the measurement gathering techniques, specifically in the frequency of measurements and in how customer satisfaction surveys are gathered, as well as in the interpretation of the metrics, since they depend so much on the type of software you support.

We will start with the routine metrics, and within them with the process metrics, without implying they are any more important than the customer satisfaction metrics.

4.1   IMPORTANT PROCESS METRICS

In this section we concentrate on the internal metrics of the support center—that is, how well processes work. What you want to measure is how well the call flow processes are being executed.

4.1.1   Metrics Inventory

You need to define a small, yet meaningful set of data that you will use as "dashboard data"—data you glance at on a regular basis as a monitoring tool. Some you will need daily or hourly or even in real time, such as call load; some you may need on a quarterly basis such as support engineer productivity.

Picking a small set of data is important. If you have an on-line call tracking system, you can run from it more reports than you can possibly absorb, so you want to focus on the meaningful ones. On the other hand, if you have to get the data manually or if you need to customize the data from the call tracking system, you want to determine the minimum set that will meet your needs before you start creating the reports.

Let's start with an inventory of possible metrics for a support center:

- *Call volume*: how many calls are coming in and how many are being closed. This gives a rough idea of how busy you are and gives you essential information to develop or test your staffing model. If taken at a detailed level, hourly or by day of the week, it gives you information necessary to schedule staff. The difference between incoming and closed calls represents how much the backlog is growing or shrinking. For high-volume environments, the backlog should be very small as a proportion of incoming calls. In complex support environments, the backlog could run at two week's worth of incoming volume.

Interestingly, unless there is a large overload (or underload), the volume of closed calls tends to match the volume of incoming calls; that is, support engineers tend to naturally work more calls when the load is higher and to work fewer calls when the load is lower. This is not to say that increasing the load is always the way to go, since there are side effects: even though the volume of the backlog may not increase in step with the incoming load, it will contain more complex calls in overload situations. That is, complex problems will tend to get ignored in favor of urgent ones.

- *Response time*: how quickly calls are attended to. Under a callback model, response time is the time between the placing of the call and the time a support engineer gets back to the customer. In a direct call system, what counts is the hold time. Response or hold time is the first variable to suffer when load increases and is therefore an excellent early warning sign. Response time is also a key factor of customer satisfaction, since "getting through" is perceived, and rightly so, as an essential first step toward problem resolution. Use the response time metrics as an early warning sign of customer satisfaction problems.

  Response time is usually measured by the percentage of calls meeting published or internal goals (as in: 80% of calls are responded to within published guidelines or 90% of callers spend less than two minutes on hold). If your support contract does not define response time guidelines, you will need to define what is meaningful in your environment. You may want to analyze response time by call priority, since a timely response is even more important for emergency calls. Significant variations in response times as well as failure to meet published goals need to be examined and addressed.

  Do not use average response or hold time as a measurement, as it can be deceiving. It's much more meaningful (in terms of customer satisfaction) to measure the percentage of calls meeting your targets.

- *Resolution time*: how long it takes to resolve problems. This is the time between when the customer places a call and when an answer is provided. Resolution time varies greatly, from minutes for easy questions to days or weeks or months for more difficult topics. Work time (the time it takes to actually work a problem to resolution) depends mostly on product complexity, although the skills and load of the support engineers and the efficiency of the processes and tools are also important. If most problems are resolved with just one call, resolution time is essentially the same as call length.

Resolution time is often expressed as a percentage of calls resolved within a certain amount of time. Depending on call complexity, it could be the percentage of calls resolved within 10 minutes, within a day, or within two weeks of the first call. Pick a target time meaningful to customers, such as calls resolved within the same business day or within the first call, and make sure that your target is neither too low nor too high (if you resolve 4% of calls within 10 minutes, 10 minutes is not a good benchmark, although it may be a good target; if you resolve 99% of calls within 2 weeks, 2 weeks is not meaningful for you, pick a shorter target). You may want to have two measurements against two target times to capture both the easy calls and the more difficult ones. As for response time, avoid using average resolution time, as it obscures the real issues.

Unless load varies greatly, resolution time is an extremely stable measure—unlike response time, which is very sensitive to even small variations in load. Resolution time goes up when load goes up, which is fairly obvious, but it also goes up, at least in complex software support environments, when load is low, since the support engineers then attack the old and difficult calls, temporarily inflating resolution time.

Do not look at resolution time performance for individuals over a very short period such as a day or even a week: it's not meaningful, since a single "long" call can change the average. Use longer periods such as a month when looking at individual performance.

- *Backlog*: how many calls are being worked at some point in time. Backlog, incoming calls, and resolved calls are all related. The size of the backlog is an indication of how well the support center is doing to handle the load. Although we can all agree that a good backlog is a small one, the minimum size of the backlog depends on call complexity, with more complex calls creating larger backlog. Managing the backlog down is always a good idea, however.

At a detailed level, the size of each support engineer's backlog gives a good idea of how busy they are. Most support engineers can juggle 15 or 20 calls without problems, but larger numbers translate into neglected customers and frantic support engineers.

A descriptive and useful way to look at the backlog is to measure it as a ratio of calls taken or closed to obtain a measurement in days (or weeks) to close. For example, if you take 100 calls a month and you have 50 calls in your backlog, you have a two-week backlog. Especially in a growing support center where the backlog in pure numbers is always going up, using a ratio allows you to scale it to reality.

- *Call aging*: how old the calls in the backlog are. This is a more detailed measurement of what is happening in the backlog, and it allows you to distinguish between having 100 calls that came in yesterday and have not yet been closed, versus having 50 calls that came in six months ago and still have no solution, and another 50 that are a year old.

  Call aging is more complex to analyze than the other measurements we have mentioned so far, so you need to experiment a bit. First pick a target for "old" calls that works in your environment, using some multiple of your average resolution time. It could be a day or two for low-end software, a few weeks for complex software. Then, count calls older than the target and examine them individually so you can help expedite their resolution. You may want to measure the backlog against two milestones for a more detailed analysis.

- *Efficiency or productivity*: how many calls each engineer resolves in a given time period. This is an indication of how each support engineer is doing, as well as an overall validation and input to your capacity model. Productivity numbers can be used at the engineer's level to monitor individual load as well as at a general level to track productivity improvements. If you are using an ACD, you may want to also track the percentage of time available on the phone.

  Daily individual productivity numbers, especially in complex support environments where a support engineer can get "stuck" working just one call for an entire day, vary widely, so do not draw conclusions about the productivity of a particular support engineer based on a very short period. Look for trends over long periods of time, such as a month or a quarter, instead, remembering that senior support engineers often have lower efficiency based on call volume, since they are often handling the more complex calls. Daily average numbers should be quite stable if you have more than a handful of support engineers (and if load is stable).

The metrics above are fairly routine. More exotic metrics can be run as well, such as the following:

- *Calls that missed response time*: this is useful to analyze why your response time statistics are not where they should be. You would probably want to run the list every once in a while and go through each call as a spot check. Most of the time, the problem is either an unexpected high load on a particular day or a particular time, a breakdown in staffing levels (e.g., a flu epidemic), or poor call flow processes that do not allow support engineers to quickly grab incoming calls.

- *Reopened calls*: if your environment allows calls to be reopened, how many calls are closed more than once? Presumably, this is because the support engineer closed the call prematurely the first time around, so the number or percentage of reopened calls is an indication of the quality of call resolutions. Since calls may be reopened for a variety of reasons, however, you will need to analyze why calls are reopened rather than simply count them.

- *Calls worked*: in a complex support environment where many calls can be worked on a particular day without reaching resolution, it is useful to know how many calls a particular support engineer worked in addition to how many calls were opened and closed, and how many calls are in the backlog.

- *Status reports or contacts with customers*: especially with long calls (complex software), you may want to measure the intervals between customer contacts and to analyze those calls for which no contact has occurred within a set period of time, either a week or your average resolution time. This is another way to look at call aging.

As you can see, there is a wide variety of metrics, and your imagination is the only limit. To be really useful, however, metrics have to be run and analyzed, so you need to define a core set that you will attend to each day or week or month so you don't waste resources producing data that is not used.

4.1.2 Core Set of Metrics

The best strategy is to define a small set of meaningful metrics to run on a regular basis; this will allow you to make comparisons between various results and to study trends. You can always run additional metrics when you want to analyze a particular area. Regularly review your routine reports, discard what you don't use, and make necessary changes. Make it very easy to generate metrics and to make them available to those who need them, or you won't make time to study them. Ideally, set up some automatic method to generate them in real time.

What do you really need to run the business? Here is a minimum set suitable for most environments:

- Volume of incoming and closed calls, backlog (as a ratio of incoming calls).

- Response time or hold time statistics against your target, expressed as a percentage of calls meeting the target. You may want to break out response time for emergency calls.

- Resolution time against the target you choose.

- Efficiency or productivity per support engineer.

- Aging calls: as a monitoring mechanism, review a list of old calls on a regular basis so you can analyze why they are not resolved and expedite resolution. You can skip this if you do not have a backlog, as in many high-volume centers.

You probably do not need more than this minimum set. A good test of whether you have too many metrics is whether you can remember the results. If you cannot recite your key metrics from memory, you have too many.

4.1.3 What to run and when

You need to run metrics every day and every week to run the business, every month and every quarter to plan the business. You also need to look at individual performance and group performance.

If you can and if your environment requires it, run the volume and response time metrics in real time. Most ACD systems allow you to set them up on a supervisor's console.

Run daily metrics overnight, so you can look at them first thing in the morning and make adjustments as needed. If you don't do it right away, you'll get caught up in the whirlwind of daily operations and you will never get to it. After a while, you will develop a good feel for the metrics, so you will be able to draw conclusions from them in a few minutes. Try to get all the information on the same report if possible, although you may have to juggle reports from your ACD and from your call tracking system.

Every day, look at incoming and closed calls, or better yet, graph the results so you can glance at them and know whether the load is heavy or light, and how well you are doing with it. Check to see if anyone is particularly loaded (or not), and take corrective action. How are you doing with response time? Your performance on any particular day is not very meaningful, but variations should be noted and analyzed. To help you, you may want to run a report of calls that missed response time. Look for patterns: is there a particularly busy time during your day? Can you adjust staffing? If you work on a callback system, is someone not picking up calls when they should? Response time statistics may not be meaningful at the individual support engineer's level; if you are letting support engineers pick from a queue, good cherry pickers are able to avoid calls that have gone past their response time, so either use a group measurement or (better) go to a random assignment model.

Daily resolution time and productivity by support engineer are not very meaningful, although with time you will develop a feel for the normal variations.

Table 4–1 is a sample daily report.

Table 4–1.   Sample Daily Report

14 January 1996
Daily Report for: Server 1

Login	In	Out	Backlog	% met Response	% met Resolution
anna	10	8	24	80	75
bridget	3	0	34	70	N/A
chandra	10	11	44	90	85
daniel	0	0	21	N/A	N/A
eliza	5	4	67	90	42
All	**28**	**23**	**190**	**84**	**74**

At a glance, and without knowing anything about the operation of the center, the report suggests:

- Daniel was apparently out that day.
- Backlog is high; if calls are complex, it may be OK, otherwise it's too high.
- Response time is not fantastic.
- Efficiency is all over the place. Are anna and chandra assigned to easier calls?

Each week, run the same metrics you run daily (volume in and out, backlog, response time and resolution time), running the reports over the weekend so you can study the results quickly before they become obsolete. Whenever practical, post the reports and graphs in a public place, electronically or on paper. It helps support engineers to participate in the running of the center and to get a first-hand impression of how things are going.

In addition, every week, run aging call reports. Zero in on calls that seem neglected and follow up with their owner to expedite resolution. This can be a tedious exercise, but it is necessary if you want to maintain control over your backlog and customer satisfaction, not to mention avoid escalations. "Stuck" calls may require management intervention, transfer to a support engineer with more appropriate skills, or both. With practice, you will be able to define a meaningful period beyond which you need to intervene. When you first get started, if you have too many calls to follow up on, temporarily pick a longer target so the list is manageable, and work your way down. On the other hand, if your aging target is very short, run your aging call reports more frequently than weekly.

Table 4–2 is a sample weekly report.

Table 4–2.   Sample Weekly Report

21 January 1996
Weekly Report for: Server 1

Login	In	Out	Backlog	% met Response	% met Resolution
anna	50	40	34	80	75
bridget	15	25	32	70	44
chandra	48	55	34	90	85
daniel	0	0	21	N/A	N/A
eliza	28	20	69	90	42
All	**141**	**140**	**180**	**84**	**69**

This weekly report raises the following observations:

- Daniel was out all week.
- Efficiency is uneven: either different support engineers have different roles or there is a performance issue with some of them.
- Anna let her backlogs grow quite a bit this week; she needs to watch out.
- Eliza seems to be overwhelmed by her high backlog; she may need help reducing it.

Table 4–3 is a sample report of aging calls.

Table 4–3.   Sample Aging Report

21 January 1996
Aging Call Report for: Server 1

Login	Call #	Opened	Last Ctr Contact	Last Note	Status
anna	12345	12/5/95	12/6/95	12/6/95	CUST
eliza	2345	12/5/94	7/28/95	12/20/95	RES
	12321	11/15/95	1/11/96	1/15/96	CUST
	12359	12/14/95	1/1/96	1/17/96	RES
	12369	12/21/95	12/21/95	12/22/95	ENG

This particular report shows calls older than 4 weeks and those for which the customer has not been contacted in more than 2 weeks. We can assume this is a complex support operation. The Status column refers to status of the call as recorded by the call tracking system ("RES" means research, "CUST" means the customer owns the next step, "ENG" means the call identified a bug or required other help from the Engineering group.

Now what about reports for longer time periods such as a month or a quarter? Monthly and quarterly reports and reports for longer periods are useful for planning and evaluating performance. Measurements over longer periods of time become more meaningful, because they are less subject to random variations. We recommend you run the same metrics each month and each quarter as you run each week.

Accurate reports and metrics require accurate data. Be conscientious about keeping track of staff and assignments on a daily basis, so that the reports match reality. To build accurate reports over long periods of time, you need to keep detailed tabs on when staff was added or removed from each team. You may choose to bypass the extra steps, but think about the implications of your decision on the accuracy of the metrics, especially if your staffing is very dynamic.

If you have multiple teams within the support center, create "Russian-doll" metrics so that each manager can see his or her team and also see the overall results. There's nothing wrong with seeing other teams' results, but a short report is more efficient. Think about the groupings you need ahead of time; it's quite difficult to retrofit reports for individual teams from a global report (the opposite is easy). Global reports are valuable for looking at trends but useless for analyzing the causes for success or failure, especially with large groups. Take the analysis down to the individual support engineer whenever possible.

Table 4–4 is a summary of recommended metrics and how frequently you should run them. Feel free to adapt them to your own needs, keeping in mind that it's preferable to have a small set of meaningful metrics rather than an extensive set of metrics you won't look at.

Table 4–4. Recommended Metrics

Metrics name	Frequency	Notes
Incoming calls, closed calls, backlog	Daily, weekly, monthly	Express backlog as a ratio of existing calls to incoming
Response time or hold time	Daily, weekly, monthly	Percentage of calls meeting target; can break out emergency calls
Resolution time	Daily, weekly, monthly	Percentage of calls meeting target
Productivity	Daily, weekly, monthly, quarterly	Per support engineer
Aging calls	Weekly (snapshot)	List of calls that exceed target resolution or time without customer contact

4.2 CUSTOMER SATISFACTION

Your customer satisfaction ratings may well be your more important metrics. After all, if you have great response time, great resolution time, and strong productivity results, but your customers are not happy, you won't be successful. The reverse is more unlikely, but it's conceivable that your customers be very satisfied without your doing well on the process metrics. Certainly, at the individual level, you will have support engineers who take longer than others to resolve issues but whose customers are more satisfied.

The only way to find out how your customers are feeling is to listen to them. There is no substitute. Measuring response time, resolution time, and others are just proxies. There's nothing wrong with process metrics, and since you can get instantaneous answers for them, you should gather the measurements, but it's not enough.

If you run a small support center and you know your customers well, finding out how your customers feel is as simple as sitting down with them and asking them. If your customers are more than a handful, however, or you don't know them personally, you need to survey them. There are many ways to conduct surveys, and while we are not survey research specialists, we do have some practical recommendations on how to proceed so the surveys are useful to you and to your group.

There are essentially three types of customer surveys, with lots of possible variations, and you can consider using more than one type:

- *The competitive survey*: an independent company conducts a periodical survey, usually yearly, which asks customers about their overall satisfaction and which contrasts results for competitors.

- *The overall satisfaction survey*: you initiate a periodical survey, which may be conducted by you or by an outside entity, to gather information about your customers. No information about customers using competitive products is gathered.

- *The transactional survey*: the survey is made for one transaction (one call to the support center), usually on a sample basis (not every call is surveyed).

Let's take a more detailed look at each kind of survey, describe the advantages of each, and make recommendations on what you should use.

4.2.1 Competitive Surveys

Competitive surveys make sense only for independent software vendors. This section does not apply to internal help desks.

Competitive surveys are conducted by a number of survey specialists such as Prognostics, usually yearly. The organizations survey a carefully researched sample of hardware and software users, typically MIS directors, and study customer satisfaction with a number of variables such as the quality of the software, performance, price, and also the quality of technical support.

To receive a detailed analysis of the data for your company, you must purchase a contract with the survey company. You will be asked to provide a representative sample of your customer base, which will receive the survey questionnaire either by phone or in writing directly from the survey company. Once the data are analyzed, you will receive scores on the different categories being surveyed both for your company and competitors. Many surveys also include a so-called gap analysis that contrasts customer satisfaction with the relative importance of the various factors in the customers' eyes. The difference between the importance to customers of a particular area and their satisfaction level shows you where you need to put your efforts. For instance, if your customers think that the performance of the product is very important and they are not satisfied with it, the gap will be high, indicating a problem. If, on the other hand, they think that price is really important and they are satisfied with it, the gap will be small, you don't have an issue with price. Finally, if they think electronic support services are not important and they are very satisfied with them, the gap will be negative, as you are overperforming in that area.

As you can see, the scope of competitive surveys is much greater than technical support proper, and they yield information that is very important to the Marketing group. You may find that your company already subscribes to a competitive survey, or you may find that you need to champion the cause of subscribing to one. We strongly recommend you subscribe to a competitive survey, since it's the only way to find out how you are doing compared to competitors. Results are especially meaningful when seen over a period of some years to determine whether changes and improvements are being felt positively by customers (it can take many months, even a year before results can be seen; be patient). Try to share the (relatively modest) cost with other departments, since the information will be useful to them as well.

Although competitive surveys are very useful to benchmark your support center against competitors, they are limited for other uses. In particular, they measure performance only at a macro level: how are you doing in general? They cannot give much information about why customers feel the way they do, and in particular they cannot pinpoint problems or strengths at the level of the support engineer. Therefore, they will give you a score each year, which may be better or worse than last year, and better or worse than your competitors', but it's up to you to interpret the scores and the improvements or lack thereof, which can be very difficult. The survey companies give good advice on what to do with the scores, and the main lesson is not to take each specific number too seriously, but rather to concentrate on large gaps and large differences from one year to the next, and to tackle only a few improvements at a time.

Another drawback of competitive surveys is that they pretty much lock you into the questionnaire the survey company wants to use and do not allow you to probe for specific issues. If you want to know what your customers feel about the new software patch downloading service you just implemented, you'll have to find out another way.

Finally, competitive surveys target decision makers, not necessarily the people who actually call your support center. This is a double-edged sword: it's good to know what the decision makers are thinking, since they sign the support contract checks (or at least the software purchase checks, if you do not charge separately for support), and their opinions are shaped by the support contacts who do call you, but they are removed from the action—and that, in part, explains the lag between changes in services and changes in opinions mentioned earlier.

4.2.2 Overall Satisfaction Surveys

Overall satisfaction surveys are very common, and you may have started reading this section thinking they were the only kind of surveys you could use. An overall survey is conducted at some regular interval, usually every 3 to 12 months, with all or more often a sample of customers. The survey asks them to rate the service they are getting for a number of characteristics. For example, you could ask customers to rate:

- The time it takes to reach someone on the phone.
- The time it takes to resolve problems.
- The courtesy or professionalism of the support engineers they talk to.
- The technical skill of the support engineers they talk to.
- The overall level of service.

It's relatively easy to do an overall survey, and even easier to do it badly, so plan well. A poorly executed survey will create unreliable results, which can inspire all kinds of bad decisions through their pseudoscientific look. Incorporate the following points in your plan:

- Use a proper sample of customers. If you survey a portion of customers, make sure you select a diversity of customers representative of your overall customer base. Consider size, geography, application type, experience with the product, even the level of usage of technical support. Apparently innocent techniques like surveying all customers whose name start with "A" can lead to biased samples. Even if you decide to survey all your customers, not everyone will respond; typically the very unhappy and the very happy ones will respond more than the ones in the middle.

- Choose the best medium to do the survey. Direct contact (typically telephone) yields the best response rate, often close to 100% of correctly identified contacts, but requires people resources and, thus, is expensive. You may want to consider having each staff member collect a few surveys each day. Regular mail is the cheapest way to send a survey but yields low response rates, often in the low one-digits, so it can end up costing more per returned survey and it can introduce biases because of that low response rate. Electronic mail can be an excellent method for software support surveys if you have customer email addresses, and in particular if you are doing an in-house survey. Monitor the survey response rate relative to the technique you use. If you are getting very low returns, say a few percentage points for an electronic survey, you may be getting biased results. Read on for ideas on increasing return rates.

- Make the survey very easy for the customer. Keep it short. Use a simple rating scheme. Make sure that the questions are unambiguous. This is particularly important for surveys that will be completed by the customer alone; you have a bit more latitude for phone surveys, since the person conducting the survey can provide additional information. Testing the survey with real customers is always a good idea. They will tell you if the wording uses jargon that they do not understand (for instance, most customers do not differentiate response time from resolution time) or if the rating system is obscure. Test the final survey with at least a few customers using the medium you plan to use for administering it.

- Have a plan for collecting and analyzing the data before you do the survey. Sending the survey is the easy part. You don't need to get fancy, but you need to know how you will tally the data (who will do it and with what tool) and what kind of simple analyses you will conduct. With an electronic survey you can build in the capability of entering response data directly into your analysis tool. With a mail survey you can use a scannable form to facilitate data entry. Do not do a survey if you don't know how you will analyze the data: it's a waste of time for you, and even more for your customers, who will have no incentive to complete future surveys.

- Plan a way to give feedback to customers on the survey. It's a good incentive for customers to respond to surveys. You should respond to customers who are dissatisfied and who identify themselves (we do not believe anonymous surveys make much sense, anyway), and also give all customers the overall results of the survey, with a few comments on how you plan to keep what's working and change what needs to.

- If you are doing a survey that was done before, try as much as possible to keep the administration and scoring the same, so you can compare results in a meaningful way. Do change questions that you know created problems in the past, and feel free to conduct additional analyses, but compare what can be compared.

A basic survey with a few questions and simple average ratings is probably sufficient for your needs. If so, you can do it in-house with few resources. Sophistication is not always better in this domain. However, if you feel the requirements exceed your resources, you can easily outsource customer surveys. Survey specialists can help you maneuver the complexities of sampling, wording, and analyzing. Use the checklist above when selecting the company.

Results from an overall survey are meaningful at a high level and require an analysis to be really useful. Small variations up or down shouldn't be cause for rejoicing or alarm. You should, however, always try to define why ratings are good or bad, or why the trend is up or down.

Should you do an overall customer satisfaction survey? The main advantage is to give you a "score card" on a regular basis so you can chart your progress. An overall survey will give the same weight to customers who call you a lot and customers who seldom or never call you. Also, if you have an internal help desk, it's the only way to get an overall rating.

Compared with competitive surveys, overall surveys give you a lot of freedom in what you survey. You can word items exactly how you like, and you can ask specific questions about your service that may not be captured in a competitive survey. For instance, the competitive survey may ask whether the customer likes electronic service, but you can ask if they know about and what they think of the new patch downloading system.

However, overall surveys, like competitive surveys, lack the level of detail necessary to make complex analyses. They do not refer back to specific people or groups. Also, like competitive surveys, they are not timely enough to spot problems or improvements quickly.

Therefore, if you participate in a competitive survey, we recommend you do not spend the time and resources it takes to conduct an overall survey, but you use transactional surveys instead. If you do not participate in competitive surveys and you have the resources to do both an overall and a transactional survey, do both if you feel you are getting results from the overall survey that you are not getting from a transactional survey.

4.2.3   Transactional Surveys

Transactional surveys are very different from either competitive or overall surveys in that they focus on a single interaction with Technical Support, as opposed to collecting a general feel for it. Because of their narrow focus, transactional surveys come with specific constraints:

- A transactional survey should be administered very quickly after a transaction is completed. Otherwise, the customer may have forgotten the particular interaction, especially if the customer is a frequent caller. Wait no more than a week before surveying customers; within 24 hours is best if the transactions are frequent.
- Transactional surveys should be extremely short. Surveys of all kinds should be short to increase the response rate, but transactional surveys, because they are frequent, should not have more than a half-dozen questions and should not require more than a rating for each.

- The data from transactional surveys should be inexpensive to collect and analyze. You will handle hundreds or thousands of surveys each month, so you can't afford to spend more than a few dollars processing each of them.

Table 4–5 is a typical, very short transactional survey.

Table 4–5.   Sample transactional survey

Case Contact: Peter Jaffe

Case Number: 17003

Case Description: Question about defining a language rpc. How do I send an rpc request using language program to a netgateway (MSG)?

Case Resolution: If using isql (or other language program) must start language request "exec rpc" in order to have MSG convert the request. This parsing logic is different from SQL Server.

Close Date: Jul 10 1996

For this particular case, please rate the performance of the Technical Support Engineer, JOHN AUTROS, on the six measures below, using the following scale.

Very dissatisfied   Very satisfied

0   10

[ ]   Professionalism

[ ]   Initial callback time compared with commitment

[ ]   Follow-up on commitments made to you

[ ]   Technical knowledge

[ ]   Time taken to resolve the case

[ ]   Overall handling of the case by the Technical Support Engineer

Thank you for taking a few moments to help us improve our service.

Becky Smith

Technical Support Manager

Corporation, Inc.

Note that the survey is generated directly and automatically from the call tracking system, extracting case details including descriptions and names directly from the system and without human intervention.

Transactional surveys may be done for each interaction, or for some representative sample. In most settings doing a survey for each call is too much, both in volume for the support center and for the customers. However, if you are doing complex support, you may need to survey each call in order to gather enough data for each support engineer. You should aim to collect a few surveys for each support engineer each month so you can use the data to evaluate performance (take into account the response rate; collecting three surveys may require you to send ten.)

You can conduct transactional surveys by phone, email, fax, or regular mail. Response rates are optimum by phone surveys, worst for regular mail ones. We strongly recommend email as a good compromise for software support settings. You can even build the survey mechanism into your call tracking system and have it automatically send surveys each night. If you have to use mail, try to scan the responses for easier, faster data collection.

You can have a transactional survey for nontelephone interactions: simply offer the survey as an option at the end of an electronic interaction. Survey results will be collected automatically.

We have already said that we are strong proponents of transactional surveys. Why? Transactional surveys focus on the unit of work: the support call, or more properly the support incident, and therefore allow you to correlate the results with specific interactions. Not that overall opinions are not interesting, but being able to track results down to the individual call allows you to pinpoint problems and successes, and to take specific action based on the survey. In particular, we recommend that goals and objectives for everyone in the support center include the ratings from the customer satisfaction survey. Contrasting the ratings for the different questions allow support engineers and managers to pinpoint individual strengths and weaknesses.

If you conduct your survey other than over the phone, you should have a system in place to identify and respond to "bad" customer surveys. The system should allow the customer to hear back from a support manager within days of the receipt of a poor survey. The idea is to acknowledge to the customer that you do read and act on the survey, and to determine whether anything can be done to improve the situation. During the follow-up call, probe for specific details on what went wrong during the call so you can use the information to coach the support engineer if appropriate.

A wonderful benefit of transitional surveys is that they bring results quickly. If, as we recommend, you send the survey the night after the transaction, and you use phone or email, you should get results within a couple of days, allowing you to keep tabs on customer satisfaction on a weekly basis. Since you also get detailed information that allows you to know where variations are coming from, you can correct problems very quickly.

To be fair, however, there are a few areas where transactional surveys are weak. First, they only go to customers who are placing calls, so you cannot know what everyone else is thinking. You will need to use overall surveys, competitive or not, to get that information. Since you run the support center primarily for the customers who do call, a transactional survey should be a good tool for you, unless customers cannot get through to place calls in the first place.

Another problem with transactional surveys is that customers can receive lots of them and may get tired of getting so many. Keep the surveys very short and easy (they should take a couple of minutes to fill out at the most), design a good sampling method if customers complain they are getting too many, and design a feedback mechanism both for problem surveys and in general to show customers that the surveys are read and acted upon. Withdraw the names of customers who request not to be sent surveys from the mailing list.

Finally, transactional surveys are often difficult for the staff to accept, since they clearly relate to a call, hence a support engineer. It's an educational challenge for you. You need to show the engineers that surveys are used in a positive manner as a coaching tool and that a handful of bad surveys are expected and will become invisible when lumped in the average. Share the actual surveys with the support engineers to help reduce the fear.

A special note to those of you who choose to conduct more than one survey: It's intellectually satisfying to check that the results of the various surveys match. However, since the questions, the respondents, and the frequencies differ, correlating the results can be a real challenge, and some survey specialists feel it cannot be done at all. Don't fret about matching each and every piece of information; go for the overall feel. First, be aware that transactional surveys tend to yield higher ratings than other surveys. That is, if you get a score of 8 out of 10 on your transactional survey, you may get "only" 7 out of 10 on an overall survey. This is no cause for concern, only a normal psychological artifact that makes people rate individuals higher than organizations. Variations up and down should match, however: you should not see a large (more than a point) upswing in one survey and not in another. If you have a situation like that, one or both surveys is using unreliable surveying techniques. Talking directly to unhappy and also to particularly happy customers is a good way to gather additional correlation data. For instance, unhappy respondents to transactional surveys may indicate they are very happy overall, but that the particular call they just experienced was a disaster. It could be that a few support engineers are pulling down your overall average. If you can compare results on specific areas, do so. In short, do a sanity check and don't worry about matching everything or matching perfectly.

To conclude, as soon as your customer base is too large for direct contact, we recommend you put in place a transactional survey that will with one instrument give you overall information as well as individual and group information. If it makes sense for you, look at participating in a competitive survey as well. Consider overall satisfaction surveys if you can spare the time and resources, but they are less important because they are less detailed. If you do conduct more than one survey, check that they correlate, and if not, study why not. Customer satisfaction surveys are worth the trouble because they give direct information, so invest in one rather than relying on indirect productivity metrics such as response time or resolution time as indicators of customer satisfaction.

4.3 ANALYSIS METRICS

In this section we discuss what kinds of metrics you may want to use to analyze the workings of your center. Typically, such metrics are not run on a routine basis, both because, as discussed above, you want to keep your routine metrics spare, and also because they would be very boring, since they tend to not change much from one day or week to the next. What are those metrics?

Essentially, analysis metrics look at the type of questions that are coming in and at how they get resolved. They cover areas such as:

- *Call distribution by product:* how many calls are coming in for the various products you support. Watch for significant changes in distribution and correlate them to their causes. For instance, a new release will usually be accompanied by a spike in calls. You also want to match the distribution of calls to the distribution of licenses, so you can tell which products create more problems than others, proportionally speaking. With that information, you can decide to stop supporting a particular product, to charge extra for it, or to lobby the Development group for a more robust product.

- *Call distribution by type of call:* what kinds of questions customers are asking. Do you get installation questions, questions about usage, questions related to bugs? Are you getting lots of consulting-type calls, which can drain your resources? Would better documentation alleviate a whole category of questions? Create your own categories for what's meaningful for you and find a way to collect the information as calls are logged into the call tracking system (modern call tracking systems have a flexible way to record the causes of calls).

  Integrating this analysis with the analysis of calls by products gives you good insight on what kinds of problems occur on the various products you support.

- *Call distribution by customer:* how many calls are coming from various customers. Tracking the top ten support consumers can give you insight into who is in a busy development phase, who needs more training, and who may be abusing your service. You may want to contrast usage from high-paying customers and low-paying ones. With the right customer database, you can even determine what the effect of training or certification is on support usage (you may even decide to bundle some training with the cost of support or to offer a discount to certified customers based on that information).

  If you are supporting internal customers as well as external ones, typically supporting your technical sales force or your consultants, sharing the list of the top ten internal callers with their managers, can help you target appropriate training and process change so you can concentrate on external, paying customers.

- *Call resolution analysis:* how calls are resolved. When we discussed routine process metrics, we recommended to track resolution time—that is, the time elapsed between the receipt of a problem and its resolution. What we propose here is to analyze the actual work time that your staff devotes to resolving questions. We will see later how this analysis can be essential when cost-justifying support tools, but it's always a good idea to understand the resolution process in finer detail than with a simple average of time elapsed. What's the average work time on a call? How many calls are resolved in half the average work time? Twice the average? Can you tell what causes them to require so much time? Can you correlate the type of questions and the time to resolution?

With modern call tracking systems, there is almost no end to the analyses you can run, but you must make sure that you collect the data you will need down the road. For example, you cannot analyze call types if your staff is not entering them at some point during the call. You cannot analyze resolution time if your staff is not tracking time spent on calls. We cannot emphasize this enough: collect the data you need, and make sure the data's "clean."

On the other hand, resist the tendency to run analyses on all the pieces of data you are collecting. The main categories above are probably all you need. Run metrics with a goal in mind. Start with a business question such as: How many staff members do I need to support product X? and put together the appropriate metric.

Going forward, we will see many examples of business questions that require simple analyses to be run on the call tracking data.

CHAPTER **5**

PACKAGING SUPPORT PROGRAMS

In this section we will describe in detail how to package support programs. Careful packaging of support programs is important both for internal and external customers, and whether or not you charge for support. In many cases, it's best to create more than one support package, so we will discuss when to offer multiple packages and how to differentiate them from each other. We will also discuss whether and how to charge for support services.

The implementation strategies for packaging services depends on the nature of the software (low-complexity versus high-complexity) and on the kind of customers you have (external versus internal), so we will clearly distinguish between the various categories and strategies.

The focus of this chapter is on the needs of a support manager. Defining support programs requires professional marketing help, so we will give you the tools you need to define your requirements and to work with a marketing professional.

We will start with general considerations on why create packages, then move on to a more detailed discussion of how to create and market successful packages.

5.1 WHAT IS A SUPPORT PACKAGE AND WHY CREATE ONE?

There are two ways to approach packaging support services: from the customer advocacy side and from the marketing side. From the customer advocacy side, defining deliverables in advance helps to create a setting in which you can undercommit and overdeliver. On a more theoretical plane, as described in Chapter 2, "Call Management Models," a successful Basic Action Workflow depends in part on how well service commitments can be negotiated, hence how well they can be defined and internalized ahead of time. Well-designed packages help speed up the acceptance phase of the Basic Action Workflow so a mutual agreement can be reached quickly between the support engineer and the customer. Support packages contribute to efficiency, and they provide a good start to keeping customers satisfied.

From the marketing side, defining packages is a prerequisite to creating customer interest. Services are notoriously difficult to sell, since they are intangible, and furthermore software salespeople are usually more comfortable selling tangible products. Defining packages puts some reality around them. Selling support services is a particular challenge when the sale is essentially an insurance sale: the customer hopes never to have to use support, but needs to have it available if needed. (Some support packages can be sold as value-added services rather than as insurance.) In any case, defining what can be expected helps to make the sale and to foster positive customer relations down the road. Many support marketers now position support packages as support **products**, complete with product numbers, to make them seem more tangible.

Even if you are not charging separately for technical support, support packages help you differentiate yourself from the competition. And if the end-user is not choosing your product or service directly, as is the case for an internal help desk, defining packages is a first step to presenting an attractive image to your customers.

Finally, well-defined support packages help minimize disagreements and legal battles with your customers, and they define a joint understanding of what support can and cannot provide to everyone inside the company, from the support engineers to the salespeople.

You should define at least one, perhaps several support packages, and you should communicate them in a variety of media. First, they will be the core of your formal or informal Support User's Guide. Second, if you are selling your services, use the package definitions to create data sheets and other collaterals to help you sell them. Finally, and especially if you charge for your services, we recommend you describe your support packages in the legal agreement your customers sign.

5.2   DEFINING SUCCESSFUL SUPPORT PACKAGES

In this section we will cover what to put in a support package, how many different packages you should offer, and the sensitive issue of charging for technical support.

Defining support packages is essentially a marketing activity and includes the following components:

- Define the audience(s).
- Define the audience's needs or the problems that are being solved.
- Define the features or the deliverables of the packages.

- Determine the benefits to the audience of the features of the packages.
- Based on the activities above, price the packages.
- And, finally, distinguish the packages from each other and the competition—that is, position them.

Although you should understand the basics described here, the perspective from a marketing professional is very useful. For smaller environments, use a consultant for a few sessions.

5.2.1   Ingredients of Support Packages

A support package details what you will provide to customers (that is, what customers should expect to get from you). Therefore, all aspects of Technical Support can enter into the definition of a support package:

- Electronic services such as access to a bulletin board, patch download services, call logging and monitoring, bug alerts, and the like.
- Proactive support services such as technical newsletters.
- All features of the phone support service: hours of access, number of contacts who can call the hotline, alternate ways of getting service such as using the Web to enter questions, response time, availability of emergency services.
- Expedited bug fixing services.
- New functional releases: we will see later that new functional releases are usually bundled with support for complex products and usually purchased separately for low-complexity products, although the trends are changing.
- Account management services, such as account reviews and technical account planning: this is a rare, very much value-added feature.
- Special emergency services, such as onsite help: also a rare value-added ingredient.

To determine the components of your support packages, you need to analyze what services you can provide versus what the customer wants or will benefit from. For instance, you may be able to offer an on-line bulletin board, but if your customers cannot dial out, the benefit is nil for them, don't bother. Or your customers may want to have onsite support, but if you cannot build the appropriate infrastructure, you will have to find another way to meet the need. Balance realism and boldness. If your customers have requirements you cannot meet today, keep them in mind for later.

In most cases, you will want to design Russian-doll style packages, where each higher level of support includes all the features from the package at the next lower level. Be sure to define customer profiles for each package—that is, make sure that each package fills the needs of a real category of customers. You need to translate each feature into a tangible benefit for the customer: a faster response time means a faster answer, monitoring calls on-line means easier communications, and so on.

5.2.2   How many packages do you need?

The number of packages you should offer depends on what your customers want, what you can deliver, and what the competition is doing. One size does not always fit all. Almost all organizations would do well to have more than one package. The upper limit is a function of how many packages you can differentiate and sustain. Don't overextend yourself: one good basic package is much preferable to four badly defined, badly understood, and badly executed packages. You can easily add packages as you grow, provided that you don't blindly promise and deliver everything from the start. A good time to add a package is when you introduce a new service.

If your customers generally have similar needs, then one package is all you need. In particular, start-up ISVs who have a fairly homogeneous customer base can get away with just one package. However, in most settings, customers demand a larger array of more customized services. In particular, the complex support world pretty much requires multiple support packages. Even with an internal help desk, you will probably find that some departments require—and are willing to fund—different levels of service.

In many organizations, a basic and a deluxe package work well. The basic package fits the need of the budget-conscious or undemanding customers, while others can get top service. Adding a pay-as-you-go option rounds out your offerings quite nicely.

As your Support group becomes more sophisticated, your ability to sustain more packages will grow and you will be able to add a larger variety.

5.2.3   Supported Products and Versions

A key, but not immediately visible ingredient of support packages is a definition of what you will support. Restrictions on what products you support are a healthy part of doing business as a support center under the "Big is beautiful" motto. Each additional product means additional investments in equipment, software, training, and people resources, so consider carefully what you support. If you are adding a product to your portfolio, consider the cost of adding it. If a product has a shrinking customer base, consider terminating support for it, with an appropriate warning period and migration path for the customers. A typical retirement or end-of-life period in the commercial market is a year. Specialized markets may require five years or more. All customers appreciate additional warning beyond these guidelines, however.

If you are an ISV, the range of products you must support is governed by the Marketing group. Analyze what product lines (and what platforms) are particularly costly to support and work out special arrangements, including retirement paths, for them. Sometimes it makes sense to continue to offer support for waning products, but to price the service higher while decreasing the benefits. For instance, you can discontinue regular maintenance releases while increasing the cost of the support contract. Hardware vendors have used this strategy for years. Be careful, though, that you can maintain knowledgeable staff on board. Keeping an experienced support engineer who can answer calls about an old version is not an expensive proposition. Training a new support engineer on an obsolete product can be extremely difficult and costly.

If you have an internal help desk, you and your users determine what to support. Negotiate with the users for products with small audiences. Present the cost versus benefits analysis to them.

Even if you cannot have free reign in determining the range of products you have to support, you can often control the number of supported versions. Supporting several versions is very expensive, so most support centers restrict their support to a handful of releases, typically the most current one and the one before that. Take care to define exactly what will be supported, distinguishing between maintenance releases, patches, and functional releases. Typically, bug fixes are available only on the most current release; if that's the case, say so. Also take care that customers can upgrade the other parts of their systems such as hardware and operating systems in step with your requirements.

Define reasonable time frames for customers to upgrade to a supported version. Some customers with tough testing or policy requirements may need many months or even years to upgrade. Give the longest notice you can when requiring upgrades.

Once the policy is in place, you may choose to accept calls on obsolete versions on a "best-effort" basis. Be careful with those, since customers often feel that you are taking full responsibility for calls you accepted to work in the first place, even on the best-effort standard.

In short: Be very specific on what is supported, including, whenever appropriate, the exact configurations and version numbers.

5.2.4   Building Support Packages

A budget support package offers only the more inexpensive, non-personnel driven electronic services, typically access to a bulletin board and other on-line forums.

Moving up, a basic support package would offer the following ingredients:

- Access to an on-line bulletin board, including access to technical tools, electronic software delivery, and bug status capability (that is, the features of the budget offering if there is one).
- Business-hours access to the phone hotline for one contact.
- If working with an ACD, normal priorities (lower than for higher-level packages); if working on a callback system, response times of one hour for emergencies, a business day for routine requests.
- Definition of what software and what version of the software are supported.
- Basic commitments for bug fixing, such as: patches available for priority bugs (with a definition of priority bugs adequate for your environment), access to existing patches and maintenance releases via an on-line system.
- Ability to log calls and to check status on-line.

A higher-level support package would include, in addition to the above:

- Extended hours for access to the hotline.
- Availability of multiple technical contacts for the customer.
- The ability to jump to the front of the line if you work with an ACD, or faster callback commitments if you do not.
- Immediate access to a call dispatcher to bypass the ACD when required.
- Remote debugging through dial-in.
- (Possibly) support for an extended variety of software and versions.
- Faster and more extensive bug fixing commitments up to onsite assistance.

Each package can also have options, typically pieces of the higher-level offerings. For instance, customers with a budget package can be offered access to the hotline for a per-call fee. Customers with a basic package can be offered emergency or scheduled help off-hours for a fee. Especially with the options, make sure that you are defining something that is at the same time attractive and valuable to the customer and feasible for you as a provider.

Sample support packages are shown in the last section of this chapter.

5.2.5   Naming Support Packages

Spend the same amount of care and time picking names for support packages as you would for any other product. Make sure that

- The name is clear and precise.
- If you have a suite of packages, the names are both consistent with each other and differentiated.
- The names stand up well to competitors' packages. Choose unique names.

Use your marketing resources to find appropriate names with an eye toward the future. Remember to copyright your names.

5.2.6   Communicating Support Packages

Customers, salespeople, and everyone in the support center need to know what support packages exist and what they contain. Once your packages are defined, you need periodically to reinforce the information, and each time you make changes, you need to educate all three audiences.

For customers, you will need to put together a set of collaterals that present the features and benefits of the packages. In a small company, you don't need funding for a four-color glossy brochure. What's important is that you show both the features and the benefits of the various packages. Use the collaterals for new sales and send them to existing customers. If you are making changes and your customers have yearly support contracts, remember that the changes won't affect the entire customer base until all existing customers have renewed, so you will need to remind customers of the new programs when they renew during the upcoming year.

Salespeople will also need to use the collaterals, and they will need to be trained on the specifics of the packages as well as how to sell them. Pay particular attention to how to differentiate between the packages, how to qualify a customer for a specific level of support, and how to convince a customer to purchase the appropriate level of support. Direct, face-to-face contact with the sales force is best to convey the message, although a written backup document never hurts. Plan to reinforce the materials periodically. Collect success stories to show how selling support and in particular selling high levels of support can make the sales force successful.

Members of the support center staff must understand what's behind the packages, so they know what the organization has promised the customer— which is, of course, what they will have to deliver. Give them copies of the collaterals the customers see, so they can relate them to their day-to-day duties. Although support engineers tend to be good at assimilating written information, face-to-face discussions are more effective. Remember to ensure that new hires are also given the information.

Even when your support packages are stable, refresh everyone's memory from time to time.

5.2.7 Service Contracts

Service contracts are legal documents, often addenda to the license agreements for ISVs, which spell out service terms and conditions. Once you define support packages you have the logical content of the service contract. The only difficulty is to phrase them in a way that is acceptable from a legal point of view. Make sure, by the way, that your collaterals including Support User's Guides are reviewed by your lawyer, since they could be used in a legal disagreement.

Depending on the kind of support you provide, your service contract can range from a formal part of the license agreement, signed by the customer when the purchase is made, to a short paragraph packaged with the software agreement for consumer software.

Most of the specifics of support agreements, such as response time, access to electronic services, and hours of service, are easy enough to write. Be sure to include any restrictions on the services available, such as what you will do for obsolete versions and what is considered a consulting issue rather than a support issue.

Problems sometimes arise for wording problem resolution commitments. Be very careful not to promise specific problem and bug resolution times, since software fixes are unpredictable. Most often, support agreements contain language such as this: "Within 24 hours of the report of a defect that prevents the Software from functioning at all, the Company shall assemble an appropriate technical and management team to resolve the issue. Using reasonable commercial efforts, the Company shall pursue a fix for the defect . . ." Work out the specifics with a legal specialist, staying away from resolution commitments and using instead commitments to give status, including by the executives of your organization and to the executives of your customers, and even refunding the cost of the software.

Another interesting legal area is that of authorized technical contacts. If you sell service contracts, you will probably want to limit authorized contacts so as to force the customers to funnel questions through a small number of individuals. Besides limiting the volume of questions, especially trivial ones, which is good for you, this encourages the development of technical expertise at customer sites, which is beneficial for you and for them. From a legal point of view, it's also useful to clearly designate authorized contacts in case you ever direct them to make potentially dangerous changes to the software or you dial into the customer machines directly as part of problem resolution. Your legal advisor may recommend that you seek specific permission from your customers when gaining direct access to their machines or even when obtaining code excerpts or data samples from them.

5.3 PRICING AND SELLING SUPPORT PACKAGES

This brings us to the loaded issue of charging for technical support. Until recently, most of the low-end software products have been sold with "free" access to Technical Support. Buying the package entitles users to call support at no extra charge, once they have filled out the warranty card. Both software vendors and customers are now switching to fee-based offerings, the vendors being clearly motivated by a desire to recoup costs or make a profit from support, the customers because the so-called free support is after all embedded into the cost of the software, obscuring real costs, and because free support may involve long waits on a support hotline, which are not conducive to the productivity they were hoping to get from the software. In many cases, fee-based support coexists with free support.

Complex software products, on the other hand, are usually sold with support and maintenance contracts that are priced separately from the software, are mandatory, and include new functional releases. In that arena, there is a push to unbundle the support features and in particular to separate the support per se (hotline) from the software maintenance.

We will start by covering issues common to both worlds before concentrating on the particular challenges of the low-end and complex software worlds. Although this section is targeted directly to ISVs, internal help desk managers may benefit from the ideas surrounding pricing for outside customers, and we devote a special section to pricing help desk services.

5.3.1 Costing Out Support

Before we plunge into the world of support pricing, let's cover some basic considerations about determining your cost. You can't really define a good pricing scheme until you know how much it costs you to provide the service. You can decide, as many companies do, to provide service for free or for less than the cost, but you cannot make an informed decision until you have worked out the numbers.

Determining the total cost of support should be relatively easy. Here's a checklist to make sure you don't forget anything:

- Staff costs, including salaries and benefits.
- Management and company overhead.
- Training, travel.
- Facilities.
- Phone costs.
- Machines, including hardware, software, documentation, mainte-nance contracts, staff and facilities necessary to maintain the machines. Include both machines used by individual support engi-neers and shared machines used to replicate problems.
- Bulletin boards, on-line forums, Web sites.
- (For ISVs) marketing and sales costs. This is very important for low-price offerings; you don't want to spend more selling and mar-keting your packages than you receive in revenue.
- (For ISVs) software maintenance costs as separated out from new functionality costs.
- Profit margin required by your company.

Note that the costs may be neatly grouped together in your budget or dis-persed in a variety of other accounts, as is often the case for the phone and machine costs.

Once you have the total cost of support, you will want to factor it out in a num-ber of ways, most probably to calculate your cost per call or your cost per cus-tomer. Define carefully what you are including in your unit cost. Leaving out large chunks such as machine maintenance or management overhead can lead to costly errors.

You will often have to figure the cost of a particular kind of call, such as calls on a particular software product, or calls on a particular platform. To accom-plish this, you will have to investigate two areas:

- The cost of specific hardware, software, and training specifically required by the platform or the product. It's not uncommon to spend more to maintain the machines for an expensive but unpop-ular platform than you collect in support fees for it.
- The staff cost for the platform or product. If such calls are taken exclusively by some groups of support engineers who do nothing else, your task is easy. Most often, however, the interesting cost-ing questions arise for products and platforms that are supported together with others, so you will need to figure out the relative dif-ficulty of calls for the platform or domain. Your main weapon

should be to compare resolution times (actual time worked) for the various categories of calls. Modern call tracking systems allow users to track their time automatically, so be sure you enforce tracking times as a routine part of the job. Do not accept substitute measurements such as time elapsed until resolution. This can lead to serious errors.

5.3.2   Product Warranty

The warranty for a software product includes protection against media defects and assurance that the product works as described in the documentation. You must define your warranty period—that is, the length of time during which you will provide help with initial usage at no charge. Many warranties are void as soon as the customer opens the package (except for media defects); most expire after a few months. Of course, warranties may be as long as you choose. Service during the warranty period is free and does not need to be fancy.

5.3.3   Pricing Schemes

Assuming you have established that you want to charge for support services, the next step is to define a pricing scheme. Establish your pricing scheme with an eye on five, often contradictory components:

- *The competition*: if you decide to price higher than your competitors, you will need to show a demonstrable advantage to customers.

- *Your cost*: you may decide to price support below cost for competitive reasons, but you should always be aware of your cost, as described earlier in this section.

- *Your desired profit margin*: it may be zero or even negative, either permanently or temporarily. The margin could be different from the overall company margin (complex software support can often bring margins higher than those for the software itself, for example).

- *The value your customers see in your services*: this is the most difficult point, since it requires intimate knowledge of your customers. The basic idea is: what will the customer be ready and willing to pay in exchange for faster or better-quality service?

- *Simplicity*: pricing must be easy to understand both for salespeople and customers; obscure pricing schemes lead to errors and frustrations and end up ignored. Keep in mind that support is an annuity stream, so you want to design a system that can be used year after year with only minor adjustments.

The most popular support pricing scheme, based on the complex support world, which has always charged for support, is to charge a percentage of the software license, somewhere between 12% and 20% of the license charge, for an annual contract. The advantage of the percentage scheme is that it's simple and easy to remember (only one number). Unfortunately, that's about the only good thing that can be said about it. Its drawbacks are numerous:

- *It does not fare well with discounts.* Although most companies define support pricing as a percentage of **list** price, in practice the guideline is often ignored, resulting in severe and sometimes unintended cuts in support revenue. Deep discounts on software products are often acceptable, since the marginal cost is almost nil, but support is a headcount-driven activity that cannot sustain deep discounts. Also, once the low price has been granted for the first year, it's very difficult for the customer to accept to pay a much higher price for subsequent years. So we create a long-lasting problem by basing the price on the actual license cost.

- *It disintegrates as software prices fall.* Falling software prices are a challenge for software vendors, but at least the marginal cost of software is low. On a staff-driven supply like support, shrinking margins become negative margins quickly. So, even if your system is working well today, think about how it will work tomorrow.

- *It does not scale well in the low end.* Let's say your support is priced at 15% of license price and you sell big systems averaging $20 k apiece. Now you introduce a new low-end product priced at $199. What support can you deliver for $29.85? It probably does not even cover your ACD costs. Most companies get around this by defining a minimum contract cost for support, but then you have a not-so-simple rule for support pricing, and one that can be forgotten and misapplied.

- *(Less of an issue) It does not scale well in the high end.* With the same example as above, let's say you sell a $2 m contract. Does it make sense to charge $300 k for support? Will the customer accept it? One way companies get around this is by upgrading their high-end support customers to a higher level of support for the basic price.

- *It makes support renewals a nightmare.* Every year, when the support contract expires, someone must recompute the costs of all the software licenses at the customer site. Then, the customer is presented with a new bill, where some items have gone up and some down, to comply with the software selling strategy du jour. The bill then becomes a fresh opportunity to haggle and disagree: a lot of work for a disappointing result.

There is a better way. Simply define your support price independently from the price of the software. It's a little more complicated, since you now need to define a support price for each type of software and configuration, but you get the advantage of decoupling software and support costs. If you have a good handle on your costs, deriving a customer price with or without a profit margin is not difficult. At the high end, you may have to define a custom price (or a discount level) for large configurations, but that is true of any pricing scenario, since large customers demand discounts. You can make high-end discounts work for you by negotiating support-friendly arrangements such as few technical contacts.

If your support price is not a percentage of the price of the software, you need to define a support price for each product configuration. You can price the support based on the cost of the support and other support-related considerations rather than the cost of the software. For instance, purchasing support for a 12-user license with one technical contact can be barely more expensive than purchasing support for a single-user license. Don't forget to assign a product number to each support package.

Sounds like too much work? There is even a middle ground between pricing support as a percentage of the software and pricing it independently of the software: you may continue to price the initial support as some magic percentage of the license price, but for subsequent years simply adjust the cost upward according to some cost increase formula. Many customers actually like this way of proceeding, since it makes support costs predictable. The only time when you will need to expand effort on renewal pricing is when a customer adds or drops licenses (and even then you can choose to simply increase or decrease the price by the current support price for those licenses).

We recommend that you either select to price support independently of the price of the software or use the middle ground of pricing initial purchases of support as a percentage and then use the previous year's cost plus some percentage increase related to support cost and benefits to the customer.

5.3.4 Logistics of Renewals

If you charge for Technical Support, you need a way to collect the fees. Fees are typically collected yearly, although you may want to give customers an option to renew for multiple years for a slight discount, maybe simply the ability to guarantee the current price for several years. You want to be careful with discounts on support contracts because of the way support revenue is accounted for. Accounting rules require that you recognize support revenue when it is provided, so if a customer pays for a yearly contract you can recognize 1/12 of the amount each month. If the customer buys two years' worth, you can recognize 1/24 of the amount each month, and so on. Therefore, giving discounts will have an effect for a long time. Keep that in mind when designing discounts for purchasing multiple years of support: a 10% discount off today's price may become a 15% or 20% discount off the price for next year or the year after. Additionally, since support sales are repeat sales (at least that's what you should aim for), discounts are likely to create expectations for further discounts down the road.

Collecting support fees requires a good process and a reliable tracking system. It all adds up. If you are not charging for support today, you may find that the cost of the infrastructure may affect your decision to switch to fee-based support.

Think of the renewals staff as a Telesales group, not as an administrative collection group. They call customers and solicit the sale, even if it's with a customer you've had for years. Set up the group like a sales group, hire sales-oriented individuals, and give them saleslike incentives based on sales quotas. You could also outsource the support selling function.

The support renewal process is typically played out in three steps:

- Three months before the support contract lapses, send the customer a renewal notice, which also serves as an invoice. Ask the customer to contact you if the information on the notice needs changing and to pay the invoice if the information is correct.

- One month before the renewal date, if the customer has not paid, call the customer to make sure that the notice is correct and has been received. Make necessary changes and send a corrected invoice if necessary.

- On the renewal date, if the customer has not paid, inform the customer that support will be cut off if the bill is not paid promptly. Set your own deadlines. It makes sense to have a short grace period, especially if the mechanism for placing and removing a customer from support hold is onerous, but beware of supporting a customer without payment for several months: it is extremely difficult to collect back fees once service has been rendered, and especially if the customer did not happen to call support during the time the bill was unpaid.

One last note about the process of support renewals: how does one handle a customer who has been a supported user in the past, but has since discontinued support, for whatever reason, for some time? This is mostly an issue if you bundle technical support and new functionality. If you don't, then no service was rendered while the customer was not under contract and you can simply resume service at the customer's convenience. (Although if the customer decides to renew when a new project is launched, the support requirements are likely to be higher than usual right after renewal.)

If you do bundle new functionality together with technical support, however, consider how to handle interruptions in the support contracts, since customers could in theory discontinue support for long periods of time only to renew a contract when a new release is announced. No harm is done from the support perspective, since no service was rendered during the time the contract lapsed, but you could end up providing very cheap functionality to those on-again, off-again users. The typical strategy is to charge lapsed customers some kind of back fee to discourage the practice, usually the greater of the lapsed period and a year. Adjust the formula up or down to match the frequency of your new functionality releases.

Charging for support also requires you have a reliable tracking system so you don't end up providing free support to customers, or, worse, denying support to customers who have paid. If you have to develop such a system, keep in mind the following points:

- The system must be integrated with the call tracking system.
- It must allow checking the status of a customer very quickly. In particular, if you plan to use your ACD as the validation engine, it will not accept more than a few seconds' delay with the validation. You may be able to work around this requirement by setting up a lookup system that is downloaded nightly from the accounting system. (This technique would not be acceptable in a per-incident environment, where the information is very dynamic.)
- Ideally, the system should be expandable to include future levels of support and per-incident pricing if you do not support it yet.

The tracking system should also provide a way to support the renewal process, such as reports indicating the contracts that are coming to expiration. Ideally, the pricing methodology should be built into the system. Finally, the system should provide a way to input purchases quickly and easily

5.3.5   Pricing Issues for Low-End Software Support

The main current issues in the low-end software support realm are switching from free to fee-based support, and whether to bundle or unbundle new functional releases.

Historically, low-end software products have been sold with "free" support, but this is changing as both customers and software vendors realize that value is associated with a separate charge and that free support gets paid for in the initial license price anyway. Also, customers who want to get better service than what is available through the free offerings are asking for premium support and are willing to pay for it. Software vendors see an opportunity to recoup costs or make a profit from support, and they know that having customers pay for support may reduce the call load.

In many cases, fee-based support coexists with free support for low-end software. Let's see how you can ease into fee-based support.

Creating a Value Proposition

A common approach is to offer free support for the length of the warranty and then to offer fee-based support. Another approach, especially if your support is currently free, is to offer special advantages for fee-based offerings compared to the free, no-frills package. You can also limit the free support along other lines than time—for instance, limit it to a small number of incidents, say three incidents, or to certain kinds of questions, such as installation and configuration questions.

If you currently offer "free" support, you need to create an attractive proposition for your customers—that is, answer the question: "Why would my customers want to pay for support?" other than with "Because they will now have to." Going back to selling support as an insurance policy, you need to present the benefits of for-a-fee support in terms of adjuncts to the basic policy. Typical incentives to migrate to a fee-based system are:

- Faster access to a support engineer through some priority scheme for paying customers.
- Priority in getting bug fixes other than through maintenance releases.
- Direct access to more skilled support engineers (if you work with a tiered support system).
- Access to a named support engineer.
- Account management services.

Some of the services are not difficult or costly to provide; however, the last three may be complex, so think twice before offering them.

One positive aspect of starting a fee-based support package in the low-end software world is that it is easy to use a pricing scheme independent from the cost of the software license, since there is no history of using a percentage scheme.

We recommend you ease into fee-based support by taking small steps in that direction, first by removing all mentions of free support in your product and collaterals (that's a big job in itself!), then by announcing the fee-based services, starting to sell them, and only later cutting off free support if you wish to. As a bonus to its beneficial effects for customers, the transition period will allow you to tune your internal processes and to make adjustments to the packages, if needed.

Bundling Support and New Functional Releases

Another issue for low-end support, also related to pricing, is the handling of new functional releases. Most vendors of complex software charge for technical support and for new functional releases together; that is, all supported customers get new functional releases without added cost. However, at the low end, technical support charges are usually decoupled from the cost of new functional releases, so that a supported user has to pay separately for new releases (almost always at a deep discount from the normal price of the product).

The advantages of bundling support and new releases are balance and simplicity. Balance, because each component is more valuable at either end of a customer life cycle: new customers need lots of support as they become acquainted with the software, and they don't need new features much, since they barely understand the ones they have. Experienced customers tend to use support less but look forward to new releases. Bundling support and new functional releases therefore allows you to create a balanced package suitable for customers with a variety of experience levels.

Also, from a company's point of view, the task of scheduling and integrating bug fixes is much easier with bundling: all bug fixes can simply go into a new release, and there is a decreased need to continue supporting old releases, and in particular to continue to supply bug fixes for them. Bundling new functional releases with support provides a handy way to fund the development of new products, something the developers of complex software have exploited very well. If you are not currently bundling new functional releases with support packages, it's easy to start offering bundles.

If customers have a choice of purchasing upgrades either as they come out or together with support, pay attention to your record keeping and do not allow individual customers to mix and match the two options, it would be a record-keeping nightmare.

5.3.6   Pricing Issues for Complex Software Support

Up to now, complex software products have been sold with fee-based support contracts that include both support and new functional releases. Buying support is usually mandatory when buying a new license of a complex support product. The pricing issues in the complex software world include requirements for per-incident pricing and a strong push to unbundle support from new functional releases, a push which is only partly related to the per-incident pricing requirement.

Per-Incident Pricing

It used to be that paying per call, or paying "per incident," since strictly speaking it may take several phone calls to resolve a single problem, was the province of low-end software. This pricing strategy is gaining ground as the distinction between high-end and low-end software blurs, driven by similarities in hardware platforms and by price.

The idea of per-incident pricing is very simple: instead of offering a yearly contract for unlimited support, customers pay a fee for each call or each "incident." Most systems offer some kind of discount for purchasing multiple incidents or call packs. The fee is most often charged to a credit card and can be paid at the time service is needed.

Some practical considerations must be addressed if you are considering implementing per-incident support. First, you must define what an incident is—that is, when one incident ends and another begins, or how to handle the "One more thing" questions at the end of a support call. Incidents are not always clear-cut, and customers can see one incident where you can see two or more. This is particularly difficult in the complex software support arena because of the nature of the questions.

Another concern is tracking the per-incident billing, especially if you offer call packs, as it is quite different from tracking the annual contracts you are used to handling. Finally, since you probably offer support over extended hours, you may want to define different, more restrictive hours for per-incident pricing as an incentive for customers to purchase a support contract. For instance, per-incident customers could be restricted to call during business hours. On the other hand, if you already have an off-hours infrastructure in place, you may want to offer off-hours service to per-incident customers, maybe at a higher price, to build up your volume off-hours.

Per-incident pricing is determined through a combination of what the market will bear and the cost of providing the service. This is another challenge for the complex software support world, where costs are high: would you pay $200 for a single incident? What about $400? Typically, margins in the per-incident business are low, as the price pressure is downward.

Note that per-incident pricing takes away from the "support as insurance" sales model. To attract customers to purchase yearly support contracts, offer them special treatment such as higher priorities, longer hours, and, of course, lower per-call prices if they end up calling a lot.

Unbundling Support and New Functional Releases

Software developers of complex products have traditionally bundled support and new functionality releases together. Bundling has served the industry well, and despite strong customer interest in unbundling, it is likely to remain the standard for the next few years. You may want to start thinking about or even experimenting with unbundling now, however.

First, the good news: bundling new functional releases together with support encourages customers to take them for granted. (It's interesting to note how many complex software support packages do not even list new functional releases as one of their features!) Unbundling per se allows you to create a value proposition for new functional releases.

The main challenge with unbundling functional releases in an environment that has used bundling in the past is the loss of the automatic funding of new functional releases. Unbundling results in the loss of your annuity stream.

Unbundling also creates a technical challenge: the entire code management process needs to be refocused to support old releases longer and more carefully than under the bundling system. No longer can you tell a customer to "simply" upgrade to the next release.

Think carefully, together with your Marketing and Engineering groups, about which method you will use. Because of the code management issues, it's very hard to change from bundling to unbundling, although the reverse is easy. And, as noted above, carefully record whether and how customers chose to purchase upgrades, and mandate that each customer choose just one method for acquiring upgrades.

5.3.7 Pricing Issues for Internal Help Desks

Many internal help desks are funded through some budget apportionment mechanism and do not really have to sell their services, even internally. However, the trend is toward internal cross-charging of services, and, with outsourcing always a possibility if the envelope is perceived to be too large, help desk managers must pay attention to costs.

Step one is to know your cost. Referring back to Section 5.2.5, compute what the average call costs you, and whether there are significant differences between categories of calls. Reflect on how you can bring the costs down: Decrease the support engineer headcount? Decrease the management overhead? Save on training or travel? Streamline the machines and software you use to replicate problems? Use proactive support methods to lower the call load? Get comparison data from similar help desks to determine whether you are competitive (or even get a quote from an outsourcing company before someone else in the company thinks of it).

Cross-charging the departments you serve may be done either on a per-call basis or by contract. This is very similar to what ISVs do when charging their customers. Typically, charging per contract is easier, because it involves fewer transactions and less record keeping in general, although it can be more difficult to justify. Per-call charges are easier to understand. In any case, you will charge either your straight cost or cost plus some margin. Present a bill to your users whether or not dollars are actually transferred between departments. It's useful to capture the value of the service.

Be sure to review your pricing on a yearly basis as your costs go up (or, perhaps, down) and your customer requirements change.

5.4 SAMPLE SUPPORT OFFERINGS

This section presents sample offerings for companies of various sizes and product complexity. Since offerings and prices change often, our main goal here is to give you ideas of how you can structure your offerings rather than trying to give up-to-the-minute descriptions. When you read the offerings, consider how the various companies approached the issue of building suites of offerings as opposed to single packages. Note the pricing differences between the packages.

5.4.1 Sample Offerings for Low-End Software

Basic Package (no charge)
- for the first 90 days (warranty period)
- unlimited toll calls

Advanced Package ($100–$200 per year)
- unlimited toll-free calls
- priority telephone access over no-fee customers
- software fixes via electronic download; physical media is extra
- on-line access to discussion forums
- possible extras: quarterly technical newsletter, development partners directory

Premium Package ($300–$500 per year)
- all features of the Premium Package
- technical newsletter on CD-ROM

Unbundled Offerings
- subscription to the technical newsletter (priced like a technical magazine)
- per-incident support ($20–$50 per incident or $2–$3 per minute)

Notice some interesting features of this suite of offerings:

- Support is provided free of charge for 90 days. An alternative would be to limit the number of calls (incidents) rather than the time frame.

- Offerings are Russian-doll style, although the basic services for support and for the technical newsletter can be purchased unbundled.

- Paying support customers have priority over the free (warranty) customers when calling the hotline.

- Upgrades are purchased separately from support, as is common for low-end software.

5.4.2   Sample Offerings for High-End Software with a Budget Offering

Budget Package ($100–$200 per year)

- unlimited access to the on-line services including a bulletin board, technical information, electronic patch downloading

- quarterly technical newsletter

- product upgrades must be purchased separately

Standard Package (12%–15% of license price, plus $2000–$4000 per contact pair, per year)

- all features of the Budget Package

- maintenance and functionality releases

- unlimited access to the hotline with callback times of 1 hour and up for two or more contacts

- ability to log calls and monitor progress electronically

- 24x7 support is available as an option to the Standard Package

Advanced Package (12%–15% of license price, plus $5000–$6000 per contact pair with a minimum of $40–$60 k per year)

- all features of the Standard Package

- toll-free calls

- 24x7 support always included

- support through a dedicated pool of support engineers

- fast, guaranteed response times (if response times are missed, the support charges for the following year are discounted)

Premium Package (custom pricing, typically 20% of license price with a minimum of $100–$120 k per year)

- all features of the Standard Package
- toll-free calls
- 24x7 support
- support through a dedicated support engineer
- fast response times (15 minutes for emergencies)
- proactive technical account management, including regular onsite visits, periodic technical account reviews and recommendations

Note some interesting features of this suite of offerings:

- The Budget Package has a very low marginal cost for the company and so can be priced dramatically lower than the others. A nice addition to the Budget Package would be a per-incident pricing offering. For complex support, per-incident pricing would probably be by the incident, not by the minute, and would be priced over $150.
- Upgrades are bundled with support except at the lowest level to allow the rock-bottom price.
- The guaranteed response time feature under the Advanced Package gives customers a nice benefit while creating minimum exposure for the company. If you manage your center and your ACD properly and you don't have a high proportion of Advanced Package customers, you should not have to issue any refunds.
- This suite is not completely Russian-doll. The top two offerings differ slightly in their definition of dedicated support. This allows catering to customers who feel they need a personal touch (with the Premium Package) while allowing customers who value speed of resolution over the personal touch to get what they need for a lower price and a lower threshold (with the Advanced Package). In addition to allowing for different features to fit different customer needs, this can be a good strategy to integrate an existing Standard/Premium model without changes.
- Customers must choose one level of support for each separate site, so that one project does not end up getting free support through another. This is straightforward to administer for a small customer. For large customers, however, you must define what a site is in relationship to the company as a whole and to an individual project. Typically you will need to be fairly close to the customer to make the determination.

5.4.3   Sample Offerings for High-End Software with High-End Options

Budget Package (25%–35% of license price with a minimum of $4000–$6000 per year)

- available only to users of designated desktop platforms
- unlimited access to the on-line electronic services including a bulletin board, discussion forums, and patch downloading function
- quarterly knowledge base on CD-ROMs
- maintenance and new functionality releases
- unlimited toll-free access to the hotline with response times of 2 hours and up for one designated contact
- no options can be added to the support package (no off-hours support, no additional contacts)

Standard Package (14%–16% of license price, with a minimum of $6000–$8000 per year)

- all features of the Budget Package
- unlimited access to the hotline with callback times of 1 hour and up for two designated contacts
- ability to log calls and monitor progress electronically
- 24x7 support available as a fee-based option
- emergency off-hours support available for an additional fee
- more than two contacts can be designated for an additional fee

Advanced Package (16%–18% of license price, with a minimum of $40–$60 k per year)

- all features of the Standard Package
- 24x7 support
- faster response times (although emergency callbacks remain at 1 hour)
- additional contacts over 2 are added automatically as fees exceed certain minimums

Premium Package (20%–22% of license price with a minimum of $200–$250 k per year)

- all features of the Advanced Package
- fast response times (30 minutes for emergencies)
- support through a dedicated support engineer if the annual fee exceeds 100 k

- proactive technical account management, including regular onsite visits, periodic technical account reviews and recommendations if the annual fee exceeds 200 k
- credits for consulting and training days

This suite of offerings has a number of interesting features:

- The Budget Package is designed specifically for low-end platforms where competition is fiercer and requires lower pricing. In addition to the platform restrictions, customers with the Budget Package don't have access to any options, including 24x7 support.
- Upgrades are always bundled with support, a common strategy for complex high-end software.
- At the higher levels, valuable options are added automatically as the fees exceed a certain level (the number of authorized contacts is increased, a dedicated engineer is made available). This is a good strategy to convince high-end customers that they are getting value for their fees.
- Pricing is designed in such a way that customers who use options heavily are incented to choose the next higher level of support. For instance, Standard customers who want 24x7 support (a common occurrence for this high-end software) should consider the Advanced Package.

5.4.4   Sample Offerings for Mid-Level Software

Basic Package

- free, unlimited access to electronic services including knowledge base, bulletin board, fax-back system
- software updates must be purchased separately
- incident packs: 1 for $150, 10 for $1500, 35 for $3995
- 24x7 access to a toll-free hotline
- unlimited contacts at single site

Advanced Package

- free, unlimited access to electronic services including knowledge base, bulletin board, fax-back system
- no software updates
- $25,000 for 150 incidents, 10 additional incidents for $1500
- 24x7 access to a designated engineer through a toll-free number
- unlimited contacts at multiple sites in one country

Premium Package

- free, unlimited access to electronic services including knowledge base, bulletin board, fax-back system
- no software updates
- $225,000 for unlimited incidents for 10 contacts at multiple sites around the world
- 24x7 access to a designated team through a toll-free number

Here are some interesting features of this suite of offerings:

- It is built around per-incident pricing.
- Per-incident pricing removes the issue of limiting the number of contacts, since you control the number of calls instead.
- Note that even at the top level software upgrades are not bundled.
- Access to the hotline is always 24x7. Pricing is not different for off-hours support. This is made possible by the very high volume of incoming calls.

CHAPTER 6
SUPPORT ORGANIZATION STRUCTURE

In this chapter we explore ways to organize the support center both within the larger organization it belongs to and internally to create maximum efficiency and customer satisfaction. There are many possible alternatives, and we will help you decide what to choose based on your requirements and preferences. Since the history of Technical Support is short, there remains much flexibility in making decisions about structure. We will also discuss the issue of outsourcing, since it often comes up when organizational questions are raised.

On the issue of choosing a reporting structure for the Technical Support group, the type of customers (internal or external) usually dictates the location of the support center within the organization, as internal help desks typically reside either within the MIS group or together with the department they are chartered to support. On the other hand, with ISV (Independent Software Vendor) support centers, the decision depends on the size of the center and where customers are in relation to the headquarters and to other existing centers. The type of support provided (high-end versus low-end) plays a minor role in determining the reporting structure.

When it comes to the internal organization of support centers, the issues are similar for help desks and ISV Support groups. They include deciding whether to provide support out of multiple centers and how to provide international support.

Structuring support centers is a politically charged decision, and many of the decisions discussed here will eventually be made for organizational reasons rather than the support- and customer-oriented rationales we present. Nevertheless, we believe that understanding these rationales will help you make and influence better decisions within your organization.

Beyond organizational and structural issues, there are many additional issues surrounding staffing and people management in a support center, which we will cover in the following chapter.

6.1   DO I NEED AN ORGANIZATION DEDICATED TO SUPPORT?

The first question you need to ask yourself is whether you need to go through all this work. When should you create an organization dedicated to Technical Support?

If you have an internal help desk, you already have an organization dedicated to support and you may skip ahead to the next section.

If you already have a dedicated Support organization, you may not wish to revisit that basic decision, but you may find it refreshing to review the reasons why a dedicated organization helps you meet your customers' needs. You may also need to address a similar issue if you must decide whether to set up a remote office, especially in a foreign country. We invite you to read on.

6.1.1   If you're just starting out

If you work for a small ISV, chances are that you do not yet have an organization dedicated to support, and you will have to decide whether and when to create a dedicated Support organization. If so, you are probably functioning with the Engineering (Development) organization responding to customer requests.

Having software developers provide support is the natural way to provide support in a start-up environment. It has advantages both because it ensures that software developers get appropriate customer input and because it gives customers full access to high-level technical skills. However, it also creates problems, which become less acceptable as the company grows:

- The skills required to deliver quality technical support are quite different from those required to deliver quality code. Customer satisfaction suffers if developers lack the customer relationship skills required to provide good support.

- There is an inherent conflict between developing software and responding to support calls. Interrupting development work several times a day to respond to customers leads to decreased productivity. When a release needs to be shipped, support time is likely to be curtailed. Similarly, heavy support loads can mean development schedules are impacted.

- Organizing and scheduling support with a crew of part-timers is difficult, and so is implementing consistent processes. This creates internal challenges, especially with scheduling. Furthermore, customer satisfaction issues as processes are not well defined.

Therefore, there comes a time when creating a dedicated Support organization makes sense. You know it's time when either the issues of skills and scheduling described above become unbearable, or, preferably, when you can anticipate the point when the support work load requires the equivalent of two full-time people. You want to get beyond one full-time person, since an organization with only one person is too small to be sustained, especially for support which needs to be up and running every day.

So we recommend that you create a Support organization once it takes two full-time staff members to handle the load. With such a small organization, you will continue to need to rely on the Development organization to provide backup and high-level assistance, but you will resolve the skills and scheduling issues inherent with having software developers provide support.

What if you have a large Development organization that also provides support and you are not experiencing any of the problems we described above? Do you need to create a Support organization anyway? First, look more closely for problems. It's very unlikely that you truly have such an idyllic situation. Our bet is that some of the developers have become specialized in providing support and others are sheltered from it, so you do have a dichotomy of some sort. Also look at process and tracking issues: are you able to determine the calls coming in and out, and to measure the effort that goes into providing support? If not, implementing a dedicated organization may help you reach those goals. Finally, consider the impact of the support requirements on crunch development periods, such as when a new release is about to ship. Are customer calls put on the back burner then?

Of course, you don't want to lose your valuable ties to the Development organization when you create a separate Support organization. Later in this chapter we will see how to preserve the ties, so that fear should not prevent you from creating a dedicated Support group once you reach a critical mass of a handful of staff members.

6.1.2   Starting a Center in a Foreign Subsidiary

Let's now focus on a different start-up situation where a small sales office remote from the headquarters office that already has a support center must decide whether to implement a local support center. In this case, the local technical sales representatives double as support engineers (and trainers and consultants). Let's explore whether and how to transition to a dedicated Support organization in this situation.

As you make the decision of whether to create a new center, take full advantage of the knowledge, tools, and processes of the existing centers. Even if the local conditions are different, don't ignore accumulated wisdom and experience.

The big decision is to determine whether you need a center separate from that other, larger one (you may want to peruse Section 6.4, "Do I need more than one center?" to help you make the decision.) Assuming time zones and language requirements prevent support from being provided from that other center, the decision to establish a separate organization is based on criteria similar to those used in the start-up situation:

- Are the competing responsibilities of the technical staff members (sales support, training, consulting, technical support) creating scheduling issues?
- Does the support workload require at least two support engineers?

If the answers to both questions are "yes," then it's time to think about a separate Support organization. It's very healthy and necessary at the beginning to continue to have support engineers play multiple roles and provide other post-sales services along with the occasional presales assignment. With a small staff, you need to make the most of your technical talent, and the support engineers will appreciate a variety of assignments to break the routine of answering support calls. Focusing individuals on the separate pieces, however, will give you more continuity and in the end will produce better customer satisfaction.

Once you decide to create a new center, take full advantage of the knowledge, tools, and processes of the larger sales and Support organization located in the headquarters office. Leverage its experience to help you avoid pitfalls so you can focus on implementation, not reinventing the wheel. Use the checklist below:

- Share problem resolution and escalation processes. The workflow model should be the same as the one used in existing centers, although its implementation will need to be modified to the local requirements and in particular to the small size of the new center.
- Give the new center full access to the knowledge base. This is key, since the new center will be too small and too new to generate its own information for a while.
- Implement the same call tracking system. Using the same system simplifies customization issues for the new center, makes it easier to share knowledge (yes, even if call notes are in German, a lot of information can still be gleaned from them), and allows for easier communication if you want to migrate to a follow-the-sun system later on.
- Especially if the new center is the first one outside headquarters, adapt your planning process for new products and upgrades to include the new center. Communication and training need to

include all support locations. This can be a difficult change to implement if casual communications among headquarters staff have been the norm.

To summarize, skills and scheduling requirements combine to recommend establishing a separate, focused Support organization once the load reaches beyond one full-time equivalent staff. Having a dedicated, professional organization will ease scheduling issues and improve customer satisfaction, both by raising the skills of the individuals who provide support and by making it possible to implement consistent support processes.

6.2 THIRD-PARTY SUPPORT: OUTSOURCING

One intriguing possibility that arises as early as the creation of the Support organization is outsourcing. Rather than provide support in-house, with its attendant requirements for headcount, phone, and tracking systems, you may consider going to an expert and outsourcing your support function.

The question can also arise after the support center is created—either as a short-term solution to handle a new release, say, or to tide you over if you cannot expand the facility or hire support engineers fast enough, or as a long-term or permanent solution.

6.2.1 When is outsourcing the right choice?

Outsourcing support may be the right solution for you as a substitute to having your own organization if you can find an organization that provides quality support at a lower price than you can. Another common reason for outsourcing is to allow you to concentrate on your core business and your core competencies (this is why internal help desks are often outsourced). Outsourcing can also be valuable as an adjunct to your organization if you need help for extremely busy periods, such as the introduction of a new product, traditionally busy times of day or times of year, or even to provide off-hours support. Also, you may choose to outsource support in special circumstances, such as a substitute for terminating support on a product. Clarify the reasons why you want to outsource, they will guide your choice: for instance, your cost requirements are different if you decide to outsource to reduce cost or to handle peak loads.

Since third-party support providers face the same challenges you do in finding, training, and retaining quality support engineers, they will be able to deliver customer satisfaction for an affordable price only if they can leverage their superior processes and the know-how they can get from you to accomplish these tasks. Therefore you will find that third-party support providers tend to follow this profile:

- They are located in an area where facilities and cost of living are affordable and where appropriately skilled labor can be found.
- They have critical mass so they can leverage better across more support transactions.
- They have established processes and systems for: call resolution, phone intake, call tracking, problem tracking, training, knowledge base, and billing.

It's hard to decide whether outsourcing will meet your need until you find a provider that meets your requirements. We will describe the logistics of finding a good third-party support provider and of making the arrangement work later on; however, here are some high-level points for predicting whether a third-party arrangement is likely to be successful for you:

- *Service as a strategic advantage:* if you view service as your core competence, outsourcing may take away the advantage by removing direct contact with your customers. If you decide in favor of outsourcing, you will need to work especially hard at maintaining the quality and the ties to your customer base.
- *Complexity of the software:* the more complex your software, the more difficult it is to find a third-party provider. Most third-party providers are excellent at supporting office-productivity packages and lightweight applications. Complex software is rarely outsourced because of the complex technical requirements.
- *Availability of training and knowledge base:* even if your software is not low-end and readily known by third-party software providers, you should be able to work out an arrangement if you can train efficiently and continuously (through a knowledge base) on your product. If you have nothing set up, training will need to be created, which will be costly. Note that you would have to train your own support people, too, but the requirements for an offsite, remote group are much higher than for in-house staff.
- *Support model:* a Frontline/Backline support model works well with outsourcing, since the third-party can play the part of the Frontline group. A Touch and Hold model requires that all support engineers be well trained, which is a challenge for third parties if your software is complex. Also, a T&H model requires you design strong processes to obtain help from technical advisers from afar.

If you are outsourcing all of your support operation, this point becomes irrelevant.

- *Processes for reporting and fixing problems:* with a third party, you will need to have robust processes to handle highly technical problems and to deliver fixes. If you are starting out, or have not yet developed those processes, the frustration and confusion around processes will become unbearable with a third party. (Starting an outsourcing arrangement might be an opportunity for you to create those processes, however.)

- *Critical mass:* big is especially beautiful for third-party support. If you have a small internal desk that supports a common word processing package, you will find that outsourcing is cheaper than doing it in-house. If you need to outsource a small Support group that supports an obscure and complex CASE package, you will find that it cannot be done properly for less than the in-house cost and that it requires months of setup. However, outsourcing a large Support group that supports a complex product may be cost effective, since the start-up costs are spread over a large number of headcount.

- *Peak scheduling versus permanent alternative:* if you are looking for help on a temporary basis, either as a one-time initiative or as an overflow mechanism, you will see that the issue of cost recedes somewhat; that is, you don't need the cost to be lower than that of your average call, just lower than your incremental cost for busy periods. The main issue then becomes: can it be cheaper for the third party to recruit, train, and retain personnel to handle the peaks than it is for you? If you support low-end software, the answer is likely to be yes, since the third party can balance your load with everyone else's for a small training investment. Also, outsourcing used in that way can be a technique for disaster recovery.

  If you have appropriate facilities and support infrastructure, consider hiring temporary help as an alternative to outsourcing for busy periods. It could be cheaper and easier to find local consultants or to train local staff, depending on how many people you need and how easily available the skills are.

In the end, once you have weighed all the facts about requirements, costs, and results, the outsourcing decision has political undertones. Outsourcing support shrinks the support center, sometimes down to nothing, and creates a lot of headcount leverage. The ultimate decision may hinge exactly on headcount vs. leverage considerations.

6.2.2 Making Outsourcing Work for You

There are four steps to a successful outsourcing partnership:

- Select your outsourcing partner carefully.
- Set service levels and include them in a mutually beneficial agreement that balances the service and quality levels you need and the profit the outsourcer needs to make.
- Define and implement a comprehensive implementation plan.
- Monitor the quality on an ongoing basis.

Here's a checklist you can use to select the outsourcing company. Use it to rate the candidates, getting first-hand accounts whenever possible. Visit the candidates, spend time with them, and check references thoroughly.

- Is the company well funded? What is the history of revenue and profits?
- Is support the company's focus?
- Is the philosophy of the company compatible with yours? This is key for many reasons, but in particular because the staff of the outsourcing company will need to be treated as your employees with respect to access to your systems, to your information. The culture of the outsourcing company, its management style, and its business philosophy all need to be compatible with yours.
- How relationship oriented is the company? Is it flexible?
- What other accounts does the company have? Will you be able to get enough mindshare?
- Are good references available? Have they ever lost an account and why?
- What offerings are available?
- What are the hours of coverage?
- What products are supported? What platforms?
- What is the expertise level of the staff?
- How is training accomplished? What training facilities exist? How quickly can they get staff up to speed?
- What is the infrastructure? Visit the call center and listen in on calls.

- What hardware and software is available to support engineers?
- What are the disaster recovery plans?
- What is the ACD used? Is it compatible with yours?
- What is the call tracking system?
- Is there a knowledge base system? What is it? How can it be augmented? Can documents in it be shared with you or your customers?
- Are electronic support methods supported?
- What is the process for communicating product defects and feedback?
- What is the call volume?
- What is the typical wait time? abandon rate?
- What is the percentage of problems resolved on the first call? the same day?
- How is customer satisfaction measured?
- What reports are available?

Define service levels in the same manner you would define them for yourself or for your customers. Include

- *Wait times:* for example, 90% of calls answered in one minute, less than 5% abandon rate.
- *Callback times for messages:* for example, callback under 2 hours.
- *Percentage of problems resolved on first call or on the same day:* for example, 80% of problems resolved on the first call.
- *Customer satisfaction ratings:* for example, 90% of customers are satisfied or very satisfied based on a random survey of 10% of the calls.
- *Aging call monitoring:* for example, daily management review of calls older than two days.

Include service-level definitions into the legal agreement and tie financial consequences to them.

Once the selection is complete, create a comprehensive implementation plan that includes: process definition, staffing, training, phone setup, hardware setup for each support engineer and for communicating back and forth, metrics reports, disaster recovery contingencies. The initial setup can take several months.

Attention to the proper setup is key, but don't stop there. You need to follow through and monitor the relationship throughout the life of the outsourcing agreement. Periodic reviews and adjustments are necessary to ensure that the partnership is working well, especially at the beginning. We suggest that you review metrics at least monthly and that you hold management business reviews quarterly. Outsourcing is a partnership. You will only get out of it what you put into it.

6.2.3   Providing Technical Support through Sales Distributors

If you use third-party sales distributors, and especially if you use them in countries that are either remote or have a different language base, you will need to consider whether to use your (sales) distributors as support centers. If you are operating in foreign territory, the considerations may be very short: they can speak the language and you can't, so they must provide support for you. Even if time zone or language requirements do not dictate it, customers or distributors may demand that you have distributors provide support to foster closer ties between the distributor and the customers.

Using distributors as support providers is different from using traditional third-party support providers, because distributors do not focus on Technical Support. Therefore, they typically have none of the systems, tools, or processes traditional outsourcing partners offer. Instead of working with a knowledgeable support provider, you will often be placed in the position of coaching the distributor on how to provide support. Moreover, turnover is often high with distributor technical people. This will affect both training and the support you need to provide to the distributor.

The main challenge is to incent the distributors to place appropriate attention on support. Since the focus of the distributor is selling, when it comes time to choose between investing in sales and investing in support, the choice is usually the former. You need to work in concert with the Sales organization to integrate the support issues into the agreement with the distributor. The issue usually boils down to how the distributor is paid: most of the time, compensation is tied to providing support per se and not to service levels. If you can include service levels in the definition of the compensation, the quality of support should improve.

We recommend you share all your tools and processes with the distributors. Give them access to your call tracking system, your knowledge base, other tools. Share training materials with them. Invite them to attend training classes. Share your approach to packaging and selling support too.

You will need to set up processes to provide second-line support to distributors. This is where having shared knowledge and systems pays off: it decreases the call load and it makes it easier to interact with them. Depending on the structure of your Support group and the level of expertise of the distributor, you may choose to have the calls come through the normal process as if they were customer calls or to bypass the first level of support for more experienced distributors.

You should arrange a royalty relationship on support revenues with the distributors if they collect support fees from their customers. The fee can be based either on a proportion of their support revenue (say, 10%) or on the support they require from you (either price this as you would for a regular, but large customer, or create some kind of custom pricing). Since distributors are often set up through the Sales force, you will need to negotiate through it to get the support terms agreed to. It's a challenge to get financial compensation added to an existing arrangement, so act early here.

The major issue with providing support through third parties is quality. Customers may well associate your name with the support they receive rather than the third party's. If you have several third parties, you may want to create a certification program (you can also use it internally, and if you have one for employees already, it's an easy matter to expand it to outsiders). Certification may either be a requirement for distributors or be used as an incentive to get more attractive support terms and conditions. Beyond that, you can monitor quality through customer surveys or other metrics.

Another issue with distributor support is how to keep track of your customers. There's a large benefit in knowing who your customers are, so you should try to include in the distributor agreement the right to get customer lists, or at least the right to use the lists for blind mailings. Accurate lists of valid support customers are important, even if you don't have access to them, to ensure appropriate royalty payments, if any, and for the future if, in a foreign country, you end up purchasing the distributor or setting up your own operation.

Domestic distributors are potential competitors if you also supply support directly to customers. Differentiate from them and find ways to be unique if you want to compete with them. Often there is a natural segmentation where customers tend to purchase support from the software vendor, but, again, if you intend to compete with distributors on support, make sure it works out well for you and for your distributors. One of the hallmarks of successful businesses today is their ability to both cooperate and compete with each other.

Foreign distributors often turn into subsidiaries: many companies expand into foreign countries by purchasing their successful distributors. If your distributor already uses the same support processes and tools you do, the integration will be much easier.

6.3 REPORTING STRUCTURE

In this section, we discuss options for where to place the Technical Support group within the company structure. If you have an internal desk, your options are limited to either the MIS department or the department that you support, so you may want to skip this section.

On the other hand, if you have an ISV support center, the options are numerous, and choosing one may make a big difference in your efficiency and your ability to provide quality service to your customers. Your choice depends mostly on the size of the group and the internal structure of the company.

Here are some options for locating the Technical Support organization:

- *In the Engineering (Development) group:* this is a common configuration for start-ups and consequently for small companies. The advantage of this setup is to facilitate close cooperation between the Development group and Support. This is particularly valuable when there is little technical expertise outside the Development group, as is the case when the company is small. It's also valuable for complex software. The disadvantage is that the focus on Support tends to be overly technical, with little attention paid to the customer aspect and the ties to Sales, including pricing and selling support. Also, Support can become the "poor relative" within the Engineering group and not receive the necessary budget and attention from executives.

- *In the Sales organization:* the rationale for this setup is that Sales and Support are both customer-oriented functions. The advantage of this setup is that the proper customer focus is placed on Support, and that escalations can be worked on as a team. There are two drawbacks to the Support-within-Sales setup: it can create a challenge for creating the necessary ties with the Development organization, ties which are especially important and delicate for complex support. Also, it can create difficult competition between established customers and prospects, where Support roots for established customers and Sales chases quotas. There is also a tendency for Support to become the poor relative in the Sales group, since the amount of revenue per head, even for companies that charge for support, is much lower for support engineers than for sales reps.

- *In the Marketing group:* having the Support group function within the Marketing group is, as with Sales, a way to provide focus on the customer. The central location of most Marketing organizations also makes it easier to mesh with Technical Support than the typical distributed Sales organization. The drawbacks are similar to those of reporting into the Sales organization, with the added challenge of having a strategic organization (Marketing) coexist with a tactical if not reactive organization (Support).

- *By itself:* Support as a separate entity is a growing trend for many companies, and especially for the ones where support is a profit center and where customer loyalty is seen as a strategic advantage. Support is usually associated with Training and Consulting to have all postsales activities grouped together. There are clear synergistic advantages to having postsales functions grouped together, since a lot of the planning and internal training requirements, not to mention the types of skills of the staff members, are similar.

  The advantages of a separate Support and Services group are to give dedicated focus to postsales customer-oriented activities as well as to exploit the synergy between those groups. Another advantage that may be particularly important to you is giving exposure and importance to the support function and to the support executive to the same degree as other functions and other executives. The drawback is that it requires special attention to create and maintain ties to the many organizations Support (and, to a lesser extent, Training and Consulting) depends on.

Let's think in more detail about the links Support must have with other organizations within the company.

- *Engineering Development and Code Maintenance:* there must be processes to plan for the introduction of new products and to resolve issues about existing products. In terms of systems, there must be a system to track problems that spans the Support group and the organization tasked to fix bugs, typically a subset of the Engineering organization.

- *Marketing:* Support is the technical voice of the customer within the company and has valuable input to give for new products. There should be a system to track enhancements, which can contain both customer-contributed enhancements and enhancements suggested internally. Enhancements can be tracked in the same system as bugs, if they can be tagged differently.

- *Sales:* both the Support and the Sales organizations take care of customers. In many organizations, a substantial proportion of software sales come from existing customers, so it's really a symbiotic relationship rather than a sequential one. It's highly desirable for sales reps to have access to the call tracking system so they can check on their customers. The major issue is usually to develop reporting mechanisms that are customer oriented rather than transaction oriented, since the sales reps must focus on the whole customer, not a specific problem.

- *Finance:* Support needs access to customer records, either to verify warranty or free support periods or to check that a customer is covered by a support agreement. This is often accomplished through a nightly download from the customer record system into the call tracking system. Since the Support group often finds out about changes in names, addresses, and phone numbers, enable your support staff to update customer records.

Regardless of the reporting structure of the Support group, it's crucial to create and maintain the various relationships and system ties described above.

Choosing a reporting structure involves political as well as factual considerations. Here are some recommendations:

- *For a small start-up ISV:* Engineering is the best choice until critical mass is reached.

- *For low-end software:* Sales is a good choice, since the ties with Engineering are less crucial and the link to Sales more crucial as support is a part of each sale, and you need to be tuned in to special promotions and the like.

- *If Support is a profit center or service is seen as a competitive advantage:* independence is best, especially if the Support group is large. It will allow independence in financial choices and will ensure the necessary focus at the executive level.

- *For a large Support group:* independence makes sense on the basis of size alone.

- *For a small Support group remote from headquarters:* Sales is a logical choice to ensure geographical closeness and customer focus. This includes support through distributors. Maintain ties to the main Support group to leverage knowledge, processes, and tools. The alternative is to have all Support groups report into a central Support organization; this is an excellent alternative when the Support organization is an independent organization, and especially if consistent international support is important to customers. If Support reports into a central location, consider strong matrix reporting to the local sales offices to facilitate coordination between these groups.

Even within the same organization, changes in reporting structure are often needed over time and should be beneficial if properly driven and executed. In the end, any configuration can be made to work, as long as the necessary ties to all other organizations are strong. The more important issue is to set up the necessary processes and incentives to focus the entire company on customer satisfaction. Structure by itself cannot replace the right orientation toward the customer.

6.4 DO I NEED MORE THAN ONE CENTER?

In this section, we discuss the wisdom and necessity of maintaining several geographically dispersed support centers. This decision hinges on four factors:

- Size
- Language requirements
- Time-zone requirements
- Disaster recovery

Size refers to the now-familiar "Big is beautiful" principle. In Technical Support, maximum efficiency can be reached with large centers because of scheduling and costs efficiencies. In other words, the size argument says that we should have as few support centers as possible, maybe even one. If all the contacts take place over the phone or through electronic means, you could have one large center located anywhere in the world. It's hardly practical, of course, to think of a place having all the relevant attributes: low facilities costs, an abundant labor supply with good language skills and willing to work odd shifts when needed. Add the requirement that the power and phone system never go down and that the region never suffers any climactic disaster, and you see that pushing for only one center is extreme.

The other factors push the decision the other way, toward more centers. Language requirements refer to what languages customers expect the support engineers to speak. This is clearly a factor of the geographical location of your customers but could also depend on other cultural factors. Language requirements are best met by locating the centers in the countries they support as opposed to having a centralized center. The alternative strategy is to recruit multilingual support engineers. If you need to use that strategy, you will want to locate the center(s) where multilingual candidates are numerous. Language requirements are usually important only in markets outside North America.

Time zone requirements can be met either by locating centers in the various time zones or by running shifts. Alternatives for providing support off-hours were discussed at length in Chapter 3, "Call Management Implementation," including implementing a follow-the-sun support model. Time zone requirements are important only in large countries or regions. Today in Technical Support, only North America and Australia support centers need to worry about time zone coverage.

Making a decision on the number of support centers to maintain involves weighing the various requirements and making tradeoffs. Generally speaking, resist the urge of maintaining multiple centers. It's a very expensive strategy. Specific recommendations for North America and international locations follow.

6.4.1   Recommendations for North America

North America is a large continent with multiple time zones and can usually be supported with just one language, English.

If your Support group is relatively small (under 40 support engineers), we recommend you have just one center, located in a convenient location for you, which would mean at headquarters if you are an ISV or in close proximity to the MIS or sponsoring department if you have an internal help desk. This setup will offer you the largest possible size. Unless your customers are content with receiving support during **your** business hours, it will require that you run shifts to accommodate remote time zones, creating potential problems if you are on either coast. It will provide no edge in terms of disaster recovery, so put effort and resources into planning for it. If you are in a disaster-prone area, you need to have a plan to handle high-priority calls should a disaster strike. Customers may be patient with you for a couple of days in case of a major disaster, but not beyond that.

If your Support group is large, we recommend you have two centers, and ideally one on each coast. Since your headcount is high, you will continue to benefit from critical mass. Having a presence on both coasts allows you to do without shifts for covering customer business hours, which in turn mean less expense and fewer headaches for you. Should your customers need a lot of after-hours help, having two centers will only help some. If you can run a follow-the-sun model, do it; otherwise, locate staff according to the hours of the customers: for instance, late hours can be accommodated more easily on the West Coast.

Having two centers also allows you to plan for disaster recovery more easily.

One of the two locations should be geographically close to your development organization, since geographical proximity is still the best way to create the close ties you need. You have more leeway in locating the second center, so pick an area where you can recruit the talent you need without spending a fortune. Plenty of locations close to good universities fit the bill. Don't hesitate to locate yourself where no other big support center is located to escape competitive pressures. And pick an area without earthquakes, snowstorms, or hurricanes.

Resist the temptation to keep a second center small compared to the original one. If you really believe that big is beautiful, make both centers big.

Even if your centers become extremely large, we do not recommend going beyond two centers in North America. We cannot see the advantage of having centers less than three time zones apart either for time zone coverage or disaster recovery.

There is no reason from the Technical Support point of view not to support the Canadian market from the United States and vice-versa. The needs, languages, and time zones are similar, and pooling the centers creates critical mass.

The one-or-two-centers model for North America works well for any other large and linguistically homogeneous region of the world. Right now for software support Australia is the only country that would qualify.

Special note if you need to provide multiple language support in North America: ascertain what languages you need to cover. Depending on your market, it might be French (for Quebec), Spanish, or Chinese (for the U.S. consumer markets). Locate your centers where you can readily recruit multilingual support engineers (large coastal cities should do it for Spanish and Chinese) or attract appropriate talent into your existing centers (that seems to work well for Quebecois).

6.4.2 Recommendations for International

The international realm is much more complex than for North America, and primarily because of the language requirements. Customers in each country will, normally enough, expect to get support in their language, which goes against big centers, since the multilingual requirements are so tough.

The usual way of providing support internationally is to have a small support center in each country, located with the sales office. The model easily meets the language requirements. The other requirements of time zone coverage and disaster recovery are usually not important in the smaller markets.

How does one meet the challenge of sustaining multiple small centers—and is there an alternative to this model? Let's answer the second question first: there is an alternative, and that is to staff one large regional center with multilingual support engineers. Some organizations have been successful at staffing such a center in Europe by locating it in an area where linguistic talent is available (the average educated European speaks several languages, unlike the average educated American). Another approach is to hire nationals from appropriate countries and to locate them in one Eurocenter.

Despite the successes that some companies are having with a multilingual regional center, we do not think it is a viable idea in the long term. You will need to add more and more languages to the pool, as your business grows together with the economies of countries that today are only small consumers of software.

Instead, we believe that for the future you need to create a structure to support and nurture small national centers. Here are two ways to approach the problem:

- A distributed Backline or Technical Advisor group.
- A centralized "supercenter."

A distributed second-level group consists of a number of high-level support engineers who are distributed among the various support centers, but report into a central location. The advantages of this structure are that the second-line support engineers are physically close to the first-line support engineers who need help, and that it provides good technical career paths in all the support centers. The drawbacks are that most second-level engineers will report to someone far away, and that it makes it difficult to leverage knowledge and equipment. Long-distance reporting relationships are easier with higher-level staff, however, and if the area is Europe, the distances are small.

The alternative, a centralized support center, takes the opposite direction by locating all second-level engineers in one location. The advantages and drawbacks are the reverse of those for a distributed group: the group is easier to manage, but it makes for more difficult communications with the first-line engineers and a stunted career path in most centers.

We favor the distributed approach, because it makes it easier to select the best minds to do the work, and the logistics can be worked around. The centralized supercenter looks very good on paper, however, and has a longer history, so be prepared to have to defend the decentralized approach if you choose it. The decentralized approach has particular advantages for complex support, where recruiting and training a second-level engineer is difficult, time consuming, and costly.

With either approach, you will need to consider the lingua franca to be used for first-level to second-level communication. Even with a distributed organization, the support engineers from one center will sometimes have to work with a second-level support engineer in another center because of expertise or availability requirements.

To conclude, outside of North America, set up small centers serving individual countries in the local language, backed up by a second-level organization, which can be either centralized or distributed.

6.5 INTERNAL STRUCTURE OF THE SUPPORT GROUP

Let us now concentrate on the internal structure of the Support group, regardless of where it reports. Internal organizational decisions are similar, whether it's an internal help desk or an ISV Support group, and whether the software is complex or not. The main ingredients are the call workflow (Frontline/Backline versus Touch and Hold, specialization by product or customer), and the size of the group. When building the structure, keep overhead at a minimum, using a large manager to support engineer ratio or fan-out, while planning for growth whenever possible so you don't have to overhaul the structure each time you add a few more support engineers. Don't plan too far ahead, however. Anticipating changes six months ahead of time is more than enough.

6.5.1 Sample Support Center Setup: Small Center

In a small support center, the main focus is to resist specialization in order to leverage as much critical mass as possible. Figure 6–1 shows a sample setup for a 20-person center.

Small Support Center

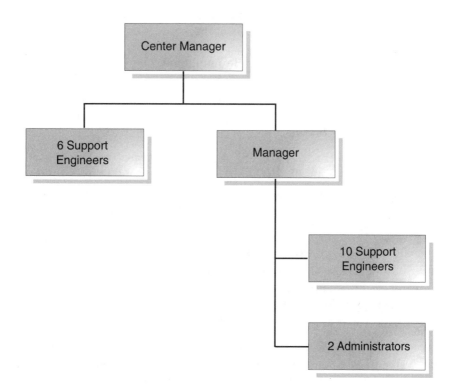

Figure 6–1

There can be no difference between the support engineers who report to the center manager and the ones that report to the other manager. Or, if you work with a Frontline/Backline model, the backliners can report to the center manager and the frontliners to the other manager.

6.5.2   Sample Support Center Setup: Centralized, Specialized Teams

Figure 6–2 shows a sample structure for a support center with specialized support teams, Technical Advisers, Dispatch, and tools support functions.

- 8 dispatchers under one manager who handle administrative tasks in addition to the standard Dispatch functions.
- 20 product-line X support engineers under two managers.
- 20 product-line Y support engineers under two managers.
- 11 product-line Z support engineers under one manager.
- 8 technical advisers under one manager.
- 2 escalation support engineers under one escalation manager.
- 7 tools, hardware support, and electronic services engineers and coordinators under one manager.

Note that even with multiple managers for the same product line (required because of the number of support engineers involved), it's a good idea not to have a second-line manager for that product line to minimize overhead. This setup will require close coordination between the managers responsible for the same product line.

The fan-out (ratio of staff to manager) is largest and most easily achieved for the larger teams. The second-level manager has 9 direct reports—quite a few, noting the diversity of issues. Note that the five product-line support managers will have most closely related concerns and may need to function as a subteam from time to time.

This setup is ideal for a large centralized center. If the center were split into two geographical locations, there would be a need for regional second-level managers and perhaps additional managers if the smaller teams were split up (most probably the Dispatch team for disaster recovery). This example highlights the overhead cost of multiple centers.

If this center were to grow more than 10%, the structure would not be sustainable because the manager ratios would be exceeded. One solution would be to group the product-line managers into a large team reporting to a newly created second-level manager position, another to spin off ancillary activities into a separate group, which could either report into the larger group or be a parallel group.

Centralized Support Center with Specialized Teams

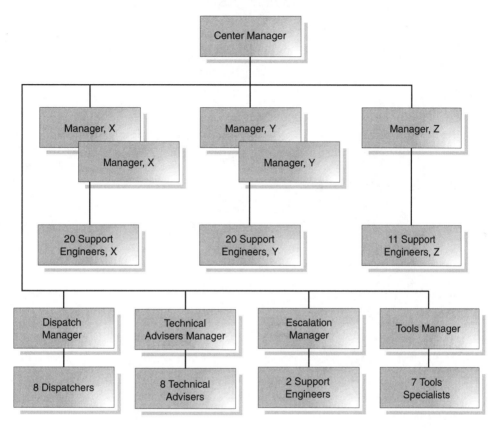

Figure 6–2

6.5.3 Sample Support Center Setup: Distributed

Figure 6–3 shows a sample structure for a distributed Support group with a Frontline/Backline model:

- 6 small support centers, each with 3–7 frontliners, one dispatcher/ administrative support staff, and one manager.

- a Backline group with 9 support engineers under one manager.

- 2 tools and hardware support engineers and coordinators, one of them is a working manager.

Distributed Support Center

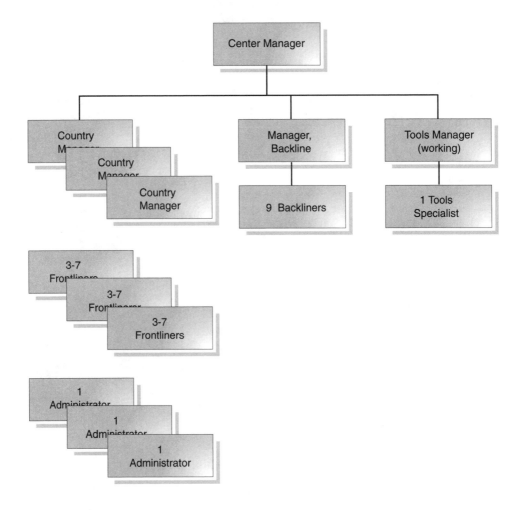

Figure 6–3

In this model, escalations are handled locally in each center by the center support manager. If more support centers need to be created, they can easily be added to the structure without changing it. This setup is most likely a regional setup for an area with multiple countries and multiple languages. Note that the fan-out is not very large for small centers, but geographical requirements make it difficult to have a different setup. Managers with small teams can be working managers, like the tools manager, or they can have additional responsibilities such as training and consulting.

6.5.4 Sample Support Center Setup: Centralized, No Specialization

Figure 6–4 shows a sample setup for a large support center with shifts, no specialization, and a Frontline/Backline model.

- 5 teams of 10 support engineers each with five managers, organized by shifts.
- 2 teams of 10 backliners each under two managers, organized by shifts.
- 2 administrative support staff members, one of them a supervisor.

Centralized Support Center

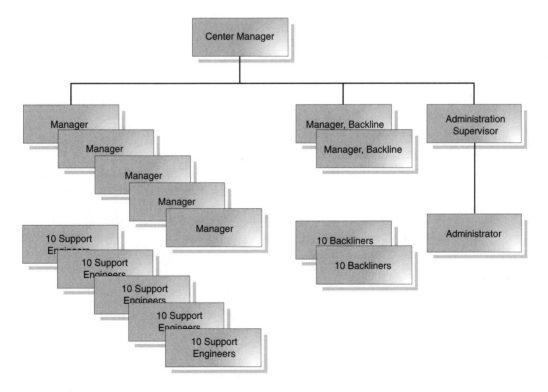

Figure 6–4

Note how large fan-outs can be achieved with large groups. The organizing principle chosen here is shifts, so that managers and engineers work the same hours. This support center has minimal administrative requirements, making it either a highly automated low-level software ISV support center or an internal help desk.

Because of the FL/BL model used, the size of the Backline team is larger than with a Touch and Hold model.

So what is important in deciding on a structure for a support center? Support centers can be located in many groups within the organization, including outside it if you select to outsource. Once the Support group is sizable, we recommend it be an independent organization for maximum visibility and effectiveness. Outsourcing can help you through a rough spot, or be a replacement for the support center entirely, although you will lose precious customer focus if you choose this solution.

Within the Support organization, aim to centralize as much as possible to obtain maximum critical mass.

CHAPTER 7
MANAGING SUPPORT PEOPLE

Now that we have discussed organizational issues of support centers, we are ready to talk about managing the people within the organization. Because support is a people business—that is, quality in support, whatever it is that produces customer satisfaction, is closely tied with the quality of the people delivering the support—we feel this issue is crucial and deserves its own chapter.

Not that managing support people is, per se, that different from managing people in other roles. All the principles of sound people management apply to managing support people, and there is plenty of literature available to discuss general people management principles. We will concentrate on issues and concerns specific to the software support environment, including hiring, compensating, scheduling, and justifying people resources. We will also discuss retaining support staff and managing their morale.

The concepts are the same whether your customers are internal or external, whether you support relatively simple or more complex products, and whether your organization is large or small. Most differences in implementation stem from the complexity of the products you support, since the kind of support engineers you will be working with depends in great part on the kind of products.

Although this chapter is billed as people oriented, we start by discussing the most business-oriented topic in it: planning for staffing needs.

7.1 PLANNING SUPPORT STAFFING NEEDS

Before you think of hiring any support staff at all, you need to examine carefully how many you require (and your controller knows it, so you might as well start working on the justification now). In this section we discuss how you can create a staffing model based on your customer base. The staffing model can then be used to justify hiring, to set pricing, and, with regular reviews and adjustments, should become a permanent tool for you. The staffing model, therefore, is one of your basic tools, and devoting your time and effort to creating a strong one is well worthwhile.

7.1.1 Utilization of Support Engineers

We will concentrate on a model for support engineers, because models for managers and administrative staff in the support center can be determined very simply based on the number (and kind) of support engineers. The first step in creating the staffing model is to create a utilization formula—that is, to determine how much time is actually available for "real" work. A typical utilization formula reads as follows:

- 52 weeks a year is 260 business days
- minus 3 weeks' personal time (vacation and sick time)
- minus 11 holidays
- usable time (actually in the office) is 234 days
- minus administrative time (meetings, email, etc.): 10% of the time is 23 days
- minus training time: 10 days
- actual time available (minus nonproductive overhead) is 196 days
- billable time (resolving customer calls) at 90% is 176 days

This is just an example. You need to adjust the formula to your particular situation. Do you have a particularly generous vacation policy? Or do you have a lot of old-timers who accumulate a lot of vacation? Then adjust the vacation number up. Do you need markedly more or less training time? Adjust that number to your need.

You may be shocked to see how a "full-time" engineer will be available to your customers a paltry 176 days a year. Let's analyze how the formula works to understand why the figure is so low and how it could be improved upon. The first items (vacation, sick time, holidays) are pretty much dictated by your personnel policies, and there's very little you can do about them. The other items—administrative time, training, and the percentage of billable time—are all under your control, and you can and should take a good look at whether you can increase the ratio of usable time.

Administrative time is often a great target for reduction. Good communication within the support center is extremely important, both as a basic characteristic of strong people management, and also because harmonious customer relationships require that the support providers themselves have appropriate information. Good communication does not have to take a whole lot of time, however. In fact, if your support engineers have to spend hours wading through mountains of information to find what they really need, you need to attend to your information system. More about this in Chapter 9, "Tools for Software Support."

In short, find ways to communicate information efficiently, by maintaining a repository of technical and other customer-focused information that is easy to search, and by devoting face-to-face (that is, resource-intensive) communication time to share personal information that cannot be conveyed in other ways. As we will discuss in the last section of this chapter regarding managing morale, personal, regular contacts between managers and engineers is key.

Training time also appears as overhead in the utilization formula, and you may be tempted to take a hatchet to it too. It could be a good move, if your training programs are not hitting the mark. Find out from the people who know: the support engineers. If they see few or no benefits from the training they receive, cancel it. You may, however, discover that some other kind of training is needed, so you may not change the number of training days at all, but at least you will get something useful for your money.

Note that, although the example cited two weeks of training, some environments with complex products or lots of new products may require much more than that amount. Environments with four weeks of training per year are not unusual. Also note that new hires may require much more than your average number of training days, whatever that is.

Since we subtracted all kinds of overhead from the number of utilization days, why are we suggesting that only a portion (90% in our example) be available for actual customer interaction. What should support engineers do in that 10%? The idea is that reactive customer contact is a high-requirement situation, even for people who have been chosen for that type of job, and that mixing in some proactive activities is good for morale and overall performance. Training and administrative tasks are part of the nonreactive activities, so what we are suggesting is that you build some time into the engineers' schedule to dedicate to nonsupport activities such as: self-directed training, including "playing" with the product, writing technical papers for internal and external use, and even brief rotations into other functions. Since the activities are in addition to formal training and administrative overhead, a small portion of time should suffice.

If you already have a support center in place, test your utilization formula. Does reality match your theoretical formula? If not, why not? Can you see opportunities for improvement? Improving your utilization ratio is the only way to "automatically" get more staff without having to justify, recruit, or train anyone. Review the utilization formula against reality once a year or so and make adjustments as needed.

Now that you have worked out your own utilization formula, let's use it to model staffing needs.

7.1.2   Capacity Models

A capacity model is a tool that takes into account your utilization formula, your products, and your customers and allows you to define on a theoretical level how much staff you need. The formula can be used at many levels: as a simple check that the actual capacity is adequate, as a tool to justify additional headcount (having a mathematical formula is a good tool to convince mathematically inclined people), as a benchmark to determine whether you are making productivity improvement, as a planning tool for new products, as a way to balance load between subgroups, and for many other uses.

If you have the luxury of a dedicated financial analyst group, you can come up with an exquisitely detailed capacity model that shows all aspects of staffing. If you are on your own, a simple spreadsheet will do. In any case, here are the ingredients of a capacity model:

- *The number of incoming calls and/or the number of customers:* there is a fairly constant correlation between the two; however, see the third point below about new releases.

- *The diversity of calls:* everything else being equal, you will need more staff if you support more products, and more versions of each product.

- *Recent products or version releases:* all support centers see an influx of calls following the deployment of a new product or the new version of an existing product. If nothing else, customers will need installation help. New products will also create new questions even from experienced users. In addition, they may be less stable.

- *The difficulty of calls:* clearly, the more difficult your calls, the more staff you will need. The most robust measurement of call difficulty is work time to resolution—that is, the time actually spent on resolving the problem (not the time elapsed between problem report and resolution, since that includes nights, weekends, and time spent on other problems). If you are not measuring work time to resolution today, do it. All modern call tracking systems make it very easy to do.

The outcome of the capacity model is the relationship between your customer base and your staffing requirement. A basic model tells you how many customers can be supported by one engineer and would run something like this: "Each customer places 3 calls per year. On the average, each call takes 21 minutes to resolve. Support engineers are available (per the utilization formula) 6 hours a day. Therefore, one engineer can resolve 17 calls per day, which is equivalent to supporting 1473 customers." You will need one engineer for each set of 1473 customers.

Unlike the utilization formula for engineers, the capacity model numbers you come up with in your operation may be extremely different from the ones in this example. If, for instance, the average customer places 30 calls a year rather than 3, the bottom line figure is one engineer per 147 customers. If the average call takes 2 hours to resolve rather than 21 minutes, each engineer can support 260 customers (at 3 calls a year).

As mentioned before, you can (or rather, your financial analyst can) create a very complex model based on all the variables above, in particular on the product type and the number of supported versions. Our advice is: keep it simple. Something very basic using only the number of calls per customers and the work time to resolution should suffice in most cases. The only area not covered by a basic model is the introduction of a new release, and you can forecast that separately by using your past experience with the effect of new releases on your call volume.

Note that, if you want to use your capacity model for scheduling purposes, you will need something more robust that simply figuring out the workload. Since calls arrive in a random pattern, you will need slightly *more* staff to handle the work. See Appendix C, "Determining Staffing Levels," for the details of the computation.

What lessons can you draw from a capacity model analysis?

- A key predictor of the staffing requirements is the number of calls per customer. Reducing that ratio has a dramatic impact on call load, hence staff. To reduce the number of calls per customer, look at ways to incent customers to become more educated on your products, maybe by offering a discount on education courses, or by offering a support discount to educated customers. Also, use proactive, non-staff driven communications methods such as electronic services to allow customers to find answers without calling your support center.

- One of the drivers of call complexity is the diversity of products you support. Keep the product and version mix as small as possible. Typical strategies include: supporting a limited number of versions, no more than two: the most current and the one immediately preceding it. For multiplatform products, support only key operating systems. If you are an ISV, you will need to work with your Marketing group to contain the diversity of products you support. If you are running an internal help desk, you will need to work with your users. If you find that a particular product is used by a handful of customers, consider implementing an end-of-life cycle with or without migration paths for the customers. The main point here is to maximize the customer base for any product you support, following the "critical-mass" principle of support.

- Another key aspect of capacity models, and one on which you have a great deal of influence, is the productivity of the support engineers. Multiply productivity by two, decrease staffing requirements by half. Your main goal should be to constantly seek to improve the productivity of your group. It's also awfully difficult to accomplish, though. First take a look at your support model (see Chapter 2). Choosing the right support model can increase productivity by an order of magnitude. Next, make sure you are hiring the right people with the right talents and motivation. Finally, look at training and information sharing. If your support engineers are spending a lot of time tracking down information that already exists, but is difficult to find, you will see dramatic improvements with the right tools and processes. Improving productivity requires that you find ways to work smarter; you can't just decree that people need to work harder.

A capacity model should be a dynamic tool. Go back and look at it every few months and make corrections if necessary. A capacity model includes many more variables than your basic utilization formula, and so it will require more adjustments. Be sure to take into account product changes, changes in the customer base (for instance, more naive customers will place more calls, but they will be easier to resolve), and productivity improvements. Question and analyze the reasons for changes. Some may be quite complex. For instance, it's been our experience that implementing proactive electronic services decreases the call resolution productivity of the engineers, although it decreases the engineer-to-customer ratio (a desirable outcome). That is because customers place fewer calls, but the calls that go unplaced are, disproportionately, the "easy" ones, Engineers need to spend more time, on average, on the more difficult calls, so their productivity appears to decrease (again, productivity per customer is increased, only the per-call productivity is affected).

A final word of caution: capacity models are meant to be manipulated at the high level and become meaningless when used at the individual level. That is, your capacity model may predict that the average engineer resolves 17 calls per day. Don't expect every engineer to resolve 17 calls a day (for one thing, with vacation and training, the average engineer needs to resolve 20+ calls per day on those days she's actually working). Even looking at engineers over a long period of time, you may find lots of individual differences that can be explained rationally by factors other than raw productivity. An engineer who specializes in difficult products, or who because of her function works primarily on difficult calls, will appear to be less productive if you consider only raw call loads. Use the model for high-level analyses and be cautious when using it for anything else.

It's extremely useful to evaluate your capacity model against others. Because of confidentiality concerns in competitive environments, it can be difficult to find a good benchmark, however. Try to find managers with operations similar to yours and compare notes. If you are one of several support managers in your company, start by using the other centers as comparison. If you are running an internal help desk, find a manager with similar requirements in a similar company (you may have fewer competitive issues doing this than for external customers). If you are having trouble finding a match, try going outside your industry, but keeping work time to resolution constant. Benchmarking against yourself over time is also useful.

When comparing capacity models, don't just conclude you are doing better or worse than the competition. Analyze the reasons for the differences and apply any insights you may come up with. Don't be afraid to undo a change that's not working (after giving it enough time).

We have spent a lot of time on capacity models for support engineers for two reasons: they can be quite complex, and they are the foundation for all the other capacity models within the support center. Make sure you get your engineer capacity model right, and the rest will be easy.

7.1.3 Capacity Models for Managers

Compared with the capacity model for engineers, the capacity model for managers is extremely simple. It contains exactly one variable: span of control—that is, the number of support engineers that can be managed by one manager. Therefore, the number of managers you need is the ratio of engineers to that span of control number.

Simple, but subtle: what is the right number for span of control, anyway? Depending on whom you talk to, it varies between 7 and 30, and the "right" number for you depends on a number of practical and philosophical issues we will summarize here.

It should be clear that your goal as a manager is to minimize overhead, and managers are overhead (usually expensive overhead). So rule #1 is to minimize the number of managers—that is, to increase the span of control. So what would be too many engineers for a manager? Here are some factors that influence span of control:

- *The experience of the manager:* more experienced managers can manage more people.

- *The organizational skills of the manager:* everything else being equal, better organized managers can manage more people.

- *The style of the manager:* hands-on managers cannot manage large amounts of people.

- *The maturity of the support engineers, both overall and on the job:* less experienced people require more management time.

- *Customer requirements:* an environment with many special customer requirements and escalations requires more managers.

- *Other managers' requirements:* managers who have multiple functional responsibilities can manage fewer people. Conversely, managing engineers who are all doing similar jobs can allow for larger spans of control ("Big is beautiful").

So the obvious goal for you is to seek out experienced managers, to train them and the engineers well, and to organize into large functional groups. Even in ideal conditions, we believe this would lead you to a maximum span of control of about 12 engineers to one manager. Are there better solutions?

The two solutions that are often proposed as alternatives are using (1) team leaders and (2) self-managed teams. Let's examine each of them.

Team leaders are individuals within the team who act as functional managers, usually without the personnel responsibilities of managers (hiring, firing, managing performance). They schedule the work, make sure it gets done, mentor new people, especially on the technical side, and help bring calls to resolution. A manager with good team leaders can definitely increase his span of control, and team leader positions can provide a strong career path to management. However, there is no free lunch: the time a team leader spends planning, supervising, and mentoring is time that cannot be spent resolving customer issues, so having team leaders increases your span of control while simultaneously decreasing your engineer productivity. The productivity outcome overall is probably neutral at best. You may choose to have team leaders as a career path or as a convenience, but do not expect to get around the span-of-control versus productivity issue.

Self-managed teams are the other popular approach. A self-managed team makes some to a lot of the basic decisions that affect the team, such as: creating and implementing schedules, selecting new members, working through day-to-day issues, and even in some settings handling performance reviews and raises. By taking over some of the traditional management tasks, self-managed teams allow for much greater spans of control. It all takes time, however, so—just as for team leaders—we are skeptical that self-managed teams can make much of a difference over productivity. Some aspects of self-managed teams are beneficial in a support environment, however, and you should consider implementing them. First, self-managed teams take responsibility for their own work. They do away with "the boss said to do it this way." and replace it with "we know it's best to do it this way." In a support environment, scheduling and shift issues can be taken over by the team with effective and team-building results. Second, the people involvement ideas behind self-managed teams are worth implementing in a support environment that needs to be team-oriented. Involve engineers in hiring decisions, ask for suggestions on resolving issues, share basic management tools and constraints, such as the capacity model and the budget.

To conclude our discussion about managers, we believe the span of control should be somewhere between 9 and 12, depending on the experience of your managers and the homogeneity of your groups. Second-level managers, if you have them, should be able to handle similar but slightly lower ratios, since they will probably manage more diverse groups.

7.1.4 Capacity Models for Administrative Staff

Capacity models for administrative staff are extremely dependent on the kinds of responsibilities administrative staff has, and in particular on the customer functions performed by administrators. If you are running an internal help desk where there are essentially no administrative (nontechnical) questions and you have an ACD, you will need very few administrators. On the other hand, if you are responsible for resolving nontechnical questions for external customers, and you are working with a full Dispatch model, you will need lots of administrative staff.

You need to set your own ratio. Count about 1 administrator for 15 support engineers in a typical external customer support environment where you need to handle nontechnical issues and have an ACD. If you have a full Dispatch function, the ratio will need to be at least 1 for 10, maybe 1 for 8 engineers. Internal help desks with few administrative customer requirements can use a 1:20 ratio.

At this point, you should have a good idea of how many people you need. It's time to talk about how to go about hiring them.

7.2 HIRING SUPPORT STAFF

Hiring good support staff is a key ingredient of your success. To keep your customers satisfied requires good staff, so you need to recruit the right people. You also need to train them well, but no amount of training can rescue a bad hire, or you from one. Hiring the right people requires that you define what talents and skills you need. In other words, you need to define a typical profile for a successful support engineer. The profile does not dictate that you always recruit the same kind of people, but it is a necessary guide to the requirements for a successful hire.

7.2.1   Profile of Support Engineers

Defining a hiring profile means to define the necessary education, skills, and experience for a successful support engineer. A lot of the definition depends on the products you support, and if you support many you may need different profiles for different products. If you already have a staff in place, part of defining a profile is to go back to the existing staff and analyze what makes the best support engineers the best (and what's missing in marginal performers). Be sure to consider minimum requirements for success. Certainly a very experienced support engineer will be more productive than a beginner, other things being equal, but you may not find experienced support engineers, and a less experienced person may do just fine.

Computer skills will undoubtedly be very prominent on your profile. Be sure to include practical experience as well as education. Define the minimum technical level you need and what you can train on. For instance, specific experience with your product is a plus, but you may be able to train someone with experience on a competitor's product. Also, if you have stiff technical requirements, you may want to consider hiring individuals with software development backgrounds, since they clearly meet technical requirements. Be sure to check that they have appropriate other skills, however, or you will end up with frustrated employees and customers.

Beyond software skills, you may require other technical knowledge. For instance, to support a financial package you may need someone with an accounting background; to support a desktop publishing package you may require publishing experience.

Then come the all-important customer service skills. Prior support experience is ideal, but also consider customer-contact experience, such as waiting tables in a restaurant, where multitasking is important even if it's not related to the software industry, as long as candidates also have the requisite technical skills.

Any profile will include at least three basic aspects:

- Technical computer and other skills, at least to the level that the candidate can master your software within a few weeks or months or whatever your training period is.
- Customer service skills.

- Organizational skills, both to be able to juggle customers and calls, and also to handle the record keeping required by the call tracking and the knowledge sharing system.

Once you have a draft of a support engineer profile, validate it with the support engineers you already have on board, using their profile at hire time. Are there any exceptions to your profile? If you have someone who initially lacked the technical background in the profile, but is very successful now, is it a signal to drop minimal technical requirements? If a successful engineer had no formal customer service background prior to coming to your group, was there anything else in her background that could predict success in that area? In most support centers, since the software industry is still fairly young, you will find a great diversity in backgrounds. Capture the diversity in the profile rather than creating an exclusionary profile.

When you use the profile, you may find that there few perfect candidates in the job market who meet it. If, after searching, you still cannot locate the right candidate, you will need to sacrifice some aspects. Most of the time, the cause is overly restrictive requirements. The profile is often weighted toward your experienced support engineers as opposed to the individuals they were when they were hired initially. Sometimes, however, even with a realistic profile, you may be faced with a tough job market. In that circumstance, our recommendation is to be flexible on the organizational skills first, then on the technical skills, but to hang onto the customer skills requirements, because it's virtually impossible to teach people skills. One, of course, can teach techniques and improve people skills, but the basic foundation must be in place. If you're not sure about a candidate's customer skills, the magic question to ask is: "What are your career goals?" If the answer has something to do with people in general and customers in particular, the candidate is probably a good fit.

Validate your hiring profile periodically. A good discipline is to look back after engineers have been in place for six months to a year at how you predicted their success versus how they turned out. A few exceptions here and there are not a problem—this is an art, not a science—but trends and patterns are a clear signal that you should reconsider requirements.

A quick note about hiring profiles for support administrators: they should be similar to the ones for support engineers, minus the technical requirements. You may find that support administrators are eager to join the technical ranks, and sometimes that can be accomplished through judicious on-the-job training.

7.2.2   Profile of Support Managers

Once you have a support engineer's profile, you need one for managers. It's somewhat less important, since there are fewer managers than support engineers, but a poor manager can have a more devastating impact than a poor engineer, so spend some time on it. The profile should cover the same topics as for support engineers, including education, skills, and experience. The basic elements of a support manager's profile are:

- People and customer skills.
- Planning skills, especially in adverse (heavily reactive) conditions.
- Flexibility and ability to function in a chaotic environment.

Managers can either be recruited from outside or promoted from within. Recruiting strategies are somewhat different for the two populations.

If you are looking outside the Support group, look for support management experience in an environment similar to yours. If you are staffing for an internal help desk, look for someone with internal help desk experience. If you support mission-critical environments, look for someone who understands mission-critical support. Level and intensity of customer interaction and software complexity are more important than the type of software per se.

We discourage hiring managers from outside the group who do not have specific support experience. Support is different from other functions, and you should be able to find an appropriate candidate. The particular industry where the experience was gained is not as important as software support management experience.

The alternative is to promote from within. There are great advantages to promoting from within: you get someone who's very familiar with the products, the processes, and the people; you have the luxury of having tested the dedication, strengths and weaknesses of the future manager, and you instantly validate the idea that there are career paths within support. We advocate to always look for internal candidates, but not to hesitate to go outside if the match is not good.

When promoting from within, you typically will need to choose people with no management experience, so you need to look for signs that the individual has the basic raw talents to be a successful manager—namely, strong people and customer skills, leadership abilities, and, foremost, the desire to be a manager. You also need to take an honest look at what mentoring and training will be available to the new manager. There are many good basic management classes available—for instance, through the American Management Association—but you need to find a way to provide mentoring, at least for the first few months. If you cannot commit to that, look outside. A failed promotion is a powerful negative message.

7.2.3   Recruiting

Now that you know what you are looking for (you have a hiring profile), you can go about looking for that perfect candidate. There are many avenues you can explore, and, depending on the local job market, your requirements, and your budget, you may consider as many as possible:

- *Internal referrals:* incent employees to refer friends and colleagues by providing a cash bonus if a referred candidate is hired. If you don't have an internal referral program, set one up. Internal referrals yield better candidates than other methods, both because employees understand requirements better than outsiders and also because they are choosy in whom they want to work with. The referral bonus should be set at about a third of your average recruitment costs through other methods. Very high referral bonuses are not necessary, since there is a powerful incentive for employees to refer quality candidates; if you get few internal referrals, the problem lies either in the job market or in the attractiveness of the group to your support engineers, and it won't be solved by increasing the referral amount.

- *Job fairs:* in areas with lots of technology companies, there are periodic job fairs, which are a good way to gather lots of resumes. The quality of leads is not always very good, so make time to attend the job fair in person to screen candidates on the spot.

- *Internal transfers:* if you run a successful department, word of mouth will bring you candidates from other departments. Don't be so flattered that you forget to apply your profile, however. If you are successful getting internal transfers, make sure you maintain positive relationships with the managers of the departments you recruit from, or you will be seen as a dangerous raider.

- *External recruiters:* there are legions of recruiters hungry for your business. For support engineers' positions, the fee is based on a percentage of the candidate's salary and is typically 20%. This is very high, and, since the fee is paid when the offer is accepted, there is little incentive for quality. Remember that you are the customer. Be picky, and if you are not satisfied, speak up. It's usually best to work with a handful of recruiters whom you can fully brief on the kinds of people you are looking for (so they do the screening for you) and who have an incentive to deliver quality candidates over a long period of time.

  It's rare for external recruiters to work on a contract basis for that level of recruiting (that is, to charge based on the success of the search, regardless of effort). You may be able to work with a success-based contract for highly paid, hard-to-find specialists.

- *Internal recruiters:* if you work in a larger company, you may have access to a recruiter within your company. Spend plenty of time educating him or her about your hiring profile and likely sources of candidates. If you are sharing the recruiter with other managers, touch base frequently so your needs are not forgotten. If you cannot afford an internal recruiter, you may use a similar strategy with an external recruiter; that is, retain one on contract and pay by the hour, regardless of how many or how few candidates are found. We recommend this strategy if you have several hires to make over a period of time, and you can find a recruiter you can trust. Over time, a good recruiter will become more skilled at spotting good (and bad) candidates, so that efficiency will improve, saving you time and money compared to using external recruiters in the traditional way.

- *Newspaper ads:* they must be mentioned in any list of recruiting methods. They tend to yield lots of low-quality responses through which you must then wade. If you want to use ads, target the right paper, the right day, and the right headings, and arm yourself with lots of patience and mail bags.

- *On-line recruiting:* this new medium is well suited for support engineers, especially at the higher end of the market. You may choose to post openings on an appropriate product bulletin board, or to maintain a Web site or part of a Web site for recruiting. On-line leads tend to be on target technically, but uneven otherwise, in particular when it comes to customer skills.

- *University recruiting:* recruiting new college graduates can be a great fit if you have high technical requirements, a good university nearby, and can afford the ramp-up time of someone new to the job market. Remember to sign up early: university recruiting programs start in the fall for graduates of the following year.

Once you have good leads, selecting a support professional is not different from selecting any other professional. Screening over the phone takes on a new meaning, since candidates will have to perform their job over the phone, so use phone screening liberally as a go/no go decision. Involve other support engineers in the interviewing process, both because they are often better able to do the technical screening and, also, because teamwork is so important in support.

Don't forget to check references. Individuals with good people skills, the ones you are looking for, can shine in an interview situation beyond their actual talents.

7.2.4 Training

Once you have hired support engineers, you need to train them. In this section we cover training needs for new hires and for existing staff. Training is a requirement for Technical Support. Even if your group is too small to warrant a formal training group, you need to put some thought and resources into training. We will cover delivery alternatives as well as content recommendations.

New-hire training should cover three broad areas:

- The processes and tools used in the support center.
- Technical product and troubleshooting information.
- Customer skills.

Processes and tools training should cover all aspects of call resolution from the time the call comes into the center to its final resolution. In particular, it should describe the call flow model you are using, stressing call hand-offs and other critical points. New support engineers must also be shown how to use the call tracking system, the phone, and any other tools used day-to-day in call resolution, such as the knowledge base system. Finally, they should understand the environment of the call center, including what customers expect, who the key customers are, and how to get help from other groups. Hands-on experience is very important to master the tools and must be part of the training program if it's delivered in a formal classroom environment. Typically, all new hires will require in-depth training in the process and tool area, since systems and procedures are unique to each support center.

New hires should also learn technical aspects of the product and techniques for troubleshooting. You will probably have wide differences in expertise in this area, since some engineers may have extensive experience with the product and others may be new to it. Even someone experienced working with the product will need some guidance in troubleshooting problems. If you have diagnostic checklists built for your product, introduce them in the training.

You may be tempted to teach "everything there is to know" about the product right away, to ensure that your engineers know more than your customers. Unless the product you support is very simple, it's usually better to limit the initial technical training to a few weeks to give new staff time to assimilate the information. If you really have a lot of information, break up the technical classes with other topics and provide lots of hands-on exercises. Learners do best with practical experience rather than lectures.

The third key area for new-hire training is customer service skills. We said earlier that customer skills cannot be taught, but specific techniques can. Also, devoting time to customer skills at the outset reinforces the importance of the topic. There are lots of off-the-shelf programs available to teach customer skills, although few are targeted specifically to software support. Look for plenty of role-plays in addition to lectures for maximum benefits.

New-hire training can consume a lot of time and resources. How can you implement a program that works without breaking the bank? If your organization is large enough (say, has more than 20 new hires a year), you may want to have a full-time trainer and coordinator and formal classes. If your organization is very small, you may need to choose something more flexible, such as mentoring. Let's explore the various options available to you:

- *Formal internal classes:* they require a formal curriculum, an instructor, a room with equipment, and most importantly a quorum of students. Since new-hire training should occur soon after the hire, the only way to sustain formal internal classes is to have a large volume of new hires. If you have that, then they are a good way to get everyone a lot of information quickly and to create camaraderie among newer staff.

- *External courses:* for at least some of the topics, you should be able to use classes being taught by outside groups. In particular, product information is probably taught to audiences other than your Support group, either by an outside entity or by your own customer training department if you are an ISV. Always take advantage of outside training if it meets your curriculum needs; it's cheaper than to do it yourself. The nuances of troubleshooting may have to be provided in some other way, but at least you get a basic understanding of the products. Also, you should get a lot of flexibility in scheduling. External classes can also be taught at your facility for your staff only, if you have a big enough group.

- *Videos:* if you cannot get to a class, maybe a video is available. Learning from a video that's more than an hour long is painful, but it's better than nothing. If you hold your own classes, you should videotape them so engineers can use the videos as review, or as a substitute if they cannot attend the class. Videos are precious for geographically remote centers if you are responsible for one.

- *Written documents:* reading the manuals can be a very good way to learn. Make sure new hires get a full set of product documentation, whether on paper or on-line. Document your processes and tools: no one else can do it for you, you may need written documentation if you are involved in an ISO documentation effort, and the documents are a wonderful way for new people to learn, whether or not they are accompanied by a class or mentoring. Documenting processes in writing rather than relying on word of mouth also helps you achieve consistent execution.

- *Mentoring:* learning from a senior person is an ideal way to learn. We encourage you to set up mentors or buddies for each new hire, even if some or all of the training occurs in formal classes. The mentor can show the new hire the ropes and walk her through the first few calls. Make sure the mentor has enough time to devote to the mentee, and sketch out a plan for what should be covered. If the mentor is responsible for large chunks of the training, develop detailed training plans and use written materials whenever possible to ensure that each trainee gets trained in a consistent and complete manner.

Don't hesitate to mix and match your training delivery methods so you can use the most appropriate vehicle for each topic. For instance, you may choose to get all technical training from outside courses, to bring an external instructor in-house for a customer service skills class, and to cover support processes and tools with mentors. Sketch out training schedules for your new hires, especially with mix-and-match approaches, to ensure everything is covered in a timely manner.

Beyond new-hire training, support engineers typically require a lot of ongoing training, as we saw when we described the utilization formula. At a minimum, they will need training on new products and new releases of existing products. If you support complex products, some engineers will be able to learn them in more depth than at hire time. If you introduce new tools, you will need to train on them, too, and an occasional refresher on customer skills may be in order. Most support engineers welcome additional training, so your only challenge is to find enough time and resources to do it all.

We have discussed the various steps involved in adding new staff, from developing a hiring profile and a checklist of what you want to look for, to recruiting, to training. We now move on to managing support engineers once they are on board.

7.3   MANAGING SUPPORT STAFF PERFORMANCE

There is nothing magical about managing support staff. Standard people management principles apply to support centers. In this section we will focus on the practical aspects of defining goals and objectives and managing pay and other incentives. Although most of the discussion is centered around support engineers, much of it applies to support managers as well.

We will start with goals and objectives, since they are key to obtaining the performance you want.

7.3.1   Defining Goals and Objectives

Defining goals is one of the basic concepts in people management and is beneficial in two ways: one, it communicates job commitments and standards clearly, and two, it allows for less subjective review and evaluation of performance. Because support can be a repetitive and stressful environment, defining clear goals and objectives for each engineer is particularly important.

What should the support engineers' objectives include? The first step is to look at the overall objectives of the support center and as much as possible to push them down to the individual engineer's level. For instance, if response time is a key indicator for you, then it should be part of each engineer's objectives. The only exception to the rule may be for factors that are beyond an individual engineer's control. For instance, you may have support revenue requirements for which an individual engineer can do very little. You may, however, include the revenue goal as some small percentage of individual objectives to remind everyone that revenue is important. And, after all, good service should translate into revenue.

The two basic categories of engineers' goals are productivity and customer satisfaction. In other words: how much do you do, and how happy are your customers? The challenge is how to measure them.

Productivity is usually measured in the number of calls handled. Be careful that productivity requirements do not push support engineers to close problems too soon and to rush customers through. Pick a reasonable productivity goal, and balance it out with customer satisfaction or some other quality measurement. In other words, make it very clear that quality is as important as quantity. If you have productivity-based rewards, they should go only to individuals with a minimum level of customer satisfaction.

Productivity goals differ for engineers in different roles, such as between support of different products, between frontliners and backliners, and between support engineers and technical advisors. Ideally, establish benchmarks for each group, or at least be aware that differences may exist. Be aware of other more subtle differences between the engineers who "cherry-pick" easy calls and others, if engineers are allowed to select what problems they will work on.

Customer satisfaction is often measured through proxy measurements such as hold time, response time, or resolution time. There's nothing wrong per se with using these measurements, and you probably want to track them for other purposes anyway, but nothing replaces the customers' actual opinion. We strongly advocate that you have a formal customer satisfaction survey, as discussed in Chapter 4, "Measuring Support Center Performance," and that you use the results of the survey to rate engineers' performance. You will, therefore, need a way to get information from customers on what they think about a particular engineer. Set the threshold for customer satisfaction rating based on what you are currently getting with some stretch. Ideally, you want to shoot for a rating of 8 or 9 on a 10-point scale.

Other areas of the goals might include quality of work, which includes an evaluation of how well the engineer resolves issues, and, especially, how problems are documented for others to see. Teamwork, a qualitative measurement of how well the engineer works with others, might also be included. Both areas are more elusive than either productivity or even customer satisfaction. So if you choose to use them, it's important to have an evaluation or rating scheme that the support engineers perceive as fair.

A sample set of objectives would run as follows. Note how the quality measurements include both quantitative and qualitative aspects, and how they balance out the productivity requirements.

- *Customer satisfaction (30%):* based on the customer satisfaction survey rating for the engineer; "outstanding" for 9.1 and over, "very good" for 8.5 and over, "good" for 8 and over, "fair" for 7 and over, "not acceptable" for under 7.

- *Quality of call handling (30%):* based on a qualitative evaluation by the manager of the call resolution process, including quality of resolution, adherence to the call resolution model, and the quality and completeness of the call notes and other documentation.

- *Productivity (10%):* based on the support engineer's productivity compared to the average for one's group; "outstanding" for more than one standard deviation over the average, "very good" for more than half, "good" for within one-half, "fair" for below one-half, "not acceptable" for under one. *Note*: This seems like a complex measurement, but the beauty of measuring against a peer group is that it automatically takes into account the ups and down of load.

- *Response time (10%):* a team measurement of response time; "outstanding" for 98% and above, "very good" for 95% and above, "good" for 90% and above, "fair" for 85% and above, "not acceptable" for under 85%. You can refine this measurement by weighing the response time for priority calls higher than response time for other calls. *Note*: This would be for a callback model; use hold time instead for an ACD-based support center.

- *Resolution time (10%):* based on the engineer's achievement in resolving problems quickly (in less than 4 business days for that environment); "outstanding" for 80% and above, "very good" for

76% and above, "good" for 66% and above, "fair" for 55% and above, "not acceptable" for under 55%. The rating system used allows for a sizable proportion of problems to take much longer than a week to resolve while focusing engineers to resolve easier problems within a week (this would work well for a complex support environment).

- *Project work (10%):* based on the results of project work as defined on an individual basis.

If augmenting the knowledge base is an important objective, you may choose to use a measurement which we have found very helpful: the number of problems documented in the knowledge base system weighed by access by other support engineers. This requires a sophisticated knowledge base system that makes it easy to get that kind of statistics, but the end result provides powerful incentive for support engineers to share their knowledge.

As you define objectives, make sure you put in place the necessary measurements to rate the objectives. There must be some reality built into the goals. Sometimes, you may find it necessary to slightly change a goal so as to make its measurement easier. Also remember to define the ratings associated with the measurements, so everyone knows what it takes to get an "outstanding" rating.

Objectives for managers should be similar to the ones for the engineers, both for consistency and to ensure teamwork. Two areas you may want to add to managers' objectives as compared to engineers' objectives are revenue and expense goals on the one hand, and some kind of employee satisfaction or employee retention goal.

For example, a retention goal might be to function with less than 10% unwanted turnover among engineers with less than 2 years' tenure. Such a goal encourages judicious hiring and retention practices without getting in the way of managers' helping engineers grow into other positions. Specifying "unwanted" turnover allows managers to exclude performance-based terminations, and therefore does not incent managers to delay taking action for poor performers. Another way to measure employee satisfaction might be to use so-called 360-reviews, through which an individual's subordinates, peers, and managers all give structured input on his or her performance.

Here's a sample set of objectives for managers. Note how they fit with the support engineers' goals above.

- *Customer satisfaction (60%):* based on customer satisfaction survey ratings, response and resolution time metrics, turnaround time for responding to substandard customer evaluations, and the number of service-based escalations for the manager's team, using ratings similar to those used for support engineers.

- *Budgetary control (20%):* based on achieving revenue and profitability goals (group objective), keeping within the allocated salary budget (for the individual group), and making a business contribution to the management team (qualitative goal).

- *Management skills (20%):* based on employee retention (the goal being to keep unwanted turnover of support engineers with less than two years' tenure in the group below 15% for the year) and a qualitative evaluation of the manager's skills including feedback by peers and subordinates. *Note*: This is where you could use a formal 360-review.

The main point is that you should have clearly defined objectives for engineers and managers. You can always refine them if they turn out to be difficult to work with, so put some in place.

One way to evaluate the quality of an engineer's work is by listening to conversations between the engineer and customers. You can do that by simply sitting in an engineer's office. However, with an ACD, there are more technically advanced ways to do it, which we will cover next.

7.3.2 ACD Monitoring

Monitoring conversations using an ACD may be done to evaluate performance, as just mentioned, and also, and more importantly, as a counseling tool. The advantage of using an ACD as opposed to sitting in the engineer's cube is that you get both sides of the conversation.

Most ACDs allow you to monitor calls either by letting the engineer know that you are listening, or in blind mode. Both methods have their proponents. Most people have a negative reaction of being "spied on" with blind monitoring. On the other hand, some very competent support engineers find the listening signal very stressful and would rather not know when the manager is listening in.

Whichever method you decide to use, make it very clear that you will monitor calls and give detailed feedback to the engineers on what you heard. Make sure you listen long enough to get a feel for the style and content of the conversations. Also, if you choose to record the conversations (as opposed to simply listening to them), you must let your customers know that they may be recorded as part of a quality monitoring system.

Again, if you don't have an ACD, consider sitting in on calls. You should get the same kind of information. Be sure to provide some counseling to new engineers.

Another interesting idea you may want to implement is an executive listening-in program. The executive could be you or your boss, or anyone else in the company. The idea is to take some time (as little as 30 minutes is effective and fits easily into an executive's schedule) to listen to support conversations. We have found that executive listening-in programs are great tools to expose executives to the real world of support, to demonstrate how difficult it is to provide good support, to highlight some of the common issues in support such as a particularly buggy release, and, also to showcase your star performers. Get a commitment from your executives to participate on a regular basis, perhaps every quarter, and pick the right support engineers who will make you proud and feel recognized by the event.

7.3.3   Pay and Other Forms of Compensation

In this section we will discuss pay and other aspects of compensation. They are only one part of the larger topic of motivating and retraining support engineers, which will be discussed at more length in upcoming sections.

The actual pay of support engineers is extremely variable and is based on your industry, the technical complexity of the products you are supporting, your location, and your competition. Check with local experts for implementation details, but here are some general guidelines.

If you are an independent software vendor, pay particular attention to how the salary ranges for Technical Support compare to the salary ranges for Software Development. Although the actual salary averages may need to be higher for software developers, it's a big morale hit when the theoretical ranges are obviously different. This is a problem that is easy to fix.

If you have access to job salary survey figures about other support jobs, be sure to compare your jobs with others in the same range of technical complexity. Technical requirements are the largest factor in determining pay ranges, especially at the high end, where the geographical location becomes almost irrelevant.

Once you are comfortable with the compensation ranges for your engineers, you need to decide how to distribute that compensation between base pay and bonus. If you decide to use a bonus, there are certain steps you should take:

- Tie the bonus to something meaningful. Tying bonuses strictly to productivity or strictly to customer satisfaction could lead to lots of unhappy customers, either way. If you have well-defined objectives, you could very well tie them to the bonus.
- If you find that everyone tends to get the same bonus, consider rolling the bonus into the base pay; it's a lot cheaper to administer.

- Bonuses should be large enough (after taxes) to matter. If your bonuses are less than 5% of engineers' compensation, consider rolling them into the base pay.

- Frequent bonuses are preferable from a motivation point of view, but they are costlier to administer, so you will need to make a decision on frequency based on the trade-off. Smaller bonuses will need to be more frequent in order to be meaningful.

- Some support centers use retention bonuses to attract support engineers to stay for some period of time (typically a year or two). Given the cost of training new hires, a retention bonus seems very inexpensive. However, you may find that support engineers stay the one or two years to get the bonus and then leave right away anyway. It may be better to use a training reimbursement close in the hiring letter to get to the same goal. Alternatively, you could pay yearly retention bonuses to support engineers who have been with the group more than two years.

- Support center or company performance-based bonuses are also a good idea.

In short, bonuses can be a good tool if they can be large enough and tied to real performance differences. If you cannot achieve sizable, meaningful bonuses, stick to base pay and use your creativity elsewhere.

Awards are another popular way to recognize support engineers. They may be given at random intervals or on a regular basis, from monthly to yearly. Define what it takes to get an award; it's important that engineers feel that winners are picked through some predictable process. Since winners will be seen as examples, make sure you select role models whom you would like others to emulate. Also, make sure that heroics, although they are most visible and easier to recognize, are not the only way to get awards. Reward and set as examples steady performers. In the same vein, make sure that at least some of the awards are related to the basic job (resolving customer problems) rather than additional project work.

Awards do not need to include money, although that's always appreciated. Do take advantage of the occasion to recognize recipients publicly, and try to have some tangible plaque or other memento that engineers can display in their cubes for all to see.

Don't forget to take advantage of general company awards to showcase your people and your group in general. Nominate your people, and have others such as satisfied customers or salespeople nominate them. It's great recognition and visibility for the chosen individual and the whole group.

Finally, although compensation and formal awards are very important tools in recognizing and motivating support engineers, there are many other ways to motivate (or demotivate) support engineers. Many support engineers, especially those at the upper end of salary scales, are not in it for the money. Issues such as quality of life and training become more important, and that's where you would need to focus your attention.

7.3.4   Nonstandard Work Schedules

An interesting area for motivating support engineers is to offer nonstandard work schedules. The advantage of nonstandard schedules is that you can often implement them at no or little cost, while significantly increasing employee satisfaction. We will discuss flexible schedules, including part-time schedules, compressed schedules, and telecommuting.

Flexible schedules allow employees to choose when they are in the office. In a support center, where staffing requirements are tough, flexible schedules need to be planned in advance but can often be worked into the overall scheme to everyone's satisfaction. For instance, if you have a West Coast center where the load is heavier at lunch time, a support engineer who chooses to take a very short lunch break could help you balance the schedule. Also, if your calls tend to be short and support engineers have a small backlog, part-time schedules may be accommodated easily. In a complex support environment where many calls require long resolution cycles, it's much harder to accommodate part-time schedules. In any case, the key is that schedules can be flexible, but they need to be planned out in advance.

Compressed schedules are another intriguing possibility: the idea is to work longer hours each day so that each Friday or every other Friday can be off. Compressed schedules are attractive to a variety of support engineers and are particularly desirable in areas where commutes are long. Again, this kind of schedule is easy to accommodate with short calls, a bit more challenging for complex calls. In a complex support environment, you need to reserve compressed schedules to individuals who can manage their backlog very well so that nothing slips on the day they are not in the office. We have seen the system used as a reward with good results.

Telecommuting used to be a poor match for support centers, since one had to be in the office to pick up the phone. No longer. With modern ACDs, it is possible for geographically remote support engineers to hook into the system as virtual operators. Telecommuters will need a solid hardware setup at home, and the usual challenges of telecommuting apply, but virtual ACD networks open a new era for support centers.

In short, nonstandard schedules can often be accommodated and create powerful motivation for support engineers for minimum effort on the part of the manager.

7.3.5   Shift Differentials

Although support engineers are almost always exempt employees (that is, do not account for their time), some aspects of their compensation are closer to what one would expect of hourly employees, and in particular they are often scheduled and paid according to shift schedules. Since they are exempt employees, shift work does not mean they should leave the minute their scheduled shift is over, but punctuality at the beginning of a shift is paramount and needs to be enforced.

As discussed in Chapter 3, "Call Management Implementation," shifts are often necessary to cover extended hours required by the customers. Regular shifts are usually handled through a pay differential proportional to the extra constraints placed on individuals working the shift. The idea is that individuals working the shifts will receive an additional compensation compared to those working normal hours. That way, you keep the idea of "base pay" and you can continue to compare individuals' pay using the base pay, but you have a flexible amount of money for people working different hours.

Shift compensation is usually expressed as a percentage of the base pay. Typical shift differentials are as shown in Table 7–1.

Table 7–1.   Typical Shift Differentials

Shift Start Time	Differential Percentage
4 a.m.	10%
5 a.m.	8%
6 a.m.	6%
3 p.m.	10%
11 p.m.	15%

Note that, as in the sample in the table, there may be additional shifts, such as 7 a.m., 8 a.m., and 9 a.m., that do not carry a differential because they are not deemed to be inconvenient enough.

If you have regular shifts that fall on weekends, you may have to define differentials for them, too.

One of the management challenges with shift pay is that engineers can get used to the extra income and find it difficult to get off the shift and its accompanying differential. Make sure to remind engineers that business requirements change and they may be reassigned if necessary.

Additional shifts, such as weekends and holidays, for which you do not have dedicated staff can be assigned on a voluntary or rotating basis. Additional shifts may be paid for separately or through some kind of compensation time scheme. The advantages of compensation time are that no additional funding is required and some engineers are eager to add to their vacation time. However, you may find it a real drain to have engineers off during regular hours, so make plans to limit or at least track compensation time so it does not become a burden. Compensation time is typically administered informally and is "lost" if an individual leaves the group.

If you decide to pay for additional shifts, expect to pay about .5% of base salary for an eight-hour shift (or a 25% premium compared to a regular workday).

If your engineers carry beepers, you should also consider paying them for beeper duty. The only exception might be if beeper calls are extremely rare (less than a call a week) and beeper duty does not occur more than once every couple of months. Your options are

- *Flat rate:* some set amount regardless of the number of calls. This works well if the amount of calls while on duty is small. The advantage of this method is its simplicity. It can break down if the person on duty gets a lot of calls, or if there is a great unevenness in the call volume from one week to the next. Typical flat rates are $100–$300 per week, higher for busy beepers and highly technical products.

- *Per-call rate:* pay per call handled while on duty. The advantage of this method is that you pay only for actual work performed. The disadvantage is that there is no incentive to carry the beeper faithfully at all times. This is also somewhat of an overkill for really easy calls. Make sure you specify whether you are paying per problem or per call, since the same customer may need repeated help with the same problem. Typical rates vary from $25 to $50, depending on complexity. A popular variation of the per-call rate for complex calls is to pay per hour.

- *Combination:* We recommend this method for busy beepers as it combines the advantages of both methods. For nonbusy beepers, stick with a flat rate.

Changes in beeper pay are very difficult to implement (except, of course, if you are offering an increase), so take some time to create a system that will work for you. When in doubt, start on the low side.

7.3.6   Rotation Schedules

We now give some guidelines on scheduling project time. When we talked about capacity models, we stated that your support engineers should be interacting with customers, whether directly on the phone or doing research on customer problems, about 80% of the time. Here are some suggestions on how to schedule the project time.

Schedule according to your average call resolution time. With short calls (a few minutes), schedule off-time everyday, say 6 hours on and 2 hours off. Schedule the off-time to accommodate your peak load. Schedule training and other activities during the off-time. This works well when calls are short and support engineers have little or no backlog.

On the other hand, if your calls are long, if resolution often takes several days, and if engineers typically carry a sizable backlog, do the rotation over weeks, say 6 weeks on, one week of cleanup time, and 1 or 2 weeks off. The cleanup time is a time during which support engineers get no new calls, so the backlog is minimal at the end of the cleanup time and the engineer can go on to projects after accomplishing only a few hand-offs. If you schedule rotations ahead of time, you can work training and vacation time into the schedule.

To conclude this section, we recommend you define clear goals and objectives for support engineers and for managers both to set a common direction and to make it easier to evaluate staff performance. We urge you to ensure that pay is perceived as fair, while remembering that other areas, such as training and overall quality of life, are just as important in determining your staff's level of motivation and satisfaction. We have given you some guidelines to implement beeper pay and shift differential. Use the rotation schedules we recommended to provide the project and off-time necessary. We now move on to a key issue in Technical Support: employee retention.

7.4 RETAINING SUPPORT STAFF

Technical support is a stressful job. Listening to customer problems all day while being able to solve only a portion of them quickly can be difficult even for folks who love helping others. At the same time, retaining (good) staff is extremely important because of the high cost of having to replace people. Do you know how much it costs you to replace someone? Compute it now. Add up:

- Your average recruiting cost (recruiter fees, internal referral bonus, management and staff time for interviewing).
- New-hire salary during the ramp-up time before a new hire becomes productive.
- Out-of-pocket expenses for training.
- Mentoring time from manager and peers.

Is your bill higher than $30 k? higher than $50 k? Remember this figure. It is your incentive to keep turnover low.

What can you as a manager do to keep folks around longer? First and foremost, hire well. Maintain a strong profile and use it for each and every hire. When you recruit, define the retention expectation before you make an offer. If you expect support engineers to stay for two years, say so in advance of hiring them. Some companies even write it down in the offer letter, with financial consequences if the employee quits of his own accord before the time is up. In any case, bring it up as a topic and as a moral requirement for the job.

At the other end of the story, conduct exit interviews with each and every individual leaving your group, regardless of tenure. Find out why they are leaving. By the time someone resigns, it's usually too late to do anything about the root causes of the departure, but you can learn about what to do for the support engineers who remain. Conduct exit interviews yourself even if your Human Resources group offers exit interviews. Because you know more about the group, you should be able to ask more detailed questions and to elicit more detailed answers. Keep statistics about why people leave and use them to adjust your hiring and management practices and the pay scales.

Besides hiring the right people, there is a lot you can do as a manager to retain support engineers. The key idea is that employee retention is not a "project" in and of itself. Retention is mostly a consequence of what you do day-to-day to make the work environment challenging and pleasant. Don't expect miracles if the workload is crushing: use your staffing model to secure enough staff.

In addition to workload, a very important concept in support center is employee career development. Make career planning a part of any formal performance reviews you have with the support engineers. Classic career paths for support engineers include: all other branches of customer support such as consulting or training, product development, MIS, and management. The possibilities should be explored with the support engineers together with the requirements to get there.

You should also make it very easy and attractive to grow within the support center. Your main tool to accomplish this is to create a job ladder that defines a progression through the ranks of Technical Support. A job ladder formalizes the various levels of expertise within the group and will look something like this:

- *Associate Support Engineer:* can resolve basic problems, and needs help from others otherwise. An associate is not ready to work in Backline if you have a Frontline/Backline model, or to be a technical advisor if you have a Touch and Hold model.

- *Support Engineer:* can resolve many problems independently. A support engineer is not yet ready to be a backliner or a technical advisor.

- *Senior Support Engineer:* can resolve most problems independently and can mentor others. Participates in improvement programs. A senior support engineer meets the requirements to be a backliner and may meet requirements for technical advisor.

- *Staff Support Engineer:* this is a "guru-level" position. A staff support engineer must be able to mentor others effectively and to lead and suggest improvement programs. Staff support engineers are found in the Backline group for FL/BL model and probably in the technical advisors' group for the T&H model.

Your own ladder could be longer or shorter, as long as you can distinguish clearly between the levels. Criteria for promotion include: technical skills, customer skills, productivity, mentoring skills, and influence beyond one's own particular duties. It's very important to define and uphold clear standards, so don't hesitate to spend some time refining them. If your group is large, make sure that different managers use consistent standards. If you have difficulties evaluating technical skills, ask the more technical support engineers to prepare technical evaluations. For the higher levels, using peer or board reviews can help you cope with evaluating high-level technical skills, as well as capture the elusive mentoring and leadership abilities.

Most of your hires will be in the lower levels of the career ladder, with advancement to the higher levels occurring internally, since the requirements for the higher levels can probably be met only by individuals who have experience working in your particular group. You may be able to attract intracompany transfers qualified for the higher levels, however. As long as you have the capability to mentor support engineers, hiring relatively inexperienced staff can be a good strategy: they should stay longer, since they have a lot of room to grow.

7.5 MANAGING MORALE

Typically, we see morale as something that happens, like the weather—important, but fundamentally beyond our control. As with the weather, we enjoy it when it is good, but resign ourselves to it or complain about it when it is bad. But what if we could manage morale? If we could take effective action in this area, wouldn't the outcome be increased productivity—people working more and complaining less? And wouldn't this in turn lead to increased profitability? In this section we lay the groundwork for you to attack the issue of morale in your organization. It will also allow you to show your employees how to manage themselves in this area.

There are two fundamental approaches for managers to take to build and maintain good morale in their organizations. The first is to coach their people to manage their Basic Action Workflows (see Section 2.1.2 in Chapter 2). The second is to become partners with them in creating their futures and, most importantly in this context, their careers. These approaches are not tips to be applied at particular times, but rather ways for you to orient yourself in working with your people day-to-day and over time.

Let's look at the first approach. Every day your people are engaged in Basic Action Workflows, both with customers calling for technical assistance and with their co-workers (fellow support engineers, you, and so on). These workflows deal with requests for something to be done, agreements about what exactly will be done, who is responsible for doing it, when it will be done, and whether the customer or co-worker is satisfied with what has been done.

Incomplete Basic Action Workflows are obviously a crucial productivity issue. Problems or breakdowns with any of the steps of the cycle, particularly those dealing with fulfilling agreements, create inefficiencies or waste. In addition, incomplete workflows are a primary source of customer escalations (service and technical) and lead to poor customer satisfaction. They are just as crucial for morale, because they result in the very moods we associate with poor morale: frustration, resignation, resentment, and distrust. Unclear requests, missing promises ("I'll try to call you tomorrow"), unfulfilled promises, missed deadlines, and so on, all contribute to bad moods and, over time, to bad morale.

Completing these workflows, or more colloquially, getting the job done, requires successful completion of the Basic Action Workflows that comprise the "job." It is not much more than a cliché to say that when work is successful, the people performing the work are likely to be satisfied. What we are saying that is more than a cliché here is that by enabling and coaching your support engineers to complete their individual Basic Action Workflows successfully, you contribute greatly to their morale and to the morale of your organization.

Helping support engineers complete their workflows successfully requires not only that you train them to complete them, but also that you have the necessary departmental and interdepartmental Basic Action Workflows in place so that they can complete them. Indeed, if you do not, then the morale of your department will be low. Some individuals may maintain a good mood in the face of incomplete workflows for reasons of personal history (which is part of why you hired them). But since they are people who have career options (which is also why you hired them), they will tire of an environment that thwarts satisfying work and transfer to another part of the company or move on to another company altogether earlier than they otherwise would. One, perhaps obvious, cautionary note: It is vital that you complete your own work-flows with your support engineers. This is the very foundation for building trust with them individually and in your organization as a whole.

The second approach—becoming partners with them in creating their futures, and most importantly their careers—is also critical. In the previous section, "Retaining Support Staff," we talked about developing career ladders. The specifics of that discussion are relevant here, too. Now we want to make a couple of more general points. When the future is open, when people see possibilities for advancement for themselves, morale, no surprise, goes up. Conversely, when your support engineers don't see anywhere to go, often feeling stuck in their present positions, morale declines. So it is essential that you work with your people appropriately on seeing where they are, defining where they want to go, how they are going to get there, and how long it will take. This not only includes providing ways for them to advance in your organization. It also includes preparing them, when the time is right, for a move onto a different career ladder. Remember, no one stays anywhere forever any more—acknowledge this; it furthers trust in your relationship with them.

Work with each support engineer individually in this regard. Consider tailoring training to their needs as well as the department's. Support engineers further along in life or in their support career will have different concerns than younger and junior support engineers. The former may want coaching to enable her to go into management. The latter may be happy with a piece of new technology as a step in building her skills and thus her career possibilities. Keeping their eyes on the future and supporting them in making it happen forges and strengthens both their ambition and their trust in you and your company.

Working appropriately with your staff on completing their Basic Action Work-flows and forwarding their careers will help build and maintain ambition, trust, and resoluteness in the morale of your organization. Of course, pervasive low morale takes time to turn around. But consistently coaching your people can provide the foundation for that turnaround. If your organization already enjoys high morale, this helps ensure that it stays that way.

In the previous section we talked about the virtue of "hiring well" for staff retention. This will put you ahead of the game in managing morale as well. Few of us are trained and fewer still have the time to work with people to shift their fundamental outlooks. If you hire a cynic, almost certainly a cynic you shall have until he leaves your organization. Negative moods are particularly contagious. One bad apple can spoil the whole barrel, unless most of them are sound. On the other hand, we can learn to manage morale and show this possibility to our people who are not thoroughly entrenched in negativity. If we are successful here, we will have a stronger, more successful organization.

We all enjoy work more when we are "at work." When we are engaged in what we are doing, work is enjoyable and we are more productive. We don't waste time in idle chatter and gossip, in resigned and cynical assessments about colleagues, managers, executives, and the company as a whole. This engagement occurs when morale is good, and, as a direct consequence of good morale, the productivity and profitability of your organization go up.

CHAPTER **8**

MANAGING SOFTWARE BUGS AND CODE FIXES

In this chapter we plunge into the world of bugs, and more specifically how to track them, fix them, and deliver fixes to customers. Bugs, sometimes politely referred to as "product defects," are unfortunately ubiquitous, so you need to think about bug and fix management regardless of the complexity of software you support and regardless of who your customers are, although your strategy will depend on your specific requirements.

Although the vast majority of calls into your support center should involve usage or documentation questions rather than bugs (the percentage of bug-related calls is usually less than 5%), bug-related problems are likely to create customer satisfaction challenges and also to create a disproportionate amount of work for you. Customers, of course, are not pleased to find that the software they purchase is not working properly, and if they have to wait days or weeks for a diagnosis and a solution they are likely to be even less pleased. From your point of view, bug-related problems are likely to consume more time than other kinds of problems, especially when they require extensive investigation—that is, when they are not already known. Therefore, having good processes for diagnosing bugs and getting fixes to customers is important to all support centers.

We won't go into great detail about what is required from the code maintenance organization, but instead will cover the basics of bugs and code fixes to help you make support decisions and influence the code development and maintenance process as needed.

We have already stated that any piece of software, like any other human enterprise, contains bugs, and we will devote the rest of this chapter to a discussion about fixing bugs. However, we feel the software industry too often uses this as an excuse to cover up sloppy design, sloppy coding, and sloppy testing. The best way to fix bugs is to have few of them to begin with, and good-quality code that can be patched without destroying it. Partnership between the Technical Support group and the Development group is crucial so that the latter does not release products before they are ready, with the resulting disastrous consequences for the customers. A large part of the bug fixing process can be used to strengthen the partnership, so existing bugs can be fixed faster and future ones avoided.

Strategies for fixing bugs are covered in the first two sections of this chapter and will be of most interest to ISVs (Independent Software Vendors) and internal help desks that support applications developed in-house. The last section covers third-party support, so it will be relevant for internal help desks, for anyone who supports products developed by an outside entity, and for ISVs that use outsourcing for providing technical support.

8.1   DEFINITIONS AND MODELS FOR BUG FIXING

Let's start with a brief overview of bug fixing terms and models, so that we all use the same terminology.

A **bug** is a defect in the product, that is, a deviation between the stated specifications of the product and its actual performance. The important thing to note here is that an "odd" behavior from the point of view of the user is not necessarily a bug. The product may well have been designed to work in a way which is not intuitive for that user, or even for most users.

A desired behavior of the product which is outside current product specifications is an **enhancement request**. As we just saw, the line between bugs and enhancement requests is not always clear. Implementing an enhancement request changes the functionality of the product. Be aware of who in your organization has the authority to declare whether specific product behavior constitutes a bug or not. Frequently this is not clear and much time and effort goes to the decision about how to characterize particular product behavior.

A **bug fix** is a change in the code to repair the bug. Bug fixes can consist of a single change in a single line of code or can involve large chunks of new code. Bug fixes can be packaged either singly as **patches** or **updates**, depending on the kind of software you are working with, or in groups as **maintenance releases**. Patches and updates need to be installed in addition to the existing base release (they are not self-contained). Maintenance releases sometimes, but not always, require the base release for installation.

Bugs are usually ranked by priority, which depends on their technical severity. A typical priority scheme would classify bugs into three categories:

- Disastrous bugs (the system cannot stay up).
- Severe bugs (the system is up, but some important functionality is affected).
- Mundane bugs (anything else).

Note that bug priorities are not necessarily the same as the priorities of the support calls they are associated with. An emergency call associated with a bug could eventually give rise to a severe, but not disastrous bug if there is a good workaround for the problem.

8.1.1 What is a maintenance release and why is it a good thing?

A maintenance release is a release that, compared to the last one, contains only bug fixes. It does not contain any new functionality. Occasionally, fixing an existing bug will look very much like creating new functionality, especially when you are dealing with one of those bugs at the boundary between bug and enhancement request, but the intent stays the same: to make the software incrementally more stable, as opposed to adding new bells and whistles. A maintenance release typically receives (and should receive) the same level of testing as a base release; that is, customers may install and run it with the same or higher level of confidence as a base release.

Beside offering high quality without functionality changes, the advantages of maintenance releases are that

- Most customers' internal processes allow them to replace the base release with a maintenance release with only minimal testing on their part because of the comprehensive testing done by the provider.
- They allow the code maintenance organization and the support center to deliver fixes in a predictable manner, keeping costs down.
- They are much easier to track than individual fixes.

Despite their advantages, maintenance releases take time to produce and package, so that even if they are available on a regular basis, there often remains a need to create fixes quickly and to deliver them through a patch or an update mechanism.

8.1.2 What is a patch and when is it a good thing?

A patch (also called an update in the low-end world) usually contains a single bug fix, although it could bundle several fixes. It usually receives a lower level of testing than a full maintenance release and, partly for that reason, it can be made available to customers more quickly. Patches are also much smaller than maintenance releases and so can be downloaded electronically much faster. Patches must be installed on top of the existing release and cannot be used without it.

Patches are inherently riskier than maintenance releases because of the lower level of testing they receive. In some environments, single patches are fully tested and there, of course, this limitation disappears. In partial test environments, however, patches are not made available to customers on a broad basis because of the risks involved. Typically, in these cases the support engineers make the decision of whether to share a patch created for a given customer with another customer experiencing a similar problem.

From the point of view of the software developer, patches are costly, since they essentially involve custom work for one particular situation, require special, albeit abbreviated testing, and require special distribution to the customer. From the software developer's point of view, therefore, patches should be restricted as much as possible.

Since emergency patches create issues for both customers (quality) and the company (cost), when should they be used? We see two main guidelines for deciding whether to create a patch: the technical severity of the problem, and the customer's business requirements. Since patches are risky, you and your customer should not choose to use them unless the problem is severe. Even if the problem is severe, a workaround, if there is one, is almost always preferable to using an incompletely tested patch. The second part of the decision hinges on an evaluation of the risk of using the patch versus the risk of staying with the current situation. If the software is an office-automation problem and the worst that could happen if the patch does not work is to lose 30 minutes of one person's work, then installing the patch may make sense. On the other hand, if your customer is running the back office of a New York Stock Exchange trading house, taking a risk may put millions of dollars at stake, and a cumbersome workaround may be worth the peace of mind.

8.1.3   Bug Fix Models

When and how customers can obtain bug fixes should be an essential part of your service contract; spell this out in the support agreement or the Support User's Guide.

First, customers with a valid support agreement should have access to patches, updates, and maintenance releases. They should be able to either download them through electronic means or to get a copy on hard media upon request, perhaps for an additional fee in "free" support environments. Define the length of time during which maintenance releases will be available for a given release. This depends on your overall business model. In most low-end environments, new functionality releases must be purchased independently of support agreements, so you need to define how long you will create maintenance releases for an old release, once a new functionality release is available. In most high-end environments, on the other hand, new functionality is bundled with the support agreement, which may alleviate the issue of having to continue to maintain separate code lines once a new functional release is out. (Discontinuing support of old releases prematurely may not be a smart business move, but that is beyond our scope here.)

Ideally, maintenance releases should be available on a regular schedule. The buggier the software, the more frequently releases are needed. A quarterly or semiannual schedule is a good goal, and in this case more is always better. Regardless of the schedule, regularity and predictability score high marks. All other things being equal, it's best to have a regular schedule for maintenance releases, and, barring that, to have a firm schedule of when the next one will be out. With the schedule and the list of bugs scheduled to be fixed in upcoming releases, support engineers and managers can work with customers to determine whether the customer should wait for a maintenance release or request the fix through emergency patches. If patches are fully tested, the need for regular maintenance releases recedes (although it's more practical to install one maintenance release than a collection of patches).

Customers with a support agreement should also have access, electronically or not, to existing patches. At a minimum, customers must be able to know the list of patches available. The decision of whether to make all patches available to all customers without a prior consultation with a support engineer hinges on a number of factors:

- *Testing:* if patches are fully tested, a good argument can be made to make them available to all customers without restrictions. If not, prior consultation with a support engineer is preferable.

- *Type of software:* if you support low-end software where the risk of a bad patch involves limited negative consequences, you may have to choose to make all patches available to customers. If you support mission-critical software, you should require consultation with a support engineer.

- *Timing of maintenance releases:* if you have frequent maintenance releases, the pressure to make patches available on a large scale diminishes.

Many support agreements do not spell out when and how customers may obtain emergency fixes for newly discovered problems, although they should. At a minimum, define an internal procedure so you are able to handle requests for emergency fixes quickly and efficiently. Typically, emergency fixes should be reserved for top-priority bugs that cannot be worked around. Everything else can be fixed in maintenance releases. Ideally, there should be a commitment to fix all priority 1 bugs in the next maintenance release (in other words, maintenance releases should contain no known priority 1 bugs), and priority 2 bugs should be fixed within the next two maintenance releases.

Your support documentation should also specify how fixes can be obtained, whether on hard media or through electronic means.

8.2 BUG FIXING PROCESS

Let's now move to a more tactical level of how bugs are isolated, tracked, and fixed. Regardless of your delivery vehicle (patches or maintenance releases) and of your testing model, define and communicate to all support engineers and as needed to your customers the basic workflow for fixing bugs.

8.2.1 Isolating Bugs

The first step in fixing bugs is to isolate and confirm that there indeed is a problem. Sounds simple enough, but especially in complex environments it could be the most time-consuming part of the process. The responsibility for isolating bugs is usually the responsibility of the Support organization, and, for difficult situations, most particularly the domain of the second-line support engineers, either the backliners or the technical advisers, depending on which support model you chose.

Isolating bugs revolves around reproducing the behavior within the support center. Sometimes the problem is sporadic even in the customer's environment, so the first order of business is to work with the customer to reproduce the problem there. Even when the behavior is reproducible at will at the customer site, reproducing in-house can turn into a lengthy and frustrating process if the customer's hardware and software environment is complex (do you have 20 gigabytes of disk handy to load a large database?). As much as possible then, the strategy is to create a small test case that exhibits the problem.

Creating an in-house test case is not a delaying tactic prior to creating a fix, as some customers may see it. The test case can then be used to check that the code changes **do** fix the problem, and ideally can be integrated in the product test suite to prevent regression problems. Therefore, test cases are an essential quality tool. They are worth the time and effort. Although there is nothing wrong with reproducing a complex problem at the customer's site, the ultimate testing and integration of the test into the test suite requires an in-house reproduction.

With well-trained staff you will be able to reproduce most problems in a timely manner with support resources. Occasionally, however, you will need to engage the bug fixing or even the development organization into the bug diagnostic process. Define a process which ensures that

- You exhaust support resources before turning to other groups, so as not to waste efforts.

- You stay involved with the diagnostic process, so the expertise goes back to the Support group for the next similar situation.

- You can get help in a timely manner to preserve customer satisfaction. This includes having a good call aging mechanism in place, so you can spot potential issues early, and also having a system to summon outside help quickly.

Appropriate call and bug tracking systems can help you with this process; we'll see how later.

8.2.2 Fixing bugs

At this point, you have reproduced the problem or otherwise documented its existence, perhaps working with the bug fixing or development organization. The next steps are confirming that the behavior is indeed a bug and creating a fix.

Who should fix bugs? There are two possible answers to that question: the Support group or the development group. Having the Support group take ownership of fixing bugs allows for a good flow of information within all customer-related functions, and it can be a good career path for support engineers. On the other hand, getting developers to fix bugs ensures that they fix their own mistakes, so they can see them and they have a powerful incentive to produce better code. It can be faster, too, since a development engineer remembers not only the code but the reasons behind its architecture and its implementation. This may be an advantage in theory only, since developers who are working on new projects may forget what they did months ago, and the original code writers may have moved on long ago in any case.

So which should you choose? Most high-end software companies choose to have the bug fixing function within the Development group to take advantage of the higher technical knowledge of developers. Some low-end software companies choose to have it as an extension of the Support group because of the lower technical requirements. In the end, what matters most is that the bug fixing organization work well with the Support group.

Even in organizations where the bug fixing function is part of the Development group, it is often a separate group from the development function per se. Having a separate group allows for more predictable staffing of the bug fixing function. Very much like combined Support and development organizations split up under the pressure of competing scheduling demands, bug fixing and creating new releases can be strange bedfellows. In that type of environment, the link between development per se and bug fixing is key.

Bug Fixing Workflow

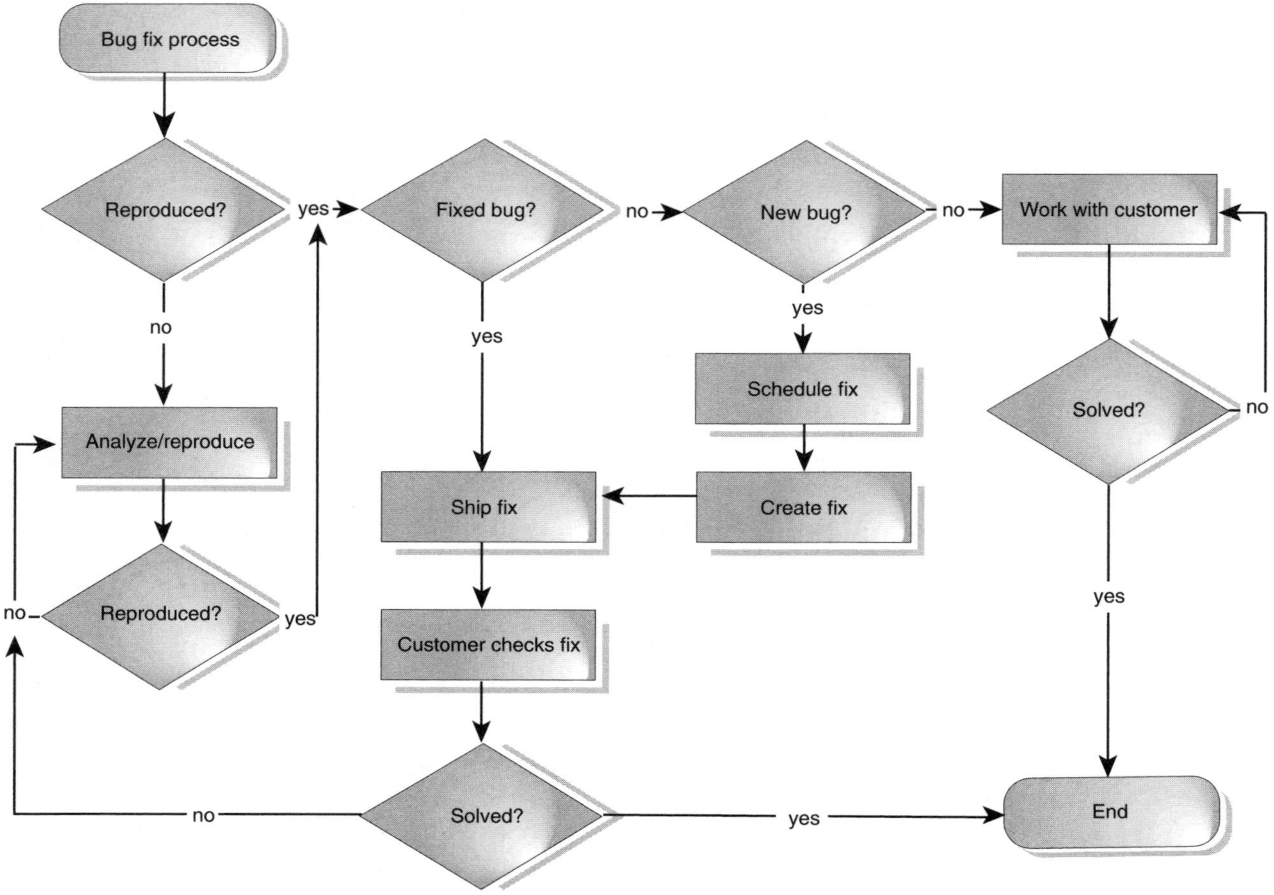

Figure 8–1

Whatever the structure, a bug fixing process is essential (see Figure 8–1):

- First, confirm whether the problem is indeed a bug. Execute this key step as quickly as possible and report back to the customer. If it's not a bug, tell the customer right away and offer alternatives to work around the issue. If the problem is a bug, define when a fix schedule will be available to the customer. It could be that the fix is already available in an existing patch or maintenance release. If so, work with the customer to upgrade to that fix level.

- If the problem is a bug, define a time frame for a fix. This depends on two factors: the technical difficulty of the fix and the business commitments and requirements of the customer. The technical difficulty of the fix dictates the minimum amount of time required to create the fix. Don't forget to take into account the testing requirements as well. If the fix is particularly complex, you may need to define scheduling in terms of steps: first, determine what module of the code contains the defect, then code the fix, then test the fix. Make sure to stress that all dates are targets, since the fix will need to be reworked if it fails.

- Create the fix and perform in-house testing.

At this point, the fix is ready for packaging, either as a patch or as a maintenance release, depending on your fix model and the severity of the bug for the customer. Once the fix is delivered, the customer will need to perform his own testing to confirm that the problem is indeed resolved.

We strongly advocate that the Support organization should manage the customer interface throughout the bug fixing process since it has ownership of the customer and the appropriate skills to interface with the customer. Some support managers, frustrated by their experiences with the code maintenance organization, may be tempted to have it take over the customer interface instead of functioning as a punching ball. We sympathize with the frustration, but we stick to our guns: you should own the customer interface throughout the entire process, while lobbying internally for better processes and service.

After the fix is created, and ideally after its viability is confirmed by the customer, then it must be integrated into the code tree so it can become a part of future releases.

Keep in mind the key point that most problems can and must be worked around, at least temporarily, while a permanent fix is created. The Support organization cannot abandon the customer while the fix is being created. Instead, the support engineer's mission is to alleviate the pain immediately by creating a workaround acceptable to the customer. The effort to find a workaround should continue while the bug is being diagnosed and fixed, especially if the bug is severe and the fix will take time (and severe bugs unfortunately tend to take a long time to fix). Many times, the bug fixing organization must be engaged in the effort of finding a workaround. As noted above, the entire process should be owned and driven by the Support organization.

Finally, some minor bugs may not be fixed for weeks and months or, even, at all. Make sure that customers understand what bugs are low-priority and what time frames are attached to their fixes. If a bug is not going to be fixed, bite the bullet and say so. As unpleasant as anticipating this conversation may be, real partnership with the customer requires it.

8.2.3   Tracking Bugs and Fixes

In this section we will discuss how to track bugs and fixes, both internally within the company and with customers, without going into details about the particular tools used (which we will do in Chapter 9, "Tools for Technical Software Support").

Plainly put, you need to maintain a database of all bugs known for the product, whether or not they are fixed. The bug list should be available to everyone within the Support group and also to customers, although the customer list can be edited to remove potentially dangerous bugs, such as security bugs, and, on a more mundane level, to make the bug descriptions easier to use from a customer's perspective.

The ideal use of the bug database is for support engineers to enter all new suspected bugs into it and to have the bug fixing organization use it as its input. The bug fixing organization can then update the database to confirm whether a particular problem is indeed a bug, schedule the fix, and then confirm the fix vehicle (patch or release identification number). To accomplish the timely results required, a service-level agreement between the Support group and the bug fixing organization is mandatory. In particular, turnaround times for confirming bugs and scheduling fixes must be defined, as well as escalation procedures for those situations where standard time frames are not sufficient. Here's an example of a service-level agreement:

- For disastrous bugs, confirm/deny the bug within 24 hours; deliver an action plan for resolution within 24 hours, including target fix date; update status daily until the fix is complete.

- For severe bugs, confirm/deny the bug within 2 business days; deliver a target fix date within a week; update status weekly until the fix is complete.

- For mundane bugs, confirm/deny the bug within a week; deliver a target fix date within a week; update status weekly until the fix is complete.

- For escalation situations: the manager of the code maintenance group is available on pager for situations where standard time frames are not sufficient.

Measure performance against the goals of the service-level agreement to ensure it is complied with.

To be useful, the bug database should contain clear descriptions of the bugs, preferably from a user's perspective (actually, it's best to have both a user description, as in "command x does not work," together with a developer description, as in "module xyz branching incorrect"). The descriptions allow reported problems to be matched against known bugs.

Include in the bug database detailed information pinpointing the releases and environments in which the bugs manifest themselves. If you are supporting multiple platforms, you may want to define a hierarchy of platforms, so bugs are always reported and tested against the base platforms unless they only occur on more exotic ones. Again, ease of search is key to avoid the waste of time and work inherent in duplicated efforts.

Track fixes together with the bugs they match. Maintenance releases should also document what bugs are fixed in them and what known bugs they contain. All this information should be available to customers with the possible exception of security-related bugs, which may need to be handled separately so as not to cause problems for customers who are running the affected releases.

More details about the implementation of the bug tracking tool can be found in the next chapter.

8.3   FIXES FOR THIRD-PARTY PRODUCTS

In this section we will apply the principles and techniques described above to the situations where the support provider and the fix provider are in different organizations. If you are providing support for a third party product, as most help desks do, or if a third-party supports your product, as when you out-source support, this section is for you.

Let's start with an inventory of situations where your Support organization is dependent on another entity in another company to create fixes.

- You are running a help desk for products built by an outside company. In this situation you are a go-between with the ISV on behalf of your customers.

- You are a support outsourcing company. Here, end-user customers may be customers of the ISV rather than yours directly, and your role may be to be a conduit or a facilitator for getting fixes, or your customers may depend on you for providing them with fixes very much as if you were running an internal help desk.

- (On the other hand) You as an ISV are outsourcing support to a third party and work with that third party to deliver fixes to your customers, either directly or through that third party.

- Less obviously, you may be indirectly providing support for third-party products, if, as an ISV, your software is used in conjunction with hardware and software for which it is difficult to quickly distinguish boundaries between it and your products. At least until the diagnostic process demonstrates that the problem lies with a product other than yours, you will be engaged in supporting a third-party product. We will cover this special situation separately.

8.3.1   Conduit between the End-Users and the ISV

If you provide support for the end-users of an ISV, your task is to make the connection back to the ISV as transparent to the users as possible. Therefore, your main focus should be the process for isolating bugs and getting fixes back from the ISV. The process should be fast and robust, and you should have ready access to the known bugs and the bugs being fixed. Ideally, you want to be able to provide bug information to your end-user customers.

Consider yourself a high-level customer of the ISV. Negotiate expedited treatment for your problems, since you represent many customers. Pay particular attention to how problems that are difficult to diagnose will be handled.

If, as an ISV, you use third parties as conduits between you and your end-users, pay particular attention to sharing bug and fix information with them.

8.3.2   Support Provider (Only) for an ISV

In this situation a third party provides support, but fixes come from the ISV directly to the end-user. The difficult part of the process is to determine when and how problems are handed from the third party to the ISV. In particular, is the third party tasked with complete problem reproduction, or are contingencies developed to engage the ISV in diagnostic and problem duplication? Note that the same dilemmas occur in the case when the third party is a conduit between the ISV and the end-user, but they are easier to resolve, since the third party is clearly set up as a customer of the ISV. Here, the lines are harder to draw.

If you as an ISV have an outsourcing arrangement with a third-party support provider but continue to be responsible for providing fixes to customers, be especially vigilant about the interface as well. Your customers will rate your service in part on how quickly and smoothly they can get fixes.

8.3.3 Multivendor Support

In many cases, and especially if you support a complex product, you will find yourself providing support for products that are not yours. Here are some steps you can take to boost your chances for success:

- Develop diagnostic tools to help determine where the problem lies. It's not a good use of your or the customer's resources to diagnose a problem only to find that the issue is with a product other than yours.

- Train your staff on the third-party products.

- Maintain appropriate third-party hardware and software for bug reproduction.

- Keep a list of third-party bugs and fixes that impact the way your software functions; share the list with customers.

- Engage the third-party vendor in a cooperative arrangement before you need it. It can be an informal arrangement, where the two support managers simply exchange phone numbers so difficult situations can be escalated quickly. You can also choose to formalize the agreement into a cooperative support agreement that spells out contacts and obligations on both sides. Reciprocal access to the other vendor's knowledge base and training program is valuable. Support engineers' exchanges are another way to build both expertise and teamwork. Remember to consider both management and technical contacts. If you are a customer of the third party for your internal usage, leverage that relationship. If you have a formal marketing or engineering agreement with the third party, leverage that.

- Consider multivendor alliances such as TSANet. With more and more interactions between products, complex situations arise where competitors also need to be partners in some situations. Because of confidentiality requirements, simple exchanges of technology and information are difficult or impossible, so participating in multivendor alliances can be an especially valuable solution.

We believe that multivendor support is a trend for the future, so much so that customers will seek out suppliers willing to support the whole family of products they use, saving them from having to interface with several Support organizations. Multivendor support is difficult, but it is also an opportunity for success.

CHAPTER **9**

TOOLS FOR
SOFTWARE SUPPORT

The right tools can dramatically increase the productivity of a support center. Tools are particularly important in the support arena for three reasons:

- Support work is process oriented, so tools can be found and customized or designed to match and enable the processes.

- Support is a repetitive business: calls are very rarely truly unique, so it is possible and helpful to capture interactions in a structured manner.

- Support involves sharing dynamic information among a large number of people. The proper tools can make the knowledge distribution easier.

In addition to the short-term benefits of making it easier to perform support work and to share information, the right tools also allow you to increase the collective knowledge on a continuous basis, providing significant long-term advantages. We will see that this goal is best accomplished when the various systems are linked together in a unified environment. In other words, the way the various tools interact can be more crucial than each individual tool. We urge you to keep this in mind when making selection decisions.

Since specific requirements differ widely, and since technology changes very quickly, we make no specific recommendations for particular tools. Instead, we help you define a checklist for what you need so you can make the right choice of features, size, and cost. In recent years, many good support tools have become available, so it's very unlikely that you would need to develop your own tools. Purchasing tools from a third party is almost always the right option, although some customization will usually be necessary. We will discuss what customization work is necessary or worthwhile, but in general we recommend you limit customization to a minimum, since it creates headaches with implementing updates from your vendor.

Choosing support tools is an important decision, not only because the cost of the tool itself and of the implementation is high, but also because the cost of failure is extremely high. Switching away from an inadequate tool takes tremendous time and resources. Meanwhile, customers cannot be serviced properly. Spend time making the decision and always consider future needs, so you are not forced into a system that cannot grow with your operation.

All support centers, regardless of size, type of software, and type of customers, need tools and you can find the right tools for them. Some particular tools may not be applicable in your environment: for instance, tracking customer licenses may not be important in an internal help desk setting. However, every single support center needs a call tracking system and some strategy for a problem reproduction environment.

We start our discussion with general considerations on how to select, justify, and implement any type of tool. The rest of the chapter is organized by type of system.

Since we present and discuss a lot of information in this chapter, you may want to target your reading strategy to your needs. Specifically, if you are considering the purchase of a new tool, start with the section on selecting tools and then read the one about the particular tool you are interested in. If you want to review your existing tools, focus on the appropriate sections for the tools you are reviewing. If you are starting from scratch, concentrate on the phone system and the call tracking system. Finally, since the connections between the various systems are so important in a support environment, spend some time thinking about how all the systems you need interact, so you can one day implement a fully integrated tool strategy.

9.1 CHOOSING, JUSTIFYING, AND IMPLEMENTING TOOLS

This section covers general strategies for choosing, cost-justifying, and implementing tools—all topics that do not depend on the type of tool you are investigating.

9.1.1 Choosing Tools

When selecting support tools, take your time and be thorough, since both the financial investment and the productivity impact are large. Proceed as follows:

- *Create a list of requirements:* To define the requirements, you must first understand to a detailed level how your current processes and systems function. Spend some time watching and listening to support engineers resolving customer issues, and interview a cross section of the staff on what is really happening out there. Gather the statistics you have about call volume, response time, resolution time, and so on. Consider the existing processes that are good and you want to keep, as well as new processes that you would like to implement but are not easy or not feasible with the existing tools.

In addition to technical requirements, include business requirements, such as the size and reputation of the vendor, the quality of its technical support, the existence of other customers of the vendor's similar to your support center, and compatibility with existing systems. Be exhaustive.

Organize the requirements into an evaluation matrix that lists the desired features and will include ratings for both the importance of each feature and how well each product meets the requirement for the feature. This kind of matrix is called a Kepner-Tregoe matrix and will be used down the road to compare competitive products (see Table 9–1).

Rank the importance of each factor on a scale of 1 to 4: not needed, nice to have, important, required. To determine the importance ratings, evaluate the impact of the feature (or lack thereof) on your operation. All other things being equal, a feature everyone uses dozens of times every day will rate higher than some far-fetched, albeit clever, feature that will be used only once in a while.

Rank performance on a scale of 1 to 4: not supported, minimally supported, fully supported, and supported beyond the requirement. At this point, define the minimum performance level required for each factor. You will fill in the actual product performance during the evaluation.

To get the maximum possible score of a product, multiply the importance of each factor by the maximum possible performance rating (4) and add up the results. To get the minimum required performance score, multiply the importance of each factor by the minimum performance rating and add up the results. You can also calculate maximum and minimum scores by categories for a finer analysis.

Conduct an internal review of the matrix by senior support engineers.

Table 9–1.   Tools Evaluations Matrix

Factor	Importance	Minimum Performance	Maximum Performance	Actual Performance
Vendor Stability				
Financial performance				
Stability				
References				
Product line				
Reputation				
Compatibility				
With corporate standards				
With other installed systems				
With vendor's vision of product future				
Product Functionality				
Hardware platform				
Hardware requirements				
Documentation				
Quality of support				
Training				
Performance				
Scalability (for future growth)				

Table 9–1. Tools Evaluations Matrix (Continued)

Factor	Importance	Minimum Performance	Maximum Performance	Actual Performance
Ease of use				
Degree of customization required				
Average transaction time				
Detailed specifications by product				

Cost

Initial license				
Installation				
Training				
Support				
Maintenance				
Upgrade				

- *Prepare a request for proposal:* Despite its fancy name, an RFP is simply a document that presents your requirements and asks detailed questions about how well the product fulfills them. Include a short overview of your support center, your call resolution process, and relevant statistics as well as your evaluation matrix, complete with importance score for each feature.

  Define what you want as a response, typically a description of the solution, a high-level implementation plan and ratings for all the requirements in the Kepner-Tregoe matrix. You also want a cost estimate for the initial purchase, customization and installation.

- *Select vendors for evaluation:* As you prepare your RFP, use the support associations' directories, trade journals, as well as your business contacts to gather names and information for potential vendors. Narrow down the list based on your basic requirements: for instance, if you have a small help desk, don't include high-end vendors; if you run on Windows, screen out vendors who don't support it. Check references at a high level. You don't want to have to evaluate more than four or five vendors in depth; it's simply too time consuming.

- *Evaluate the vendors:* Ask each vendor on the short list to respond to the RFP in writing. Make it clear that you want a short and complete response and that the quality of the response is a factor in your decision. Set a response deadline. Make someone on your staff available as a contact in case the vendor has questions.

  You may want to use a competitive evaluation for critical features. That is, ask the vendor to describe how the product would handle the requirement, while making it clear another vendor can also handle it. The answers will help you determine who has the best mousetrap.

  In parallel, or after you evaluate answers, schedule a demo of the tool and a visit to a reference site. Bring support engineers and managers with you and ask questions. If your requirements are complex or require lots of customization, ask for a proof of concept or a prototype for some subsystem of your choice, preferably one that appears particularly difficult to implement.

  Check references thoroughly. If you can find blind references, all the better. Target support centers similar to yours in size, complexity, and requirements. Check that the vendor uses its own product as a production tool in-house. If not, find out why.

- *Make your choice:* Evaluate the responses to the RFP and your own direct observations. Evaluate the results of your reference checks and other observations of demos and site visits. To get final scores from the Kepner-Tregoe matrix, multiply each factor's importance rating by its performance rating and add up the numbers. Compare the scores to the minimum and the maximum score. It's also useful to calculate intermediate scores for each category by adding up the weighed scores for that category and dividing the total by the sum of the importance ratings for that category.

  Analyze what makes certain products better than others: a product that has everything you need and more except for one crucial requirement may not turn out to be the best suited after all.

  This last phase is a good opportunity to check for overdemanding requirements. If none of the available products can do everything you want, look at the requirements again. Do you really need each and every feature you thought you needed? Weigh your requirement against the heavy cost of customization and pare down the requirements list as much as possible.

Look at price last. Make the features decision first, because you can't afford to buy a product that does not fit your needs, and also because the final cost often depends on exact requirements, since many desirable features are packaged as extra options.

9.1.2   Cost-Justifying Tools

Once you have chosen the tool you want, and preferably before then, you will probably need to prepare a cost justification or an ROI (return on investment) for your favorite controller. (It's really a good exercise to do it for yourself if you happen to control financial expenditures.)

Cost justifications are unnecessarily dreaded. With the right framework, they should be relatively painless and bring a healthy financial judgment to investment decisions.

The steps are straightforward. First, you need to gather the costs. Be exhaustive. Don't stop at the initial purchase price, but also include all costs related to the implementation, including training, customizing, even retrofitting of existing facilities. Then make an estimate of ongoing costs such as support. Contrast the cost with the additional productivity you expect to gain from the tool. Don't go overboard. No tool will triple productivity the day it's installed. If you find gains in a matter of months, you are doing very well; usually productivity dips for a while when a new tool is installed. In other words, your financial justification should show that your expense will be counterbalanced, over time, by greater productivity.

Here's a checklist of the initial costs to consider:

- *Initial purchase price for the hardware and software.* Include all the equipment, software, and options required. Determine what pricing scheme is used: by CPU, by registered user, by concurrent user, or some other method.

- *Installation costs.* Include any additional facility expense required if a special environment is required to install the equipment. It could be as simple as a lock on a door or as complex as a special air-conditioned room or special wiring.

- *Customization costs.* Include all consulting and programming costs.

- *Implementation costs.* Include conversion from legacy systems, testing, and the initial setup which is required even if you plan to use the product in its "vanilla" version.

- *Training.* Include both the out-of-pocket expenses for the training and the productivity hit for the people attending the training. Add miscellaneous expenses such as room and equipment rental and course materials. Include training for the end-users and for the system administrator if you need one.

- *Unamortized portion of existing tool.* Check with your controller on this one. It could be that the tool you are currently using has not been fully accounted for on your balance sheet. If so, you will need to account for it.

- *Add some percentage for unforeseen costs.* They will occur no matter how carefully you plan. Your controller knows this and will be impressed by your conservative outlook.

So far you have captured initial costs. Now, add ongoing costs:

- *Support fees and contracts.* Often, the fee for the first year is included with the purchase price, but not always. Check. Also try to negotiate a clause to limit the increases in support costs from one year to the next.

  To handle future growth, make sure you understand how additional licenses are priced, and in particular whether you can add users as you need them or whether you need to purchase blocks of licenses. If you forecast growth in the near future, you may get a better deal by prepaying for the appropriate block of user licenses you will need rather than negotiating again in a few months.

- *Ongoing training costs.* They can be minimal if you can deliver the training in-house, but make sure you have the expertise to do so. Can you buy or license materials from the vendor?

- *System administration, maintenance, and internal support costs.* Include the compensation for the individual or group of individuals who will perform the system administration and support duties.

At this point you have determined the total cost of ownership of the new tool, and you may be faced with a counterproposal to develop the tool in-house. When comparing in-house and third-party costs, in-house costs may appear lower because the exact development requirements are underestimated and because most often the maintenance costs are not included. Insist on realistic estimates for both. Unless you have a very large operation with very specialized requirements, buy from a third party. Although you may not be able to fulfill your exact requirements, you should be able to come pretty close, and the R&D costs, now and in the future, will be spread over many support centers, providing you with more features and quality than you could build by yourself.

Calculating costs is relatively easy. Determining the productivity boost is a bit more involved. One good strategy is to start with your cost per call. (See Chapter 6, "Managing Support People," for a full description of how to compute it.) Then determine how your cost per call will be affected by the new technology. Typically, you need to determine how much time per call will be saved by using the new system.

With an automated system your staff will be more productive, because they will spend less time on administrative activities, such as looking for the next call, looking for open calls, looking up customer phone numbers, and more significantly they will spend less time on the technical resolution of calls, because they will find the information they need quickly. The trick is to estimate the actual savings. The savings can be very small for each individual call, but with hundreds or thousands of calls they become significant.

Analyze your process and add up the savings on each step saved or simplified. For instance:

- Dialing the phone: 5 seconds (if you are installing an autodialer).
- Getting the call to the right engineer automatically: 30 seconds (if you are installing an ACD).
- Answering phone calls directly rather than having to do callbacks: 2 minutes (if you are installing an ACD).
- Faxing a document manually to a customer: 2 minutes (if you are installing a fax server).
- Finding a document through an on-line search rather than having to go to a central library: 5 minutes (if you are installing an on-line knowledge base).
- Playing phone tag with customers: 5 minutes (if you are installing an electronic customer interface to the call tracking system).

Don't be overly optimistic with your estimates. If your average call takes 8 minutes to resolve, saving more than a minute with any one feature would be a major coup. Once you add up all the savings, consider whether the composite is realistic. After all, you may be held to these cost savings.

Sometimes a straightforward analysis is not sufficient, because all steps are not present in all calls. If so, you need to refine your analysis. Here's how to proceed. Separate the calls into categories—not too many—say: short, medium, long. Determine typical length and distribution for each category. Finally, apply your cost-savings analysis to each step. For instance, with a call distribution as shown in Table 9–2, the average call lasts 19.25 minutes ($2 * .25 + 15 * .5 + 45 * .25$). If an on-line knowledge base can shorten the middle step (internal consultation) by 5 minutes, you're down to 16.75 minutes for the average call (2 * .25 + 10 * .5 + 45 * .25).

Table 9–2.   Call-Distribution Example

Call Type	Description	Time	Percentage
Short	Answer is in documentation	2 min.	25%
Medium	Requires internal consultation	15 min.	50%
Long	Requires extensive research	45 min.	25%

Once you determine your saving per call, simply multiply the figure by your call volume to determine total savings. If you are doing a long-term analysis, don't forget to factor in increases in call load as well as increases in costs such as salaries. If your figure is higher than the cost of the tool, then it's financially wise to buy the tool. If not, you may still want to decide to buy the tool, but on grounds other than pure financial savings.

When you prepare your cost justification, remember that revenue savings alone do not a good justification make. Use plenty of graphics to illustrate your point. Savings look bigger in graph form.

One last note about the cost-justifying exercise: we conducted it purely from the productivity and cost angle—that is, can you save money with your new tool? One could take a more aggressive approach and justify the expense based on increased customer satisfaction, increased sales, or even increased employee satisfaction. It could be a good strategy if customer dissatisfaction is very high and is impacting the company's financial success, or if employee turnover is extreme and you can show that employees leave because of the lack of proper tools. In most cases, we believe your friendly controller will react better to a standard ROI analysis.

9.1.3   Implementing Tools

Implementing support tools is an exercise in project management and includes the familiar project management steps (see Figure 9–1):

- Based on a thorough assessment of the situation, define requirements.
- Then, design a plan,
- which is implemented into a prototype,
- which is then tested so deployment can occur,
- which, in turn, is followed by a feedback phase.

The Project Management Cycle

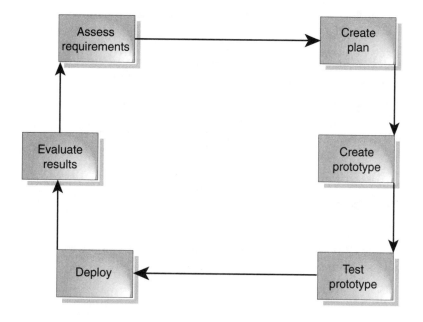

Figure 9–1

Changing support tools is a major disruption to your operation, so design a comprehensive implementation plan. Rely on the vendor for help and advice. You may never have implemented a new support tool before, but the vendor has participated in many such exercises (did you check whether it did?). Do not rely exclusively on the vendor, however. You are the one who has to live with the system, so get involved. Also, you know a lot more than the vendor about your specific requirements.

Involve some of your key support engineers and managers in the implementation cycle, starting with the requirements phase. You will be less likely to go astray and you will gain buy-in for the new system. Do keep the project within reasonable business bounds by making sure you are not unnecessarily duplicating each and every step of your current process with the new system. Often it's better to change the process as you change the tool, and even to change the process to accommodate the tool, rather than to subvert the tool to a process it's not meant to support. Plus, if existing tools do not support your processes, perhaps your process is not that great to begin with.

Pay attention to the internal marketing of the new tool. Resistance to change is very real, especially when change affects the way people go about their daily tasks. Don't build up expectations too high, however, or you will end up with disappointed support engineers. The homework you did for justifying costs can be used to share what kinds of productivity improvements to look forward to. (Use it as a test: if the support engineers don't believe your time savings numbers, they may well be too high.) As mentioned above, involving the support engineers in the planning and implementation of the new tool helps with the internal PR campaign. Participation is the first step to acceptance.

Plan the actual conversion from one system to another in exquisite detail. You probably don't have the luxury of doing a live dry run, so plan for every contingency you can think of as you go live. Don't forget to celebrate once the conversion is over.

9.2 PHONE SYSTEM

For now, the phone is the primary interface of support centers with their customers. While the advent of electronic call logging and monitoring has started to erode its importance, the phone will remain the most important interface for many years.

To simplify, the phone system for a support center can be either a PBX system or an automatic call distributor (ACD). An ACD queues calls, delivers prerecorded messages, and distributes calls to the legendary "next available agent," typically the agent who has been idle the longest. ACDs allow you to queue calls according to the type of service required or to their priorities. Some can request, record, and use information from the caller such as a customer identification number to expedite the call processing process.

There are other, older options than PBXs and ACDs. For instance, automatic call sequencers (ACS) can queue calls, alerting the agents as to how many calls are waiting, until an agent picks up the phone. Unlike an ACD, an ACS does not distribute calls to idle agents.

Another option is a uniform call distributor (UCD). One can view UCDs as first-generation ACDs. They route calls on a round-robin scenario, following a fixed list of agents rather than the more sophisticated algorithm of longest idle used by ACDs. UCDs cannot route calls through menu trees and have none of the fancy options of ACDs.

With ACDs becoming more and more affordable, there is little incentive to choose either a sequencer or a UCD, so we will limit our discussion to ACDs.

9.2.1 Do you need an ACD?

The answer is almost always: yes. The ability to greet the caller automatically, to route the call to the appropriate support engineer, to validate customers, and to direct them to route their own calls based on simply punching the right options into the key pad almost always increases both productivity and customer satisfaction substantially.

It's perfectly possible, however, to run a support center with a regular (non-ACD) phone system. In this case, the calls come in over a regular phone line monitored by one or more individuals. Once the calls are answered, they can be logged and passed on to an appropriate support engineer, either on a call-back basis or by simply transferring the call live. Alternatively, they can be handled on the spot by the support engineer who answered the phone.

The limitations of a non-ACD system are as follows:

- It limits the number of individuals who can answer the phone at any one time.

- As a consequence, it makes it very difficult to have customers talk directly to a support engineer on the first call, once the support center numbers more than a few support engineers.

- It requires that all administrative tasks related to incoming calls be handled by a human being.

- It limits the number of incoming calls to the number of available lines and staff members. At peak times, customers who cannot get through cannot choose to hold.

- It has very primitive capabilities for record keeping and gathering statistics.

Despite its limitations, a non-ACD system can be just fine for a small support center, or even a medium-sized one working under a dispatch and callback system. If you are using a non-ACD system, you will have very little to worry about, since it's so simple. The only caveats are to make sure its voicemail feature is robust (check out the size of the voicemail box; you don't want it to overflow) and also that the system is properly maintained and available, including availability in the event of a disaster. It's very literally your lifeline to your customers.

If you are working with a non-ACD system and are considering moving up, the two reasons to do it are: your center is getting too large for a non-ACD phone system, or you want to switch from a dispatch model to a direct to the support engineer model.

Let's explore what features you need to look for in an ACD.

9.2.2   Features of an ACD System

Since ACDs vary in complexity from very simple to very sophisticated, with price tags to match, it's important to determine what you really need today, and what you may need tomorrow. Your checklist should include the following items:

- *Compatibility with the existing PBX phone system:* you may choose (you may have to choose) a system that is not compatible with the existing phone system within your company. In that case you will need dedicated trunk lines, and you will also have to change the phone numbers of all support center staff. You will also have to think about how to transfer calls to other areas of the company who use a different phone system. There are no standards in telephony, so you will likely have to compromise one way or another. Make your selection on the basis of the features of the ACD rather than on the compatibility issue. Of course, all things being equal, compatibility is desirable.

- *Size:* how many incoming calls do you get at one time? How many agents do you need to support? How many incoming phone numbers do you need to handle? ACDs always have a size limitation, so check this out. Also check how you can expand the system as you grow.

- *Routing requirements:* dust off your call routing algorithm, and see how it can be modeled in the system you are evaluating. Do you require a simple queuing mechanism, or do you need several levels of branching? Do you need different menu trees based on time of day or day of the week? Do you want some customers to get priority treatment? Must the ACD handle different incoming numbers differently? Basic ACDs may not be able to handle complex routing requirements. Bring your routing algorithms with you when you meet with vendors.

- *VRU (voice response unit):* as a complement to the routing capability, a VRU allows you to collect information from the user (usually by having him push appropriate buttons on a touch-tone phone) and to act on it. With a VRU the call travels through the system together with the information collected along the way. The better systems track the call through its entire lifetime together with its record.

- *Hold time:* the most basic ACDs may limit the amount of time someone is on hold and unceremoniously hang up once the time's up. What do you want customers to hear when they are on hold? Music, recorded announcements, a disk jockey? Do you want them to choose what they hear? Would you like the ACD to give them an idea of how long they will have to wait or how many calls are ahead of them? (People wait more patiently if they are told how long they will have to wait.) Do you want to allow customers to leave a voicemail message or to request a human attendant at any time? Many systems allow branching out only at specific times, so, if the flexibility is important to you, ask.

- *User interface:* is the phone ergonomically acceptable? Note that most ACD phones are quite large. Will they fit on your users' desks? Are headsets available? What information about the system is available from the support engineer's phone? Many systems have an indicator for how many calls are waiting in the queue. Can that be customized? Another option is a wall-mounted sign displaying summary information.

- *Monitoring tools:* how can a manager see what's going on with the system? Most ACDs provide a supervisor console where one can see at a glance how many agents are logged on, how many are available, how many calls have been taken so far, and so on. If the console information is not what you need, make sure it's customizable with your requirements. On-line views are often less flexible than reports.

- *Reporting capabilities:* one of the advantages for an ACD is that it allows you to gather many kinds of statistics about your calls, including volume, wait time, abandon rate (the percentage of callers who hang up before the phone is answered), calls per support engineer, both incoming and outgoing, average talk time, and so on. If you don't have an ACD, you probably wonder whether you will ever use all that—and you're right. The main thing with reports is to see what is available, to make sure your basic needs are met, and to determine what can be customized.

The better ACDs allow you to customize the boilerplate reports, which saves a lot of time. Make sure you check how much training is required to customize or to create reports. Will you need to hire an outside expert to do it? Reports about callers' VRU information are often more complex. Check them specifically if required.

Finally, check that reports are available in electronic format, so they can be manipulated by another program such as a spreadsheet.

- *Interface with the call or customer tracking system:* if you want the ACD to perform administrative tasks such as customer validation or automatic screen popup, you need to find an ACD that can be interfaced to your customer or call tracking system. Such interfaces are always custom, but you should make sure the appropriate hooks are in place.

Using the checklist as a guide, develop your own and integrate it into the Kepner-Tregoe matrix. Be sure to distinguish your basic requirements from the extras so you can include a wider variety of candidates. Think about your future needs. It's hard to forecast growth and future needs, but changing the phone system is very costly and difficult, so you don't want to have to do it often.

Finally, think about the maintenance requirements. Who will be responsible for maintaining the new equipment and its accompanying software? What training is required? How much maintenance is required on a weekly basis? Complex ACDs tend to require better-trained staff and more tuning, although they admittedly provide more user-friendly tools to do the maintenance.

9.2.3   Interfacing with Other Systems

Let's spend a bit more time discussing the ties between the ACD and other systems. Only the more sophisticated ACDs allow interfacing for now, but it's clearly the way of the future, not to mention a productivity enhancer. Consider a few potential applications.

One is customer validation. The idea is to prompt the customer to enter a customer identification number using the numbers on the dial pad and then to check the identification against current records. If the customer entered a valid number, he can then be given a choice of menus (or even be given priority over other customers, or a different set of menus based on the level of support he has purchased). If the customer entered an invalid number, he can be routed to a human attendant for help. The same idea can be applied to a system that handles both contract and per-incident customers, where you want to route per-incident customer calls to an order-taking agent and then return them to the system for routing to a support engineer.

The benefit of integrated customer validation to the customer is that he will be routed very quickly to a support engineer. The benefit to you is that the validation is done by the software and does not require human intervention, reducing your cost.

Another possible application is to use the information collected during the call to automatically paint the computer screen of the support engineer with the appropriate information a second before the phone rings. For the support engineer, it gives enough time to get a snapshot of who is calling and maybe on what product, if that information was collected during the call. It also saves the overhead of having to enter the customer information. From the point of view of the customer, it speeds up the process. The only caveat, as we found out from direct experience, is to avoid using the information on the screen to greet the customer by name: it's simply too disorienting for the customer ("How do you know my name?").

Yet another application of an interface between the ACD and the call tracking system is to allow automatic calling from the call tracking system. For a customer callback, the support engineer directs the phone from the call tracking screen to dial the customer number. The gain of time may seem small, but it does avoid dialing errors and eliminates a most unnecessary piece of administrative overhead. This kind of capability is most valuable for support centers with a heavy load of return phone calls.

Only the more sophisticated ACDs allow for this kind of interfacing, and even then there are limitations on the number of variables that can be shared back and forth. Note that you don't need to interface the ACD and the call tracking system right when the ACD is implemented, but it's a good idea to do the planning at the beginning to make sure the ACD supports what you need, and also to be able to get help from the ACD vendor while you have your closest working relationship with the vendor.

Creating the links between the system requires knowledge of both the ACD interface and the call tracking interface. It's usually not a large undertaking and should take no more than a few weeks' programming time. Interface programming is often contracted out because of the specific knowledge required. ACD vendors maintain a roster of suitable programmers, although, as always, check their references.

9.3   FAX SYSTEM

This section discusses requirements and recommendations for handling faxes. We will organize the discussion into two segments: automatic "Fax-on-demand" systems and ad-hoc faxing to or from a support engineer during the resolution of a customer call.

9.3.1   Fax-on-demand Systems

A fax-on-demand system is an automated system that allows customers to use their phone or sometimes their desktop computer to request faxed information. It can be a valuable adjunct to your support strategy, since, although the initial cost is high, the system requires very little manpower to keep it going, and the resulting decrease in call load can be significant.

How does it work? The customer calls the fax-on-demand phone number. He is then guided through menus to select from an array of documents. This is preferable to forcing the customer to request specific document numbers, which in turn requires you to fax the directory to lots of customers. Once the document is selected, the customer can then choose to have the document faxed (or emailed) to him. No human intervention is necessary, so the operation can be done at any time.

Fax-on-demand systems are valuable if many of your calls can be resolved quickly by giving information to the customer. (Do look for alternate ways to deliver that information, however, such as on-screen help.) Fax-on-demand systems require that a database of documents be available to customers. See Section 9.5 for more details on creating and maintaining a knowledge base.

9.3.2   Fax Communication during Problem Resolution

Many times, support engineers need to either communicate information to the customer or get information from the customer that is best conveyed in writing, such as the exact steps of a lengthy recovery procedure or the exact text of a program.

If email is a possible medium, use it. It's much easier to store and edit email than faxes since it's already in electronic form. Ideally, as we will see in the next section, your call tracking system should allow you to store both outgoing and incoming email right in the system to create a complete record for the call.

Faxes are a bit more difficult, since they do not originate in electronic form. If faxes are a part of your business model, we highly recommend that you investigate a way to send faxes directly from the call tracking system, and a way to store incoming faxes on-line, ideally within the call tracking system. In particular, you should have an easy way for a support engineer to send documents that are already in your knowledge base to a customer as part of a call. It's a great time-saving strategy to ask the customer to read the information contained in the fax and to call back with questions or further instructions, rather than repeating the information over the phone. It also saves time if the support engineer does not have to print the document, walk to the printer to retrieve the document, fax the document, and make sure it was received.

9.4   CALL TRACKING SYSTEM

The call tracking system is the key system in the support center. If you are just starting out, this is where you need to spend your energy. A call tracking system allows you to keep a detailed history of each and every call, which you can then use both to run the support center day-to-day and also to analyze trends. A call tracking system

- Keeps a log of active calls, including all interactions between the customer and support engineers, so that engineers can have a record of where they are in the resolution process and so that an individual other than the call owner can quickly determine the situation when needed for a hand-off or an escalation.

- Assists the support engineers in managing their time and their queue of calls by providing lists of and structure to the work in progress.

- Keeps records for solved problems, so you can refer back to them for learning and analysis, such as: what kinds of questions do you get? what is the history of a particular customer?

- Centralizes data that can be used for metrics, such as response time, resolution time, productivity, and trend analysis.

Can you make do without an on-line call tracking system? Yes, you can function with pieces of paper or individual electronic records kept by the support engineers. You can also get by with a multipurpose system such as an on-line posting system a la LotusNotes. However, modern call tracking systems allow so much flexibility and productivity that there is really no reason not to have one, even for a very small support center. Count on spending between $1000 and $5000 per support engineer.

The rest of the section covers the requirements for a call tracking system that are related to the logging and tracking of calls, then the requirements related to reports and metrics capabilities, then the maintenance requirements. Finally, we cover the interfaces of the call tracking system with other systems.

9.4.1 Logging and Tracking Requirements

The most obvious requirement for a call tracking system is that it tracks calls from beginning to end, allowing you to record each interaction and its relevant characteristics. Use the following to start building your requirements checklist:

- *Complete, detailed action log for each call:* Look for an easy and quick way to enter new calls, including creating a second call for a new issue from the same customer. Check that all call attributes that are important to you, such as priority, product type, version, customer type, and type of call, can be recorded and adjusted (most systems allow for customized screens so ensure that your requirements can be implemented).

  Once the call is entered, you should be able to record who took each action (based on some user identification, but look for an easy way to find the name and number of the individual right off the system), when the action was taken, what was done, and how long it took.

The system should record the start and stop times for each action and allow an override, so all worked time can be logged. If logging time is important for you and your support engineers often juggle several calls, check that time can be tracked against several problems at once.

Transaction logs should allow the recording of both internal and external information, so that customers can be given a view into the call tracking system without having to share all the details. (This is somewhat less important for an internal help desk.)

- *Complete, automatic queuing mechanism:* The system should support enough queues for your needs and should offer easy ways to view queues based on various criteria such as age, type of customer, and so on. Look for how the system can signal the users that a call is waiting. Some systems allow on-screen notification, email notification, and even activate pagers. Check that the notification is activated both for new calls and for calls transferred between queues.

- *Quick and easy checks on calls* based on given criteria such as: call status (is the action with the customer or with the support engineer?), calls older than a certain threshold, calls without a customer contact in more than your target, and so on. You shouldn't have to create customized reports to get basic information.

- *Quick check of customer history:* With a click of a button or at the most a simple query, you should be able to find out what other calls the customer placed and which ones are open. This helps prevent duplicate calls on the same topic and allows quick reference to past history if problems are related.

- *Friendly and efficient user interface:* Modern call tracking systems give a GUI (point-and-click) interface and a navigation menu, both of which should be easy to use. Basic actions such as opening a call, creating a transaction, and closing a call should be very fast and in particular should not require navigation through multiple menus. The system should allow you to require certain fields to be completed before transactions are logged and to supply defaults and pick lists for various fields. Most systems allow you to customize the entry screens, so you can rename the fields according to your terminology, and also to add and delete fields as you need them. Some systems allow users to define shortcuts to get to the most popular screens. That's a nice feature; it's even nicer if the popular screens are sequenced properly to allow quick access.

Finally, investigate systems with on-screen help. It will increase productivity and decrease training requirements.

In addition to the basic capabilities we just described, there are some advanced features you may need as well:

- *Support scheduling:* allows support engineers to schedule tasks for particular days and times, and gives automatic reminders of appointments by email or through a popup window. This feature is particularly valuable if your support engineers have to do a lot of callbacks or scheduled research.

- *Work bins:* support engineers should be able to partition their work into subgroups as they wish. For instance, group calls by type, by urgency, or by type of action required. The support engineer should control the sorting mechanism; it should not be set systemwide.

- *Escalation support:* the system can be customized to automatically highlight to the manager calls older than a certain threshold, or to take particular action on those calls.

- *Links to email and other communication techniques:* allow the support engineer to send and receive email or faxes that are tracked through the system. This capability improves productivity and ensures that all records are tracked together with the call.

9.4.2   Reports and Metrics Requirements

Besides logging and tracking requirements, you want to make sure you can obtain the reports and metrics that you need through the call tracking system. In Chapter 4, "Measuring Support Center Performance," we described how to design a metrics analysis strategy. To monitor productivity, you will be looking for data on call volume, response time, and resolution time, grouped in various configurations if you have a large operation. To analyze call types, you will need call distribution data by time, product, and type of problem. Finally, your transactional customer satisfaction survey forms could be run as a report from the system itself.

First note that you cannot get statistics on items that are not logged into the system. This may sound obvious but is often overlooked. For instance, say you want to do some analysis on how long it takes you to resolve problems, perhaps to prepare a justification for buying a new support tool. If your support engineers do not track their time properly in your call tracking system (assuming the system allows to record time), your problem is with the recording, not with the reporting.

The system should give you a number of basic, customizable report templates so you can run your operation. Customization is important, because you don't want to have to write reports from scratch if all you need is a minor modification. If you can live with the basic format, all the better. If you need to customize, check what skills are required to do it; you may not want to pay dearly for each and every report. Be careful to check that the templates allow for flexible querying and grouping. Often the report format is just fine, but the system cannot easily give you subsets of the information, such as data for a particular set of support engineers.

In addition to the basic templates, check whether the system allows you to create reports from scratch, and if so, how. If your call tracking system is based on a relational database, you should be able to get anything you want, but the underlying schema may be so complex that you need a full-time analyst to crank out reports. That may be more than you want to invest.

It's often a good idea to create "stub" reports that include the basic queries you are likely to need and that prompt you for the particular data you need. For instance, say you are interested in monitoring the aging of your calls, but you don't know yet what your aging target will be or you plan to shrink it down. You could have a report written to list all calls older than the number of days specified by the individual running the report. If, down the line, you decide that you always want to know calls older than two days, you can hard-wire the two-day target into the report.

Speaking of running the reports, investigate how the system can automatically send routine reports to you without your having to take any action. Running the same report every morning gets old. Computers have rendered obsolete the performance of this kind of repetitive task by hand.

If you intend to send a transactional customer satisfaction survey, determine how the reporting capability of the call tracking system can help you. Customer satisfaction surveys are often beyond the means of standard call tracking systems, but interestingly enough smaller help desk systems sometimes do offer that feature, since the email addresses of the (internal) customers are already stored in the system.

9.4.3 Maintenance Requirements

Even after the initial setup, all call tracking systems will require some maintenance. Make sure you understand what is needed and you plan for how to do it. Maintenance includes:

- *User maintenance:* as new users are added and existing ones deleted or changed, the system records will need to be updated. How difficult is it? What about changing groupings, products, or call types?
- *Backups:* since you will be running your operation on your call tracking system, you must have a bulletproof backup and restore method.

- *Customization of screens and reports:* this is an ongoing requirement as your needs change, especially for reports (changing screens creates lots of confusion, so you won't want to do it often). Look for user-friendly features such as on-screen editing and, particularly, prepackaged templates which allow you to get most of what you want with additional tweaking still allowed.

The last item to check is who will do all this maintenance and what training that individual or group of individuals need.

9.4.4 Links to Other Systems

The call tracking system is at the heart of your operation, so you will find all kinds of benefits when you link it to other systems: the customer tracking system, the bug tracking system, the knowledge base, the ACD, and even other systems such as your HR system (to have an up-to-date list of support engineers and their managers, and, if you run an internal help desk, a list of your customers).

What exactly are the productivity benefits of the links? Look at Figure 9–2.

Tools Integration Strategy

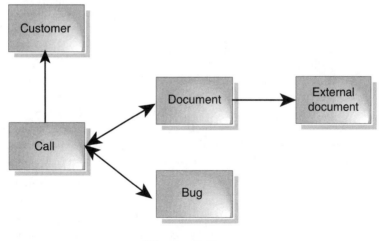

Figure 9–2

- *For the customer tracking system:* the ability to check that a customer is valid before providing service; access to logistical information about the customer, such as address, phone number, email address; the ability to check what software the customer is running (or at least what has been shipped).

- *For the bug tracking system:* the ability to link calls and related bugs. This allows you to quickly determine the bugs that are impacting large numbers of customers, and also to let customers know where there is progress in resolving the bugs they encountered. Depending on the bug fixing model, you could even close customer problems from the Technical Support point of view once a bug is confirmed and let the link with the bug system drive the completion of the loop back to the customer until the bug is fixed.

- *For the knowledge base system:* the ability to link documents and calls. Therefore, you will be able to determine what documents are used the most, and then drive changes in the product or the documentation, or weigh often-used documents more heavily for future searches into the knowledge base. We have also mentioned that you could use this information to reward the authors of popular documents.

- *For the ACD:* the ability to perform some administrative tasks directly in the ACD, if the ACD supports such activities.

- *For the customer communication system:* the ability to perform administrative functions on-line, such as logging calls, checking status, and so on.

It's difficult to create the links you want, not just because the systems are different and sometimes not compatible, but also because the ownership of the other systems often resides outside your scope of control. The customer system belongs to Sales, the bug tracking system belongs to Development or to a third party, and those outside entities have goals and priorities other than Support. Do all you can to integrate the systems within your control (typically call tracking, knowledge base, and the ACD), but don't neglect the others. One strategy is to use tools provided by the same vendor. Some of the larger vendors provide suites of products. Since the integration of the tools is such a productivity enhancer, we recommend you look at this option, even if it means settling for somewhat inferior features.

The most basic and important link is with the customer tracking system. When the customer tracking system is separate from the call tracking system, the link is most often accomplished with a nightly download of customer information into the call tracking system. Ideally, the connection should be live and two-way, allowing support staff to see real-time changes in the customer data, and to make changes on the fly rather than having to rely on an administrator or to run two systems. Live two-way connections are often impossible because of the natures of the systems, however. In any case, do not create your own customer database; plug into the corporate database.

Links to the bug tracking system and to the knowledge base will be discussed in the appropriate sections below. The link to the ACD has been discussed already.

What about linking the call tracking system to your customer communications system, so customers can view the status of their calls and enter new ones? We are enthusiastic supporters of this strategy, as it allows for better customer service (no more waiting for a status, no phone tags, round-the-clock access) while at the same time helping your productivity. There are a few caveats, however:

- *Security:* you need to make sure customers do not have access to other customers' records, and that appropriate firewalls are in place to protect your company's information.

- *Recording of confidential information:* even with an internal help desk, there is information that may not be appropriate to share with the customer. If your call tracking system does not allow you to segregate out confidential information, support engineers will either enter information that customers should not see, creating possibly difficult customer problems, or more likely will not keep complete records on-line, subverting the purpose of the call tracking system. Both outcomes are undesirable. Fortunately, many call tracking systems allow for double entries. You will probably find yourself encouraging support engineers to put more information in the external portion rather than the other way round.

- *System cost:* making information accessible to customers is expensive. Even if your customers are internal, giving them access to your system means that you need to beef up your hardware and your license pool, or even create and maintain another application. You may want to investigate cheaper read-only servers, although that would require you to put in place another procedure for logging new calls and to update existing calls. Weigh that against the productivity improvements of fewer phone tags and status calls.

9.5 BUG TRACKING SYSTEM

A bug tracking system allows you to keep records of all bugs, which you can use as a request list for the bug-fixing organization and as a reference for everyone else—and, in particular, support engineers and customers. A bug tracking system

- Keeps descriptions of bugs, together with their fix history and status.

- Assists the bug fixing organization in prioritizing work.
- Keeps records of when and where bugs are fixed.
- Centralizes data that can be used for metrics on bug frequency and the bug fixing process.

9.5.1   Features of a Bug Tracking System

Many bug tracking systems do not record enough information to be useful for Support and for customers. This is usually because they are owned by the Development organization, which is unaware of specific support requirements. For more details on the bug fixing process, refer back to Chapter 8.

From the support point of view, a complete bug system records the following:

- *Bug identification:* usually an ID number and a title.
- *Status of the bug:* open, resolved, being investigated, duplicate of another bug, and so on. The list of possible statuses reflects your bug fixing process. For instance, if the Support organization enters potential bugs and the bug fixing organization validates them (we recommend this approach), then all bugs start out as "reported" and continue on to "confirmed," "not a bug," or "duplicate."
- *Bug priority:* captures the technical severity of a bug.
- *Bug description:* many systems allow for a short and a long description, or for internal and external descriptions. Since sharing the bug list with customers is becoming a requirement, opt for a system that allows you to store a customer-viewable description in addition to an internal one.
- *Author information:* usually a login or an internal ID.
- *Date reported, date fixed.*
- *Product and platform information:* exact version(s) impacted.
- *Fix information:* where is the bug fixed? Version number, patch number.
- *Internal bug fixing information, such as:* what module of the code the error occurs in, who is working on a fix, and so on. This is key information for the bug fixing organization, but not crucial for the Support group. This is not shared with customers.
- *Associated customer calls:* this should be accomplished through a link with the call tracking system. See the next section for more details.

In addition to recording key pieces of information, the bug tracking system should support the bug fixing process. From the point of view of support and customers, here are the essential points:

- *Ability to change the status according to the bug fixing cycle:* as described above.

- *Search capability:* this is probably most important for the Technical Support group. When a suspected new bug is reported, can you quickly interrogate the bug database to determine whether the bug has already been reported? Is the search engine flexible and complete? Are version and platform differences handled smoothly? Can bugs be found through a flexible word search without requiring detailed knowledge of keywords?

- *Transaction log for actions taken, with their owner:* for instance, if the bug is marked "not a bug," is the reason why it was rejected logged together with the rejection? This kind of audit trail is rarely supported by bug tracking systems, although many will allow a copious comment field, which can be very useful to convey intermediate fix information.

- *Queue management:* for the sake of the bug fixing organization, can bugs be queued and assigned for a fix, just as calls are queued within Support?

- *Query and reporting capabilities on most aspects of the system, and at least to answer the questions:* what are the outstanding bugs in release *xyz*? What bugs were fixed in release *xyz*? These are common support questions and will need to be answered in the bulletins that accompany maintenance releases.

As we hinted, although a good bug tracking system will help deliver quick, quality answers to customers, it's only as good as the information it contains. Establish standards for recording information, especially the critical pieces such as the descriptions, and establish a bug life-cycle process to ensure that bugs are looked at and fixed or rejected quickly.

What about maintenance of the bug tracking system. It's very similar to the maintenance of a call tracking system. Since the bug database is less dynamic than the call database, the backup and uptime requirements are somewhat lessened, however. Also, most of the reporting requirements will be on the Development and Product Management organizations side rather than Support's.

9.5.2 Links with Other Systems

We will discuss linking the bug tracking system and the call tracking system as well as sharing bug information with customers.

Linking the bug tracking system and the call tracking system by recording what bugs are related to what calls (a single bug may be related to several calls, and some calls will be related to several bugs) allows you to accomplish the following tasks:

- Prioritize bugs by finding those that impact the largest numbers of customers.
- Prioritize bugs by finding those that impact "key" customers, as defined in some customer classification system.
- Alert affected customers of the existence of a serious bug.
- Notify affected customers of the existence of a new bug fix.
- Given that a particular bug fix has created a serious regression problem, alert customers who reported the bug of the problem.

Trying to accomplish the tasks above without a link between the call and the bug tracking system is virtually impossible. The cost of not being able to make such decisions in terms of productivity and customer satisfaction will be significant in most organizations.

Linking the call tracking and the bug tracking system is easiest if you purchase integrated products from the same vendor. However, you should be able to implement a link between systems supplied by different vendors if appropriate API's (Application Programming Interfaces, that is software "hooks") are available.

What about giving customers access to bug records? Once again, we are enthusiastic supporters of the strategy both for customer satisfaction and productivity reasons. Actually, sharing bug information is easier than sharing call information, since read-only access is sufficient. Require that customers call Technical Support to report new bugs so you don't find yourself with a lot of funny data to clean up.

The basic strategy is to post information about existing bugs on-line. This requires some data quality checking, as the descriptions originally entered need to be checked and occasionally translated into customer-friendly English.

A better implementation, especially with a complex product and a sizable bug list, is to allow customers to search an on-line database for the bugs that interest them.

The next level of refinement is to have a proactive alert mechanism for severe bugs. What this means is, for serious bugs, customers who have signed up for the service or customers who run the particular product and configuration get an email or fax alert that shows the bug together with a description of workarounds and fixes. This kind of notification is a great value-added service.

Expect to get some internal resistance to the idea of advertising bugs. Your argument should be that customers expect that software products have bugs and they much prefer to avoid them than run into them. There's no surer way to get a customer mad than to have him call with a problem and be told it's a known but not advertised bug. Providing security such as allowing access only to bona-fide customers and having a screening process for posting bugs should help convince inside opponents. Also see to it that although access to particular bugs is easy, generating a full bug list from the outside is difficult, so as not to expose a negative image of your product.

9.6 KNOWLEDGE BASE SYSTEM

What is a knowledge base? A knowledge base is a collection of documents that can be used to resolve customer problems. In this context, the documents will be technical ones and contain information such as release, certification, and compatibility information; summaries of past calls with their resolution; troubleshooting checklists; white papers; and so on. To be useful, a knowledge base needs to be searchable; that is, the user should be able to find the document(s) relevant to the problem quickly and easily and, ideally, without having to remember a set of cumbersome key words.

From the point of view of creating and maintaining a knowledge base, a knowledge base should make it easy to enter new documents and, most importantly, should have a robust way of supporting the review of documents, including deleting obsolete ones.

Knowledge bases are much more complex than the other systems used in support centers. They can also be a great productivity booster by:

- Shortening resolution time dramatically for known problems.
- Decreasing the amount of duplicate work.
- If distributed to customers, preventing calls in the first place by allowing customers to find their own answers.

Do not even consider a knowledge base system until you have a good call tracking system and a good customer tracking system. Go for the basics first. Also, although the payoffs of a knowledge base system can be great, the requirements for a successful system are high, since a knowledge base tool is essentially an empty shell which you must fill with information.

Some call tracking systems include a knowledge base, and many more offer add-on modules for knowledge base maintenance. As we will see, the integration between call tracking and knowledge base systems is key, so it's always worthwhile to consider what your call tracking vendor has to offer for a knowledge base.

Do you need a knowledge base system? Take a look at the information your support engineers use now. You may not think of the manuals scattered on their desks as a knowledge base, but that's what they are. So are the folders and pieces of paper stored in your senior support engineers' desks. What other sources of information do they use? What do they need? It could be that with a small help desk, where most questions are unique, the need for a knowledge base is small. But if your center is large or you have lots of new support engineers, recurring questions and inexperienced individuals will make the knowledge base very worthwhile.

Although the other support systems also require strong internal processes to be really useful, the knowledge base system is even more demanding. You can and should look for a good tool, but the first part of the equation is to think about how the information will be collected and its quality maintained; otherwise you will spend a lot of money in vain.

9.6.1   Information Collecting and Maintenance

Let's describe the process through which information is created, entered into the system, and reviewed for accuracy.

Information suitable for the knowledge base comes from a large variety of sources. The first step is to make an inventory of all the information you want to have in the system and where it resides or how it can be created. Be exhaustive. You may not be able to get everything you want in your first implementation, but you should understand the full requirements. Your list will include:

- Product documentation.
- Known problems and their resolutions.
- Troubleshooting checklists.
- Information about existing bugs, including their fix status.
- Certification information.
- Schedule of future releases.
- Engineering documentation and specifications.

The main source of information, and the one on which you have the most influence, is from the Support group itself: information gleaned directly from calls, and information synthesized by support engineers and other members of the support team, such as troubleshooting checklists and diagnostics tools.

Although all support engineers can contribute information, create a validation process to ensure that incorrect information is not propagated internally and, even worse, externally. If you are planning to share information with your customers, add another step to validate information for customers and, perhaps, to have a professional writer edit the documents.

So, in summary, you will have up to four steps:

- Create a document.
- Validate the document to ensure the information it contains is correct.
- Edit and format the document to improve readability and ensure consistency.
- Approve the document for external publication, if you have a customer communications problem.

Typically, senior support engineers are responsible for the validation and the decision to approve the document for customer access.

Information that originates outside the support center also needs to be managed. Items such as product documentation, product descriptions, release schedules, and compatibility information need somehow to be obtained and compiled. Sometimes the best strategy is to offer the groups who maintain that information access to the support knowledge base, so it becomes the prime repository of information. Often, however, other groups will maintain their own systems, and you will need to interface to them, perhaps by downloading information. If so, develop a strategy to ensure that information is kept current in the support system.

Depending on the volume of documents required, you may need to dedicate an individual or a group to obtaining and consolidating information that originates outside the knowledge base system.

Finally, you need to determine how information will be kept current. Even a document that has been validated and approved for customer viewing today may become incomplete, incorrect, or simply irrelevant in a few months. How will you manage obsolescence? Start with a systematic way of replacing old information with new: for example, keep only the current release schedule on-line, or keep no more than two releases of product documentation on-line.

For documents that are not replaced by new ones, there are two strategies to consider, usually together. One is to allow users to report questions and issues on existing documents and have an expert review the suggestions. The other is to force all documents through a periodic review, even if no one has reported a problem with them—for instance, review all documents once a year. To make the process easier, consider having authors, when they create the document, specify the date or release until when the document is valid. We recommend using both strategies together, but few tools fully support the implementation of the former today, unfortunately.

If you think this is a lot of work, it is. Contrast it with the consequences of broadcasting incorrect information. Maintaining the knowledge base tool is for the most part maintaining the quality of the documents. Maintaining the tool itself—user administration, backups, and so on—is the easy part.

9.6.2   Knowledge Base Tool Requirements

Any tool you choose will need to support the following functions:

- *Searching for information:* make it very easy for the support engineer to find what she needs without having to remember awkward keywords. Good systems have a full text-search engine that allows complex queries including Boolean operators. Better systems have complex weighing mechanisms to help users narrow down searches that retrieve lots of documents. Be sure to fully investigate this area with established sites. It becomes a problem only when there are large numbers of documents available in the system, so it's impossible to test it realistically in a demo.

- *Entering new documents:* many document retrieval systems that have great search engines make it very cumbersome to enter new documents. A knowledge base is a very dynamic system, so you want to look for ways to make it easy to contribute new knowledge. Ideally, entering new documents should occur on-line through a user-friendly interface. If documents need to be entered manually, you will have a delay between the creation of a document and its posting, during which time it won't help resolve a single call. Moreover, if it's not really easy to enter documents, the support engineers might just not do it.

- *Making changes to existing documents:* support engineers should be able to alter documents they wrote and to comment on other documents, particularly when they find errors. Ideally, users should be able to make on-line changes, so they can be reflected to all users immediately.

- *Supporting the maintenance process:* behind the scenes, you want to be able to track document attributes to simplify maintenance and publishing requirements. The average knowledge base user may also benefit from meta-information about the document she is looking at. For instance, a support engineer may need to know whether a document has been validated and whether it can be shared with a customer. She may use the name of the author to ask that person for more details or for clarification.

Someone working on the maintenance of the information has a special need for meta-information about the document. For instance, she may want to search for all documents in a particular topic area that have not yet been validated. In short, look for a system that maintains a flexible set of document attributes, information about the document such as: author, creation date, topic area, validation status, document quality (from draft to formatted to customer ready), and even a full history of the document from creation to its current version.

This area is weak to very weak in most of the existing systems.

Can the call tracking system be the knowledge base system? Some call tracking vendors claim to do just that. If all you need is information from past calls, you may find that this is indeed a workable solution; however, consider the following points:

- Will each search retrieve dozens or even hundreds of past instances? If so, how can support engineers wade through them?

- Will searches sometimes retrieve inaccurate information—for example, information recorded by an inexperienced support engineer?

When used as a knowledge base system, a call tracking system usually performs poorly on two counts: integrating information from other systems and ensuring the quality of the information. It doesn't mean you should always look for another tool. If your call tracking system allows you to integrate foreign documents such as product documentation and you don't have too many, and if searching on past problems yields tolerable results, then you may be able to make do with just one system.

If you need more, investigate dedicated knowledge base systems. You will find two broad types:

- *Expert systems:* expert systems use "if-then" rules to allow both forward and backward chaining. The simplest example of an expert system is a decision tree. Expert systems need to be preprogrammed with the appropriate logic for your environment. They are easy to work with for end-users. However, they adapt very poorly to the dynamic environments of support centers where new rules and new situations occur constantly, so more modern tools prefer other approaches. You will be happy with an expert system if your environment is stable and your scope of problems small.

- *Case-based systems*: case-based systems use past experience, typically resolved calls, so they are a step up from searching the call tracking database for past hits. Case-based systems can include all kinds of information and not only call information. They provide weighing and searching strategies to zero in on those situations which most closely match the one being researched. A big advantage of case-based systems is that the information they use grows as new problems and new resolutions are added to the database.

Because of the limitations of expert systems, you will probably choose a case-based system, so that you will need to concentrate on the quality of the information database.

Carefully model your document creation and maintenance cycle through the tools you are considering, and establish how the tool will access the various information sources you need to use. Ideally, the support engineers should be able to access all data—past calls, bugs, and all other documents—through one interface.

One last note: really smart knowledge base systems can tell you what they don't know. By recording searches, both successful and unsuccessful, they can report back on what support engineers are searching for the most, when they find answers and when they do not. By concentrating on popular but unsuccessful searches, you can either: improve the training program if the searches are not posed properly, or create documents to address them.

9.6.3   Links to Other Systems

The main links for the knowledge base system are to the call tracking system and to the customer access system.

Linking the knowledge base and the call tracking system allows the following functions:

- Support engineers can query the knowledge base directly from the call tracking system, perhaps using the description of the call they are working on, without having to open another window or retype the information.

- Support engineers can enter information from a particularly interesting call into the knowledge base system with a few keystrokes. This sounds like using the call tracking database itself as a search target, and in fact you could choose to do both, but it's much more powerful. The idea is that information can be taken from a call resolution and enshrined into the knowledge base, probably in a cleaned-up version, and that such information will be treated as more valuable than a call in the call tracking database; for instance, it can be weighed higher for future searches. You can choose not to use the call database at all and to consider only those calls which have been entered into the knowledge base. It's a process decision that depends partly on the mix of calls you have and, as much as we hate to admit it, on the capabilities of your tool.

- Calls and documents can be linked to show what documents served to resolve what calls. This helps determine areas of weakness in the product or in the information available to customers. It also helps you run the support center by showing what percentage of your calls are resolved, at least in part, through on-line documentation. If the percentage is low, you should be trying to increase it. Under 30% would be low in any environment, and you should see your percentage going up with time as the database grows (the percentage may dip with new releases, since they will introduce new, unknown problems).

A good knowledge base should make it possible and easy to share information with customers. Better-informed customers are likely to resolve more problems without calling the support center and to be happy about it, since it saves them time. We'll explore specific delivery methods in the next section.

9.7   PROACTIVE CUSTOMER COMMUNICATION SYSTEMS

Proactive customer communication systems share information with customers before they need to call the support center, with the following benefits: increased customer satisfaction, call avoidance (fewer calls), and decreased call length, since customers are better educated to start with. Note that some doubters believe that giving customers more information only creates more problems, because customers will have questions about the information and may also try more difficult things than they would have if left to their own devices. This is not true in our experience. That is, proactive information will undoubtedly generate some calls that would not occur otherwise, but with proper quality controls on what goes out you should end up with fewer calls overall and faster resolution times, because customers are better educated. Customer satisfaction will be higher, too.

Proactive customer communications systems include nonelectronic means such as paper newsletters. Newsletters are fine, although printing and postage costs are high. They are also static and may be ignored. We strongly recommend using other methods.

Electronic systems include:

- *Email:* email is inexpensive and can reach many customers (all, if you have an internal help desk). It's good for disseminating product alerts. The disadvantage of email is that, like a newsletter, it is initiated by you and not by the customer, so it could be ignored. Also, it allows one-to-many communications but cannot easily sustain discussion groups.

- *Fax-on-demand systems (already mentioned):* fax-on-demand systems can be used both as a broadcast mechanism and as a flexible self-serve mechanism for customers. It's a good fit for customers who do not have ready access to anything but a telephone. It has the same disadvantages as email, and it's expensive.

- *Interactive audiotext:* customers use their phone to access technical information. Advanced systems can guide the customer to a solution. This is good for routine issues of low complexity, such as common printing problems.

- *Knowledge base on CD-ROMs:* customers can search the CD-ROMs to find the information they need. CD-ROMs are well adapted to sharing large amounts of information and for allowing complex searches, all for a modest investment both for you and for the customer. They are static, however, so they make it difficult to share up-to-date information. Like newsletters, they may be tossed aside and never used. Finally, they have to be mailed to each customer.

- *Bulletin boards:* bulletin boards allow a variety of communication mechanisms from looking up information to participating in discussion groups to downloading software to disseminating alerts. Bulletin boards can either be maintained by you in the support center (in which case you will need to purchase and maintain an appropriate tool, along with the associated modem and phone lines) or they can be leased from a third party, such as CompuServe. In either case, the capabilities are similar, and the decision hinges on what environment is more comfortable for your customers and how much maintenance you want to take on yourself. There are on-line charges associated with either method, which must be borne either by you or by the customer.

- *The Web:* it's an ideal, flexible medium for two-way communication that outperforms most bulletin boards, in particular when it comes to capturing information from customers. Maintaining a Web site requires appropriate software and people resources, although you may be able to piggyback your needs onto your corporate Web page. On-line charges apply. Not everyone has access to the Web.

Besides the maintenance requirements of the customer communications tool, including user registration, hardware and software maintenance, you need to define a strategy for managing the information flow through the tool, namely:

- *Moderate the forum:* a support engineer should monitor the postings, remove offensive ones (they should be pretty rare), handle sensitive questions off-line, and make sure all questions get answered.

- *Post appropriate information:* you need to have an information broker who decides what information to post and, especially, what information to refresh. With a good internal knowledge base the posting is much easier, since the information is already validated and stored. The information broker should take an active role in determining what information should be posted and who can put it together, if it does not already exist.

Managing the flow of information is much easier with proper links between the call tracking, bug tracking, and knowledge base systems on the one hand, and the customer communications system(s) on the other. For downloading information to the customer system, you could make do with a simple nightly download. Uploading information into the call tracking system requires a more sophisticated (and faster) strategy.

Note that, if you have several customer communication tools, your information must keep the information stored in the various systems in sync. It's much easier to support just one interface.

Don't forget that the customer communication tools themselves will require support besides keeping them up and running, as some customers will not know how to use them. Be sure to designate the individuals or groups who will assist customers with questions about using the tools.

9.8 CUSTOMER TRACKING SYSTEM

Although the customer tracking (registration) system is often owned by the Sales group, the Support group has specific requirements, namely customer validation. It's easier if the customer support status can be stored directly in the customer tracking system, but sometimes you will need some kind of auxiliary system to track support details, including per-incident data. If your customers are internal, you will most often maintain the customer database right in the call tracking system.

The customer tracking system must be on-line to avoid providing service to unauthorized users and to avoid lengthy paper searches. The only exception is for very small help desks.

As previously mentioned, the customer tracking system should be linked to both the ACD and the call tracking system for maximum efficiency. The difficulty you will most likely face is that both interfaces require very fast response from the customer tracking system, and that may well force you to consider download alternatives rather than a full real-time connection.

Above and beyond the requirements for the tool, you need to establish who is responsible for the data stored in the customer tracking system and for its maintenance. Customer data changes quickly, and out-of-date data can lead you to provide service or even shipments without proper payment or, even worse, to decline service to a legitimate customer. Also, improper initial data entry can lead to costly changes down the road, so if you are responsible for maintenance but the order-entry group is responsible for the initial entry, make sure everyone agrees on how data should be entered.

9.9   PROBLEM REPRODUCTION ENVIRONMENT

This is the tool (or the set of tools) that you cannot do without. You simply must be able to reproduce problems in environments similar to your customers'. Problem reproduction is a key step both in the resolution process and also, should a bug be found, in the fix creation process, including integrating the problem as a new test for the software.

9.9.1   Choosing a Reasonable Equipment Set

Unless your customers' systems are all simple and all the same, the first step in creating a problem reproduction environment is to create acceptable compromises for what you need and can afford. Generally speaking, you can select smaller, cheaper versions of high-end machines, and you can select clones of high-end equipment. You may even be able to make do with a "base" platform if you support a range of platforms on which the code is essentially the same. With desktop equipment, you may be able to swap external drives to quickly load different operating systems and configurations without maintaining completely separate machines.

Whenever you take shortcuts, however, you create opportunities for problems that occur on the customer machines to be not reproducible on yours. For instance: if a problem only occurs when operating on large data sets and your disk capacity is limited, you may not be able to reproduce it in-house. If the problem is some strange interaction between the software and the microcode for a particular machine, using a different model will prevent you from reproducing it.

Not having an exact duplicate of the customer environment may occur even if you have a very complete set of equipment. Whatever equipment you have, you must plan for alternatives, if you get into a situation where the particular hardware and software configuration is simply not available. Here are some ideas:

- *Use the customer's system:* if the customer can reproduce the problem at will and you can't, some variable somewhere does not match. Maintain a set of modems and the appropriate remote-control software, if necessary, to dial into the customers' machines so you can witness the problem first-hand. This is a great strategy for customers with unusual hardware or very large data sets. The limitations are that the customer may have security restrictions for dial-in sessions, and if they are using their machine extensively, it may not be practical to share it with you for investigative purposes.

- *Look in-house:* does the Development or QA organization have a machine that's a better match? Maybe another support center has access to the right machine. Arrange to borrow it. This is a practical strategy for exotic equipment that would be too expensive to buy for limited use. If you plan to use equipment that's not yours, arrange logistics in advance of a crisis. If the equipment is shared on a regular basis, you will want to establish rules of engagement, so that a support engineer does not unwittingly shut down a machine being used to do a build (or vice versa).

- *Use your third-party contacts:* if a customer has a problem for which you don't have the platform, the platform vendor may be very motivated to work with you. After all, it's their customer, too. This works well for unusual hardware requirements, including large data sets, since the vendor can usually muster large amounts of equipment on short notice.

- *Rent the equipment on a short-term basis:* this is a good strategy if you can find the right equipment quickly.

- *Outsource:* find a testing lab that has the appropriate software and can conduct the testing for you. This is a good solution for expensive or seldom-used equipment if you can find the appropriate match.

9.9.2   Centralized or Distributed?

Once you decide what type of equipment you need, you must decide whether to make it available to each support engineer at her desk, or whether to have it available either in a separate lab room or shared over a network. Here, again, you need to strike a balance between convenience (and, therefore, productivity) and cost.

The support engineers' workstations probably match the type of hardware your customers are using, so they may be usable for problem reproduction, at least for small issues. Consider beefing up memory or disk space to provide a minimal problem testing and reproduction environment. It's the ultimate in convenience to have the machine right on one's desk and at one's disposal.

Next, consider making the necessary equipment accessible from the support engineers' machines, but shared. This is not always feasible for all equipment, but again you get access from the desktop, even if some sharing is required.

Finally, place the equipment in a shared room and have support engineers physically go to it. This can be the best setup if the testing required is destructive, so that the support engineers need to have complete control of the machine anyway. Remember that even walking across the hall takes time, so you take a productivity hit each time the environment needs to be used.

Problem reproduction equipment needs to be maintained, which requires a support contract and some system administration resources. In smaller environments, it's often acceptable for support engineers to maintain their own machines, and it can even be good training for their jobs. As the group's size increases, however, it's usually a good idea to have someone dedicated part or full time to the job to ensure consistency.

A special note for managers of multiple support centers: duplicating reproduction equipment in each center is a costly proposition and is one of the reasons why we caution against multiple centers (see Chapter 5.) Whenever your WAN performance allows it, share machines over the WAN instead.

9.10   CALL CENTER MANAGEMENT APPLICATIONS

Call center management applications are relatively new and are pretty exotic compared to the bread-and-butter applications covered so far. You certainly do not need a call center management application if you don't already have all the other systems we have discussed. And what is a call center management application, anyway?

In a nutshell, a call center management application helps you with call forecasting, call staffing, and staff scheduling. Call center management applications are also called staff planning utilities. They use techniques described in Appendix 3, "Determining Staffing Levels," to relate call volume, call length, the desired service level, and staffing needs. Refer to Appendix 3 for more details about the Erlang method, as it's called.

By their nature, call center management applications apply only to large support centers with well-known calling patterns. You must be able to provide accurate call volume and call length to predict anything. They can be very useful if you have very dynamic call patterns, so that you can quickly forecast staffing needs and schedule staff appropriately.

Look for ease of use and, if you want to use the application for scheduling in addition to forecasting, good integration between the two modules. Unlike other support tools, this one will be used by a handful of users, typically the managers, so your evaluation cycle will be comparatively easier and shorter.

9.11 FACILITIES

This section covers one of the most basic, but sometimes overlooked tools: the physical environment where support engineers work. Poor work-space arrangements can impair productivity, and good ones can boost individual and group productivity by allowing people to be more comfortable when doing their work and by enabling easier communication.

We will cover office and cube arrangements, furniture, and the ergonomics of workstations.

9.11.1 Organization of Space

The criteria for organizing work spaces include: efficient use of space, noise control, privacy, communication, and cost. Noise control is very important in support centers since you don't want phone conversations to be disturbed by others, both for the customers' and the support engineers' sake. If your office has an open plan setup, this means that you have to pay attention to the quality of soundproofing, and in particular to the quality of the partitions used to define the space. The other important factor when organizing space is balancing privacy and ease of communication. Most people value their privacy and feel exposed when sitting in an open environment, such as one without partitions or even one with low partitions. On the other hand, high partitions, walls, or doors (if you have offices) often function as a barrier to easy communication. If the workflow in your support center requires a high level of communication, you may need to weigh ease of communication ahead of privacy needs.

In most environments, the setup will be the so-called open office with cubes, often to follow corporate requirements, which themselves derive from housing employees within the smallest possible space. It's very possible to set up a support center with offices, however, and the main challenge you will have with offices is to promote easy communication. Encourage everyone to keep their door open as often as possible. Provide guest chairs to promote drop-in visits and provide shared spaces for larger groups to meet.

With an open office, you have three options for dividing the space:

- Cubes with high partitions (5 or 6 ft.)
- Cubes with low partitions (3 or 4 ft.)
- "Pods," or small groups of workstations separated from others by walls or high partitions

High partitions are best at achieving maximum perceived privacy, and, all other things being equal, also provide a good level of noise control. Communications can be a challenge, however. Place support engineers who work on similar problems in the same general location, provide guest chairs if the cubes are big enough, and provide small conference rooms close by for impromptu discussions. In addition to the communications issues, high partitions inhibit natural light and views and can feel claustrophobic when the cubes are small, so you will need to pay particular attention to lighting. High partition cubes are usually a good choice, because most employees are happier in an environment with more privacy, thereby increasing morale and the overall quality of work and service to the customers.

Low partitions enable easier communications at the expense of privacy. They are not as efficient at controlling noise, so if you use low partitions, you have to buy the very high-end kind, with better padding and a much higher price (and you may need to go beyond your corporate standards for office furniture to get that quality). Managers often like low partitions, because they feel they can better control the operation when they can see all the support engineers. Indeed, low partitions make it easier to see the support engineers, but are you relying on that kind of direct control to operate? If so, you have a trust issue, which you should address independently from choosing partitions.

Pods are a less common but attractive alternative. The idea is to have small groups of support engineers (four or five) sit together at a counter or separate tables, but within the same space. Each pod is separated from others by a wall or high partition for privacy and noise control. In addition, each pod has access to a small enclosed office to be used for concentrated study when peace and quiet is essential. The advantage of the pod is that communication is very easy, even to the extent of overhearing a conversation nearby and jumping in as needed. Conferencing several support engineers is very easy too. Privacy issues are heightened, although the available office can alleviate them somewhat.

Regardless of the configuration you choose, we recommend you treat all support engineers equally, although you may choose to provide very senior people offices when everyone else has a cube, in particular if they need to hold frequent discussions for a help desk. Managers need to have easy access to a closed-door room to discuss personnel issues, but it does not follow that they need an office—just ready access to one without a cumbersome reservation process.

We have already mentioned that conference rooms are useful to facilitate communication among support engineers. Ideally, plan for several conference rooms of various sizes so that one can be available any time it is needed (otherwise, you will have hallway conversations, which create a lot of noise). Equip the conference rooms with whiteboards and computers so that real work can happen there.

Give a thought to informal communication areas. Our experience is that the kitchen or the water cooler attracts lots of short technical conversations. In addition to the refrigerator and the coffee machine (perhaps the most important productivity tool in the support center, in our experience), consider adding a table and chairs and a whiteboard. You want to preserve a nonbusiness space where people can unwind, but still make it possible to get work done there.

Finally, consider setting up a "quiet room" for support engineers to take short breaks and regroup as needed. A quiet room requires only a few comfortable chairs and magazines (no TV or telephone). Many times, a peaceful break can restore the ability to concentrate and to deliver quality support.

9.11.2 Workstation Ergonomics

In addition to the global organization of space, think about how each workstation is organized. This is an important decision, since we know that poor ergonomics can create all kinds of troublesome health issues from carpal tunnel syndrome to vision problems.

First, make sure everyone can be comfortable when working at their computer. This usually means that the workstation is fully adjustable to the various body types. Fixed table tops and chairs are not appropriate. Sturdy adjustable furniture is very expensive, but so are disability payments and even the frequent breaks required when working at an uncomfortable workstation.

Second, consider lighting, screen orientation, and screen shields to minimize vision strain. Natural lighting costs more, but it relieves stress and eye strain. Most support engineers spend long periods of time staring at a screen; poor screen positioning can create significant and lasting vision problems.

Consider bringing in information or a consultant to promote sound ergonomics practices. Too often employees won't bother to adjust their $400 chairs and will not get any of the benefits they were intended to give. Make sure that support engineers take reasonable breaks. Even a great setup won't overcome lengthy sessions in the same position. Also consider installing software that prompts engineers at scheduled intervals to take stretching breaks and leads them through a set of exercises. Remember that the support engineers' jobs are less varied than managers', so the ergonomics challenges are heightened for them.

CHAPTER **10**

NEW PRODUCT PLANNING

In this chapter we discuss all aspects of planning for new products: training, beta programs, planning for hardware and software, and how to put it all together.

Planning for new products is important for both small and large organizations. Large organizations usually have a group dedicated to new product planning, whereas small ones do not, but the principles are the same.

New product planning must occur for all product types and all customer types, including products from a third party. The steps involved are generally the same whether the product is genuinely new (to the market) or whether the product is simply new for your organization to support. Only the section on testing and beta programs is specific to organizations releasing new products they have created to either internal or external customers.

10.1 PLANNING FOR NEW PRODUCTS

Let's start with an overview of the planning cycle for supporting new products (Figure 10–1), whether the product is truly new or only new for your support center:

- Assess the requirements, focusing on the gap between where you are and where you need to be.
- Create an implementation plan.
- Work through the plan until completion.
- Reflect back on the cycle to improve future projects.

The cycle is the same for all new products, regardless of how complex they are. Actually it's nothing more than an all-purpose implementation cycle. The scope of the cycle is, of course, vastly different when you are preparing for a "minor" new release and when you are preparing for a major new product. If your support center has to cope with the introduction of lots of new products, you will want to develop a set of practical implementations of the standard introduction cycle suitable for various levels of product complexity, as measured by their impact on technical support.

The Planning Cycle

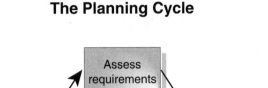

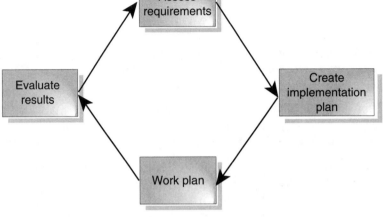

Figure 10–1

10.1.1 Elements of a Support Plan

Even with simple products and small organizations for which the support plan is reduced to a few paragraphs, you need to cover the following topics:

- *Product overview:* what is the product and what does it do?

- *General assessment of the support impact:* this topic captures how new and different the product is compared to existing products, from the perspective of Technical Support. In particular, is the technology totally new to the market, so that customers are likely to be discovering new concepts as well as the product? Is the technology new to the Support group? Are there any special requirements?

- *Support process:* can the new product be supported with existing processes, or do technical and customer requirements dictate adjustments?

  Generally speaking, it's best to use the existing processes for all products (assuming the processes are working well) so as not to create unnecessary confusion, but there are situations where it's best to alter the standard processes or to create new ones. For instance, a new Web-based product may require that you provide a Web interface for Technical Support. Be cautious when adding or modifying support processes. The changes should be motivated by a thorough analysis of the need, since they will be expensive to implement, especially if the new process has to coexist with the old one. Work through the entire existing support process for the new product to make sure that all aspects of the process can be used for the new product, including getting bug fixes.

It is sometimes necessary to use a slightly different process at the beginning, because some part of the (normal) process is not ready, or because you need to test some aspect of the process, or even because part of the training for the new product is delivered through a special on-the-job training mechanism that alters the normal process. Always try to migrate to the normal, standard process as soon as possible to avoid confusion and extra work.

- *Product supportability enhancements:* what can be added to the new product to minimize support cost and expedite resolution? Enhancements can take the form of help screens, installation help, better error messages, error logs, or diagnostics tools.

- *Training requirements:* are the requirements for the new product so different from the current requirements that you will need to recruit new support engineers with a different set of skills to support the new products, or will training the existing engineers suffice? What kind of training is required to support the new product? Beside information on the product itself, include more general requirements, if the product introduces new technology. Also include training on new processes, if any. Specify who will create the training materials, who will deliver the training, and who will handle the logistics for the training delivery. More on training in the next section.

- *Hardware and software requirements:* what is needed for the new product to run in your replication environment? Are brand-new machines required? Is a memory or other upgrade of the existing machines necessary? Beside the new software itself, are other pieces of software necessary, such as compilers, third-party products, or upgrades to existing software? Will you need to support the new product in parallel with old products? If so, will you need multiple replication environments? Finally, what are the procurement and installation lead times for new software and hardware?

- *Beta program, if any:* see the last section of this chapter for details.

- *Schedule for the various activities:* include plenty of detailed milestones, so everyone has an opportunity to check readiness at intermediate points. Include opportunities for support staff and customers to determine whether the product is ready for release as you get close to deployment.

If you work for an ISV, coordinate closely with the Marketing and Development organizations to integrate your plan with theirs. In a mature organization, you want Technical Support to be an integral part of the product-release cycle. What does this mean?

First and foremost, you want the product managers to make support part of the overall product plan, just like testing or distribution. This is the most important point. If you find new products just show up one day and you are suddenly expected to support them, establish yourself as a key player in the release game. The bottom line is that you cannot deliver quality support without adequate preparation, which, at a minimum, requires time. You must be made aware of upcoming new releases and of the ever-changing target release dates and features.

Second, you want to form strong alliances with the other players, so you can benefit from their knowledge to create and implement your support plan. For example: training the support engineers requires some assistance from the Development and Marketing organizations; many of the hardware and software decisions are much easier if you can consult the expert who set up the systems in the Development group; and you will need allies to implement your ideas for supportability enhancements.

Finally, Support can and should have a voice in the final release decision. Why? First, as noted above, releasing a product without adequate support is not a good idea if the goal is to have a successful product introduction. Therefore, the product manager should want the Support organization to be ready at release time. Second, the Support organization has special access to customers and therefore knows a lot about what customers want, what they expect, and what they really do with the product. For instance, the Support organization has expertise in determining whether a particular bug is something that can be lived with or is something that will severely impact the customer. Using the Support group as the voice of the customer adds a valuable perspective to the release decision.

Regrettably, many software developers today do not make Support a true partner in the release cycle. If you are in that situation, work on changing it. Promote the idea that customer satisfaction will be increased if Support has representation in the release decision. A good model is to have a "product team" with representatives from the various functional areas, including Technical Support, who are responsible for making decisions and communicating with their constituents during the release cycle.

Learn what battles to fight. Often, the main reason why Support is kept outside the release decision is that experience has shown that Support never feels the product is good enough to release or that the Support group is really ready to support it. Concentrate on high-level issues, be willing to take a risk, and show yourself a good business partner: you will increase your chances to be included in the release decision.

10.1.2 Who does Support Planning?

Effective support planning requires a combination of project planning skills, technical skills, and training skills. Who in the Support group should be tasked with it?

A variety of answers can be given, depending in part on the size of the organization and on the skill sets of the various individuals within the organization. One of the key decision factors is whether technical expertise is at a premium within your organization. This is often the case, especially with high-complexity products. If you are in that situation, we recommend you consider splitting the requirements for technical skills and project management skills and having two individuals (or groups) work on each new product introduction, one from the project management side and one from the technical side. On the other hand, if technical skills are not in short supply, then using one individual (or group) to shepherd the entire project is easier and simpler.

Here are some possible scenarios:

- In a large Support organization with many new, complex products, set up a function dedicated to support planning. The support planning function should be staffed with support planners with strong project management skills. Their role is to leverage the various other skills required, such as technical or training expertise, and to ensure that the plans roll out smoothly. Since they will have to interact with many different people in different organizations, some very technical, make sure you find people who can communicate effectively with highly technical individuals.

- In a small Support organization, you cannot afford a dedicated planning function. Depending on the complexity of the product, the manager usually ends up driving the planning effort either by himself or with the help of a senior support engineer for the technical aspects.

- In an organization with low-complexity products, you should be able to staff a dedicated planning organization with individuals who have the complete mix of skills required: project management, technical, and perhaps even training. If the number of new products is too low to justify a dedicated planning group, you can make do nicely by designating appropriate support engineers to champion each new project as it comes up, or you may make it a part of a manager's role.

Whether or not you have a dedicated function, clearly designate a project leader for each new product, whose responsibility it is to coordinate the creation and execution of the plan. Make sure everyone knows and communicates with that project leader.

If the project leader is not technical, leverage the skills of a senior support engineer for the technical aspects. Typically, a backliner or a technical adviser, depending on your model, will be part of the planning team (she could be the planning "team" in a small setting). Pick someone who has the specific expertise required for the product being considered. Especially for complex products, the support engineers involved in the planning will become product experts during the planning phase and will continue to play that role after the product is launched.

Particularly complex products and products with brand-new technology may require that one or more support engineers be assigned full time during the planning and early implementation phases. Rotate strong support engineers through this function, keeping in mind that they will have to deal with the stresses and uncertainty associated with a new product rollout. Make flexibility and business sense a requirement in addition to technical skills. Also, since you are investing a lot of training in these pioneers, think about how to retain them in the Support group beyond the initial period, or you will lose your investment. Finally, make sure they have strong commitment and backing from the Development organization if you work for an ISV; otherwise they will get frustrated as their planning goals become difficult to achieve.

10.2 TRAINING FOR NEW PRODUCTS

We have already touched on the topic of training when we covered new-hire training in Chapter 7, "Managing Support People." Training for new products has many similarities with training new hires, so some of the concepts should appear familiar.

When planning the training for new products, don't automatically go for the full-fledged, formal, created in-house class. Formal classes are expensive to create and deliver, require a large audience (or else they are even more expensive), and allow little flexibility in the schedule (everyone has to be available at the same time in the same place). Think about other alternatives.

CBT training is a good option for relatively simple products that can be learned without direct access to an instructor. The development cost of CBTs is very high and the delivery cost very low, so CBTs are well suited to large audiences and also to distributed audiences, since the travel costs to attend a class would be high.

Also investigate videos, written documents, and good old OJT (on-the-job training), if they can produce the desired results. Good situations in which to use mentoring rather than formal training include very complex products where shoulder-to-shoulder learning is required and situations where very few support engineers need training. Why set up something elaborate for just a few people? If you choose mentoring, make sure the mentor has enough time to devote to the mentoring, and sketch out a plan for what should be covered.

Regardless of the delivery medium, your first decision is whether you need to create the training or whether it already exists somewhere. If you are signing up to support a completely new product, you will have to find a way to create the training, whether in-house or through an outside third party. Even in this case, there may be others in the company who also need training on the new product (the Customer Education department, other internal training groups), so you may be able to leverage your efforts with theirs. If the product is merely new to you, buy the curriculum, if not the entire training package, from the outside. It's much cheaper to proceed that way. You can always add components specific to your organization if required.

If you have to develop the training yourself, the main obstacle will probably be to get the appropriate level of technical expertise, especially if your products are complex. The name of the game, once again, is to leverage that technical expertise so that the expert has a minimum burden of "pure" technical tasks. In any case:

- Create a strong training agenda with well-defined objectives to ensure topics that matter to you are covered.

- Conduct an evaluation of the training after the fact to ensure that the objectives were met.

- Think about how materials to learn about new products can be integrated into the new-hire training. Ideally, you will be able to use the same materials for both.

Here are your alternatives for developing the training materials, whether you are choosing a formal training class, CBT, videos, or written information:

- Have the Development organization do it. This is sometimes difficult to achieve, because the developers are busy creating the product. Also, the resulting materials may not be very easy to learn from, because not many developers have strong training skills.

Having developers create the training could be a good solution if you are creating standard classroom training (in most environments, developers would not be able to develop a CBT or shoot a video), if you don't have other alternatives, and also if the developers themselves teach the class, since they will be able to fill any gaps in the materials.

- Have the developers serve as "subject-matter experts" for other individuals who have the training skills required to develop the materials. This requires some involvement from the developers, but less than the previous option. The results are superior because of the better course development skills of the course writers. We prefer this option, although it's more complex than the first one. The luxury variant of this option is to have a professional course developer (in-house or free-lance) paired up with a software developer; the less expensive variant is to have a support engineer play the role of course developer.

- If the software developers are just not available, then you will need to make do with having a support engineer or a course developer put it together. Insist on having software developers check the final result for accuracy, at the very least, and if possible participate in the initial speculation about and definition of the training. Although the previous option is much preferable in our mind, this one can be quite suitable for low-complexity products.

Assuming you have a way to get materials developed, what are the options for delivery?

- Have the software developers teach a formal class. It may be a struggle to free up their schedule, and their teaching technique may be rudimentary, but they will know all the technical aspects. This is a good solution if they wrote the class. (Actually, it is the only way to compensate for potential deficiencies with the materials.) It can also be a good solution when they served as subject-matter experts. To leverage their technical expertise further, consider taping the class on video. Then show it to the support engineers who cannot attend, or use it for review.

- Have the support engineers or the course developers who wrote the class deliver it. Try to get the software developers to attend all or part of it to answer the tough technical questions. You can combine this technique with the one above by having the software developers teach the first class and seeding the class with the individuals who will redeliver it. We recommend this method, because it combines the best of the technical and teaching worlds.

- Have a professional instructor teach the class. This method should give you good teaching skills, but—depending on the technical skills of the instructor and the complexity of your products—might not provide the technical depth required. If you can get an instructor with the appropriate technical skills, go for it.

If you have a dedicated support training organization, you will naturally use it for new product training. Whether you need a dedicated support training organization is a matter of volume and availability of alternate sources of training. If other technically oriented organizations have training resources, you should consider joining forces before creating your own group, unless your organization is very large or has specific training requirements.

10.3 TESTING FOR NEW PRODUCTS

This section covers product testing per se, from a Technical Support perspective, as well as running beta programs for new products. It is intended as a checklist for support managers rather than a treatise on software testing.

This section will be of interest to any support manager who is responsible for non-third party products, whether the end customers are internal or external to the company.

10.3.1 Product Testing

Products, of course, should be tested before being released. The question at hand is: should the Technical Support group be involved in, or even own, the testing process?

There are several reasons why the Support group can bring value to the testing process:

- Support knows customer needs better than anyone. Support engineers have an intimate knowledge of what customers are likely to try with products. They also have a good eye for how a product may be misused. They have been exposed to a variety of uses for the product, and they understand how some customers will push it to the limit.

- Support engineers have the technical skills required to test the product from a user's perspective. In fact, their day-to-day jobs require them to reproduce customer problems, which is exactly what is required to perform usability tests.

- Since the Support group will have to live with the final product, it has a distinct incentive to test thoroughly. Support engineers appreciate the opportunity to find the bugs before the customers find them. From a management perspective, a great way to cut support costs is to increase the quality of the product.

- Testing a new product is a good way to get familiar with it. Testing can be seen as a part of the training process.

- Finally, having someone other than the developer test the product is always a good idea, since the developer may not have the detachment necessary to see the flaws. In particular, the developer may not be able to think up good ways to "break" the product. Whenever possible, avoid this conflict of interest.

Despite the advantages of having the Support group test the product, we recommend that testing be owned by a separate QA function, and that the Support group only have a part in the testing. Why? Because the Support group should focus on helping customers and not be pulled into all kinds of other efforts.

Although the Support group has the expertise necessary to conduct testing from a user's perspective, more complex kinds of testing are best conducted by testing experts. Building test suites and integrating regression tests as new bugs are discovered requires a different set of skills and, ideally, should be owned by a separate function staffed especially for it.

From a political perspective, it's best to have an independent entity own the testing cycle. The Support group should be a part of the release decisions, but it's best to have an independent group (the QA group) make the "go/no go" decisions.

One good way of involving Support in the testing cycle while providing some hands-on learning is to hold "bug-a-thons" for new products. Gather the support engineers after-hours and have them use the product as users would, looking for problems. In addition to finding bugs early, you will get a good team-building exercise between Support and Development.

In summary, we recommend that the Support group participate in the testing effort particularly for those areas that are close to normal customer usage such as installing the product and testing the user interface. Involvement should start early so that potential problems can be corrected with plenty of time for further testing.

10.3.2 Beta programs

Beta programs have become common steps in deploying new products. We are delighted to see them become routine. The idea of a beta program is to share software with customers before declaring it ready to be shipped. Customers test the product in real applications and provide feedback both on the quality of the products (are there any bugs?) and on its usability as well. The feedback can then be incorporated into the final product to improve its quality and its attractiveness to customers. During the beta program, the software development company has a chance to test its processes, and in particular its support processes, as they work with the new product.

In this section we discuss how to run successful beta programs. It's almost a given these days that new products will have beta programs, but let's first summarize why you would want to hold them. After all, they require quite a bit of effort.

The main goal of a beta program is to have a test run of the product so that large problems can be fixed before it ships *en masse*. Therefore, you want to ensure that appropriate amounts of testing will occur during the program, and we will see what you can do to maximize your chances here. The second goal of a beta is to give the company a chance to test its internal processes, from manufacturing to shipping to technical support. The trick here is not to make the program so special that normal processes are bypassed.

Considering the goals of beta programs, what are the steps to implementing one?

First, define in advance what you want to achieve; don't leave it to chance. Sending the software to some random customers and waiting to hear what they say is a waste of effort. At worst, you could get a ton of bad press if customers hate the product and no concrete indications on what to do to improve it. You need to control the beta program from the technical and PR perspectives.

Define what you want customers to test with the product. Starting with the features of the product, create a checklist of what customers should be trying to accomplish with the product. The checklist will be particularly long and complex for brand-new products. For long checklists, you will want to parcel them out among various customers, so that each set of customers gets a particular set of features to test. Don't stop with feature testing, however. Include technical support and other company processes. It's perfectly acceptable and even desirable to have special processes during the beta program. For instance, many beta programs allow for direct access to developers. Or, if only a small set of support engineers are trained on the new product, you may need to offer reduced hours for support of the beta product. If you choose to have special processes, use the last few weeks of the program to do a realistic test with the normal processes.

Based on the requirements, define a reasonable amount of time for the beta program. The main error here is to have a program that's too short. With external customers, a three-week beta is meaningless, since they will barely have time to install the software before time is up. The ideal length depends on the complexity of the product as well as the obstacles encountered along the way and should be flexible, depending on how it goes, but we recommend a minimum of six weeks.

Select beta sites carefully. Beta programs are expensive to run, so you want to focus on those customers who will provide high-quality testing. Using your list of requirements, recruit and qualify beta sites. Beta customers should commit to a certain level of testing in writing (again, use your checklist). If possible, they should be known to you as competent customers—the more demanding the better, sometimes. Finally, they should agree to the rules of the game, such as providing regular feedback, not using the software in production mode, and channeling feedback to you rather than the press. Despite the requirements, there are benefits for customers who participate in beta programs, most notably that they get a head-start on using the new products, an advantage that can be very much appreciated, especially by VARs.

Don't let commercial concerns determine who can be a beta customer, based strictly on business considerations. It's fine to have a few courtesy beta sites. For quality feedback, though, selecting the sites you think will participate most actively is the most important criterion. Also, experience shows that admitting presales sites into a beta program can backfire and result in losing the sale. The Support group as well as the Sales group should be able to come up with plenty of nominations from the existing customer base.

Start the program with a good-quality product. With development cycles contracting, it seems that what was once considered alpha software is often now renamed beta. This confusion with the Greek alphabet is not positive. No beta-quality testing can occur on a product that contains a number of show-stopper bugs. Define minimum quality criteria for the start of the beta program based on the number and nature of known bugs. Define the criteria and get the various parties to agree to them way in advance of the start of the beta to avoid the temptation of shipping something that is not quite ready.

While the beta program is running, check with customers frequently. Have they received the software? Did they install it? Where are they on their testing cycle? What obstacles are they encountering? The more proactive you are with beta sites, the better information you will get and the faster you will be able to complete the cycle.

In addition to personal contacts with the beta customers, we like to see regular conference calls either for the entire set of beta customers or for subgroups, if there are too many customers to have an effective call. Drive the conference call to elicit structured feedback from everyone.

And now for the most difficult decision: when to end the beta. Although you want to have a time target for the beta, the real criterion is whether the product is ready to ship. Release criteria should be defined when beta starts and include such items as number of bugs by severity. For instance, there should be no show-stopper bugs. A good strategy is to involve the beta sites in creating the exit criteria, and even to use that discussion as part of the qualification for beta sites.

Once the criteria are defined, remember that the most important one is always the feedback from customers. If customers say the product's not ready, it's not, even if your exit criteria are satisfied and no matter how much you long to release the product. Do periodic checks during the beta program to evaluate how you are doing versus the release criteria, so you can revise the release date appropriately.

Finally, be open to failure. Some products are just not meant to be. If beta customers are lukewarm about a new product concept, it's very unlikely that a larger set of customers will be any happier about it. Beta customers tend to be leading-edge customers, so they are biased in favor of new products. They must like the new concept if you are to have any success.

Practically speaking, beta programs can be run from a variety of groups, and in most cases from the Marketing or Development organization. Technical Support is also a good place to conduct beta programs. In any case, be sure to have support participate fully in the effort, since you need to test your processes before mass-ship.

In summary, although testing is not the main focus of the Support organization, we believe that the Support group has much to offer to improve product quality. Get your Support group involved in the testing cycle.

APPENDIX A
SAMPLE USER'S GUIDE

S uccess with Sybase

*Your Road Map to Training,
Support, and Consulting Services
for Sybase Enterprise Products*

SYBASE®

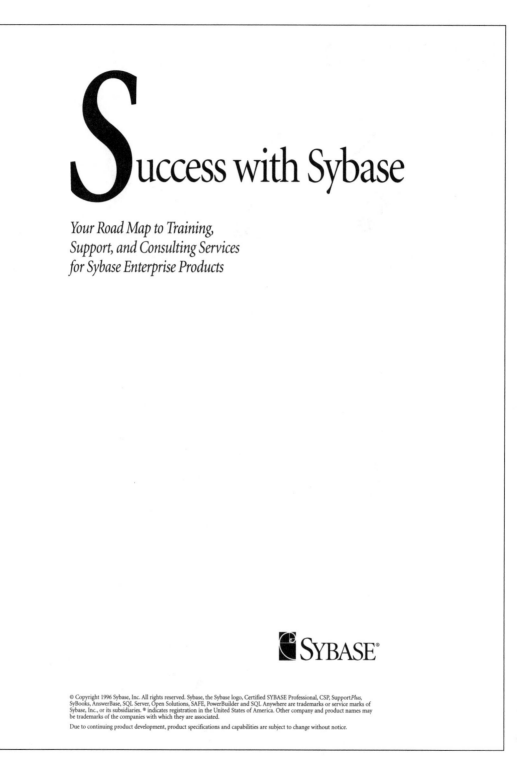

Success with Sybase

Your Road Map to Training,
Support, and Consulting Services
for Sybase Enterprise Products

SYBASE®

Welcome

It's our pleasure to welcome you to the Sybase family. Success with Sybase contains all the information you need to ensure success with your new Sybase enterprise products no matter where in the world your company is located. Each section provides practical, invaluable information. Use Success with Sybase as a road map and you'll quickly find answers to questions about training, technical support, consulting, online services, and more.

Contacts and telephone numbers are conveniently consolidated in the appendixes at the back of this guide. If you're not sure which number to call, simply try one of the telephone numbers listed on the back cover.

For additional copies of Success with Sybase, contact your Sybase sales representative or call the appropriate number listed on the back cover of this guide.

Table of Contents

1

Education Services

Education Services is committed to ensuring the success of your enterprise IT environment. To help you gain expertise and self-sufficiency on Sybase software, we offer a broad array of training programs and certification programs, which ensure that your IT professionals stay current with constantly evolving information technologies.

Skills Assessment

Sybase and Sybase Authorized Education Partners offer a full range of education solutions designed to equip your organization with the right skills, precisely when and where you need them. To help you define a comprehensive education program, Education Professionals use a Skill Assessment Method that:

- Determines the current knowledge and skill level of each employee

- Identifies educational needs to meet job requirements

- Develops individual education plans.

Training Programs

Formal training in Sybase® technology dramatically increases your staff's understanding of our family of client/server products, boosting their effectiveness while preserving your investment in this technology.

Based on the results of the Skills Assessment, you can choose the best method for completing the required training from the following options:

- Courses regularly taught at our Learning Center facilities and Authorized Education Partners' centers

- Private courses taught at your site or at Sybase Learning Centers

- Customized curriculum to meet your organization's unique requirements

- A cost-effective and flexible self-study training portfolio, which includes CBT, multimedia, and video.

Sybase is continually adding new courses and updating course materials to ensure that information on the latest software releases are covered. Courses have also been designed to make your migration from previous versions easy and straightforward. To keep your IT team abreast of recent releases, consult with your Sybase Education representative.

Certification Programs

The Certified SYBASE Professional® (CSP℠) Program offers three levels of certification designed to test your knowledge and prove your mastery:

- Certified Sybase Professional Database Administrator (CSP-DBA)

- Certified Sybase Professional Performance and Tuning Specialist (CSP-PTS)

- Certified Sybase Professional Open Interfaces Developer (CSP-IFD).

How to Find Out More

To obtain Education Program catalogs, schedule of classes, Authorized Education Partner Locations, or more information on the Certification programs, contact the Professional Services Learning Center nearest you (see listing in Appendix A) or connect to the Sybase website at www.sybase.com and select the Services and Support section.

Support Services

2

Sybase offers a range of support services to help you use your Sybase Enterprise Products effectively — whether you're installing software, designing or developing an application, or running your completed application. Sybase support programs help you gain fast, accurate answers to your technical questions through knowledge databases, interactive documentation, technical support, and online open forums. Sybase also offers software update programs that supply you with new enhancement releases and quality updates.

Support*Plus* Offerings

Sybase offers a choice of Support*Plus*℠ plans to suit the varied requirements of enterprise customers. The overview on the following page shows the key features of each plan. Additional service options are also available for many plans. Contact your Sybase sales representative for more information about these Support*Plus* plans and about their availability in your country.

Renewing Your Support Contract

To obtain all of the support services discussed above, you must have an active Sybase Software Support Agreement. You will receive a quotation for your renewal before the expiration of your support agreement. Be sure to renew it promptly to avoid delays when you require support. If you have questions about your contract, want to change support plans, or want to find out renewal dates, call the telephone number of the location nearest you listed on the back cover of this guide and ask for assistance.

How to Find Out More

To order additional Sybase support services or to obtain more information, contact your Sybase sales representative or call the telephone number of the location nearest you listed on the back cover.

Support*Plus* Features

The following table highlights the key features of the four Support*Plus* Plans.

Support*Plus* Plans				
	Preferred*	Advantage	Standard	Lite**
Telephone Hotline Access	24 x 7	24 x 7	Bus. hrs (M-F)	Bus. hrs (M-F)
Number of Calls	unlimited	unlimited	unlimited	per call or 10 pack
Support Contacts	unlimited	4	2	anyone may call
P1 Target Response	30 minutes	1 hour	1 hour	2 hours
P2 Target Response	1 hour	2 hours	4 hours	8 hours
P3 Target Response	2 hours	4 hours	4 hours	8 hours
P4 Target Response	2 hours	4 hours	4 hours	12 hours
Enhancement Releases	●	●	●	with update subscription
SyBooks™	●	●	●	with update subscription
Maintenance Releases	●	●	●	included with product
Support*Plus* Online Services	●	●	●	
AnswerBase™	●	●	●	
Sybase OpenLine	●	●	●	
Priority Maintenance*	●			
Alliance Support*	●	option	option	
Global Support	option	option	option	
After-hours Support	included	included	option	

*   Available in most locations.

**   Available in most locations, for departmental and workgroup customers with selected Sybase products, including: Sybase SQL Server™ for Workplace UNIX and DRDA Gateway products.

Alliance Support Features

The Alliance Support Program* provides the following features:

- Designated Support Team
- Two Support Contacts[1]
- Priority Response
- Priority 1 Response Time of 15 minutes
- Priority 2 Response Time of 1 hour
- Priority 3 Response Time of 2 hours
- Priority 4 Response Time of 2 hours
- Case & Trend Reports
- Orientation to Sybase
- Technical Case Reviews
- Optional Dedicated Engineer
- Optional Alliance Engineer Site Visits

---

*   Available in most locations.

[1]   Preferred customers get three Alliance Contacts.

Obtaining Answers to Your Technical Questions

Quickly Getting Answers to Technical Questions

The following diagram shows the fastest process for obtaining answers to your technical questions.

Sybase gives you three easy ways to gain answers to your technical questions: SyBooks — interactive product documentation, Electronic Support Services — a group of electronic tools that give you access to a wide array of technical information, and Technical Support — locations around the world where you can log a support case with technical support engineers.

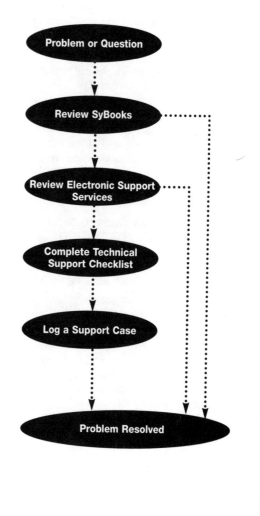

SyBooks —
Online Documentation

SyBooks online documentation for Sybase products provides convenient, easily readable and accessible product documentation. With SyBooks, all of the documentation you need is online. Easy-to-search references within each document are linked to related text, enabling you to quickly jump to the exact information you require and print whatever you need.

SyBooks is delivered on CD-ROM, so you can download it to your server and control who has access to it. If you own multiple Sybase products, you may receive SyBooks on multiple CD-ROMs, based on product categories. You can make SyBooks available to an entire work group or only to a few experts from a single workstation. Complete installation instructions are included. New SyBooks CD documentation is sent out with new enhancement releases.

SyBooks system requirements. To use SyBooks, you need a CD-ROM drive running under one of many platforms. This allows you to load SyBooks on a server or to run SyBooks on a single workstation. Consult the SyBooks packaging for details.

SyBooks-on-the-Web. Sybase documentation collections are also available via the World Wide Web. To access SyBooks-on-the-Web, connect to www.sybase.com, select the Services and Support section, click on the Sybase Enterprise Technical Support section and then on SyBooks-on-the-Web.

Common Questions

Is SyBooks available for every Sybase product? *SyBooks is available for most Sybase products. Where it is not available, you will receive hard copy documentation.*

How can I obtain additional copies of SyBooks? *Because SyBooks can be downloaded onto your server for all users to access, you may find that the CD(s) you receive with the enhancement release is enough. If you do need to buy additional copies of SyBooks, contact your Sybase sales representative or call the telephone number of the location nearest you listed on this guide's back cover.*

Where do I call for usage questions about SyBooks? *After reading the installation guide that accompanies your SyBooks CD, your Sybase technical support contact should contact the Technical Support Center with any questions.*

How can I obtain print copies of documentation? *If you want print copies of Sybase documentation, you have two choices: You can print the documentation from SyBooks or you can purchase hard copy manuals. To purchase manuals, contact Sybase at the telephone number of the location nearest you on the back cover.*

How can I find out more about SyBooks? *To find out more about SyBooks, contact your Sybase sales representative or call the telephone number of the location nearest you listed on the back cover of this guide.*

Electronic Support Services —
Electronic Access to Information

Electronic Support Services give you instant access to the information and support you need. Services include Support*Plus* Online Services via the World Wide Web, Sybase OpenLine via a CompuServe Forum, and the AnswerBase CD knowledge database. Use the electronic service that best fits your needs.

Support*Plus* Online Services —
Web-based Technical Support

Support*Plus* Online Services on the Web let you manage your cases, download software fixes, and access technical information whenever you need it. Support*Plus* Online Services are secure. So you can access and transmit sensitive information freely. Use Support*Plus* Online Services for:

- Electronic case management, which lets you log your cases directly into the Sybase Technical Support case database, view and update customer information, and close cases

- Electronic software distribution, which lets you download software fixes when you need them

- Technical information library for finding information by document type, version, topic, operating system, product or title.

Support*Plus* Online Services system requirements. To access Support*Plus* Online Services via the World Wide Web, you need a modem, an Internet connection, and a Web Browser that supports the secure sockets layer (SSL). Netscape Navigator is recommended. In addition, if there is a firewall between your system and your Internet connection, you must also use a proxy server that supports the SSL protocol or configure your firewall to support

the SSL protocol. You must pre-register online for access to Support*Plus* Online Services.

Logging on to SupportPlus Online Services

1. Use Netscape Navigator. Type http://www.sybase.com

2. Select the Services and Support section

3. Click on Sybase Enterprise Technical Support

4. Click on Register Online for Support*Plus* and complete your registration

5. Allow 24 hours for your registration to be processed.

Common Questions

Where do I call if I have access or usage questions? *For technical questions about SupportPlus Online Services, your Sybase technical support contact should contact the Technical Support Center.*

How can I find out more about Support*Plus* Online Services? *To find out more about SupportPlus Online Services, contact your Sybase sales representative or call the telephone number of the location nearest you listed on the back cover of this guide.*

AnswerBase —
Knowledge Database

AnswerBase is Sybase's knowledge database that is sent out periodically to Sybase technical support contacts. With AnswerBase, you can locate answers to technical questions right in your office. Its advanced search and retrieval system searches a wide array of technical documents, including product documentation for supported releases, trouble shooting guides, technical newsletters, technical notes, and more. You can also use AnswerBase to copy and print a document you may have lost. AnswerBase is delivered on CD-ROM, so you can download it to your server and control who has access to it. Make it available to an entire work group or only to a few experts from a single workstation. Complete installation instructions are included with the CD.

AnswerBase system requirements. To run AnswerBase, you need a CD-ROM drive running under one of several platforms. This allows you to load AnswerBase on the server or to run AnswerBase on a single workstation. Consult the AnswerBase packaging for more details.

Common Questions

How do I install AnswerBase? *The Installation and User guides that are shipped with the AnswerBase CD give detailed installation instructions.*

Where can I obtain answers to usage questions about AnswerBase? *After reading the Installation and User guides, your Sybase technical support contact should contact the Technical Support Center with any additional questions.*

How can I obtain additional copies of AnswerBase? *Because AnswerBase can be downloaded onto your server for all users to access, you may find that the CD you receive is enough. If you do need additional copies of AnswerBase, contact your Sybase sales representative or call the telephone number of the location nearest you listed on this guide's back cover.*

How can I find out more about AnswerBase? *To find out more about AnswerBase, contact your Sybase sales representative or call the telephone number of the location nearest you listed on the back cover of this guide.*

Sybase OpenLine — *CompuServe Open Forum*

Sybase OpenLine, an open CompuServe forum available 24 hours a day anywhere in the world, shares the collective expertise and experience of Sybase and its users. With Sybase OpenLine, Sybase users with CompuServe accounts can connect with other users, broaden their knowledge of Sybase products, and increase their effectiveness. Typical forum sessions involve discussion and information about Sybase products. Sybase OpenLine libraries contain the latest product and company information. And online conferences feature experts talking about exciting industry topics.

Sybase OpenLine system requirements. To access Sybase OpenLine on CompuServe, you need a modem and a terminal or a personal computer.

10

Logging on to Sybase OpenLine via CompuServe

1. To log on to Sybase OpenLine, you need a CompuServe account (see information below for setting up a CompuServe account). Connect to CompuServe either by accessing it directly or by connecting to CompuServe through the Internet.

2. Once you are connected to CompuServe, type: GO SYBASE. Then choose Sybase OpenLine from the menu.

3. You will now have two options — to visit or to join. Joining gives you complete public access to Sybase OpenLine. Visiting gives you general information about Sybase OpenLine. Typically you will want to join.

Setting up a CompuServe account.
If you do not have a CompuServe account, you will need to set one up to access Sybase OpenLine. Start by calling one of the telephone numbers below and asking for representative 532.

Setting Up A CompuServe Account		
CompuServe Numbers	**Freephone**	**Direct**
North America		
Canada	800 524 3388	614 529 1349
Mexico		+52 5 629 8190
United States	800 524 3388	614 529 1349
Europe		
Austria	0660 8750	+49 89 66 535 111
France		+33 1 4714 2165
Germany	0130 37 32	+49 89 66 535 111
Hungary		+36 1 156 5366
Switzerland	155 31 79	+49 89 66 535 111
United Kingdom	0800 289 378	+44 272 760681
Asia & Pacific Rim		
Australia	800 025 240	+61 2 410 4260
Hong Kong		+85 2 599 2788
Japan	0120 22 1200	+81 3 5471 5806
New Zealand	0800 446 113	+61 2 410 4260
South Korea	080 022 7400	+82 02 528 0472
Taiwan	080 251 009	+886 02 651 6899
South America		
Argentina		+54 1 345 3871
Chile		+56 2 696 8807
Venezuela		+58 2 793 2984
Africa & Middle East		
Israel		+972 3 638 8230
South Africa	0800 112252	+27 12 241 2530

For information on countries not listed, contact CompuServe at the telephone number listed above that is most convenient for you.

11

Accessing Special Interest Sections

For qualified users, Sybase reserves several Special Interest Sections, including:

• Sybase PrivateLine Forum — provides current technical information online, including Troubleshooting Guides, Tech Notes, Technical Tips, Installation Guides, patches and fixes, EBF cover letters

• International Sybase User Group — contains information targeted for customers interested in or active participants in the ISUG

• Sybase Open Solutions™ members — includes specific information for Open Solutions partners.

To obtain access to a Special Interest Section, choose the Sybase main menu option for PrivateLine Registration.

Common Questions

How frequently is Sybase OpenLine updated? *We update Sybase OpenLine daily —sometimes even by the hour and minute —with new questions from other users, answers to your questions, and new information about our products and company.*

Where do I call if I have access or usage questions? *For technical questions about Sybase OpenLine, your Sybase technical support contact should call Sybase's Technical Support.*

How can I find out more about Sybase OpenLine? *To find out more about Sybase OpenLine, contact your Sybase sales representative or call the telephone number of the location nearest you listed on the back cover of this guide.*

Information Directory — *Where to Find Sybase Technical and Product Information*

The following Information Directory will help you determine where to go to obtain information on Sybase and Sybase products.

Information Directory	WWW Support*Plus* Online Services	WWW Sybase Home Page	Sybase OpenLine	AnswerBase CD	Direct Mail	Sybase Magazine	Shipped with the Software
PRODUCT INFORMATION							
AVAILABILITY							
New Products/Releases Alert	•		•	•			
Customer Letters/Announcements	•	•	•	•	•	•	
Education Schedule	•		•	•	•		•
CERTIFICATION							
Product Certification Alerts	•		•	•			
PRODUCT DETAILS							
Datasheets	•	•	•				
White Papers	•	•	•	•			
Customer Successes		•			•	•	
END OF LIFE							
End of Life Letters	•		•	•	•		
PARTNER INFORMATION							
Partner Product Information		•				•	•
SUPPORT INFORMATION							
Sybase Technical News	•		•	•			
Troubleshooting Guide		•	•	•			
Technical Notes	•		•	•			
Frequently Asked Questions	•		•	•			
SYBASE GENERAL INFORMATION							
Press Releases		•	•				
Annual Report		•					
News Articles about Sybase		•			•	•	
Earnings		•				•	
Management Letters	•		•	•	•		

Technical Support

4

Contacting a Sybase Technical Support Center is another way to obtain answers to your technical questions. Sybase Technical Support Centers are staffed with technical support engineers who are ready to answer your company's technical operational questions about Sybase products. Sybase has Technical Support Centers located in many countries around the world. See Appendix C for locations and telephone numbers.

Understanding Sybase Case Management Process

Sybase records and tracks every question or request for assistance that your technical support contact makes to the Technical Support Center as a "case," each with a unique reference number (case number). This identifier allows us to prioritize and track your problem effectively as well as to share additional information as the case is resolved. Please make sure you record the case number of your question or request for assistance. You will need it to reference any future calls.

Case priorities are assigned based on the problem's urgency and its impact on your business. The priority of the case determines the targeted initial response time as shown below:

Priority 1: The software is not operational and no workaround is possible, or a workaround exists but is unacceptable because of its impact on your business.

Priority 2: The software is operational but its functionality is seriously affected. If a workaround has been provided, the loss of functionality can only be sustained for a few days. Or there is an installation problem for a Preferred or Advantage customer.

Priority 3: The software is usable, but a problem has been identified and a specific portion of the system either provides incorrect results or is not operating as documented. A workaround is available and acceptable. Or there is an installation problem for a Standard or Lite customer.

Priority 4: You have a question or a request for a product enhancement.

Technical Support Contacts

Depending on your Sybase support contract, your company may register one or more authorized technical support contacts. These support contacts, selected by your company, are the only people authorized to contact the Technical Support Center with questions. Authorized technical support contacts are established to protect your company and your software. This arrangement ensures that only people you authorize can request us to investigate or make modifications to your system. Designated support contacts also provide a focal point for the transfer of knowledge and skills.

If an unauthorized person calls, we will ask them to contact your authorized technical support contact instead. However, in an emergency, we will begin working on a case with an unauthorized support contact on an exception basis, subject to later verification.

We recommend that you choose your authorized technical support contacts carefully. They should be individuals who are knowledgeable about your technical environment and about Sybase products. They must also be readily accessible to other staff for questions.

Adding Technical Support Contacts. The number of technical support contacts depends on the Sybase support plan your company has chosen. To add more support contacts, you can either purchase the option to add support contacts or upgrade to a higher level of support that offers more support contacts. For more information, call the telephone number nearest you listed on this guide's back cover and ask for Customer Service.

Changing Technical Support Contacts. If your technical support contact leaves the company or changes positions, or if you need to make a change for any other reason, send a letter on your organization's letterhead by mail or fax to the Customer Service group at your Technical Support Center. The current technical support contact or a manager should request this change. Include the following information:

- Your organization name
- Name of technical support contact to be replaced
- Name, address, and phone number of the new replacement technical support contact
- Signature of the support contact to be replaced or of the department manager.

Site ID (customer number)

Your Site ID identifies licenses and technical support contacts at your specific site. You can find your Site ID on the packing slip sent with your software. If you do not have your Site ID number, call the telephone number nearest you listed on this guide's back cover and ask for Customer Service.

Preparations Before Logging a Technical Support Case

To expedite the resolution of questions, technical support contacts should gather as much information as possible before calling the Technical Support Center. When you call, be prepared with the following information:

• Site ID (customer number)

• Sybase server version

• Operating system type and version

• Front-end (client) product and version

• Client machine operating system type and version

• Description of the problem (include error numbers, error messages, circumstances in which problem occurred)

• Other useful information (copy of error logs, reproducible case, number of users on the system, average percent of CPU usage, any other pertinent information).

Appendix D represents a Technical Support Case Checklist, which your technical support contact can use to gather this information. Duplicate the checklist so that you have a copy handy for each question or problem. Once you have filled out the form, keep it. You may find it useful to train other members of the team on the problem and its resolution.

Logging a Technical Support Case

You can log your case electronically using Support*Plus* Online Services. Refer to Section 3 for more information on electronic case logging. Or phone your case in to the Technical Support Center nearest you or the center specified in your software license. Refer to the Technical Support Centers list in Appendix C.

Since you will need to supply detailed case information or enter it yourself electronically, be sure to gather this information beforehand on the Technical Support Case Checklist in Appendix D. By recording this information before a support engineer returns your call, we can do preliminary research on similar problems and often answer your question more quickly.

Whether you log your case electronically, or phone it in, you will receive a unique case number. Be sure to record this number on your Technical Support Case Checklist. This is your quick reference number to all information about your question.

Once your case has been logged, it is assigned to the appropriate support engineer.

Response Times

The speed of our response is determined by the severity of the problem as well as by the terms of your Sybase support agreement. Shown below are target time commitments for providing a response: (Depending on current case volume, actual times may be less.)

Target Response Time				
Support*Plus* Plan	Priority 1	Priority 2	Priority 3	Priority 4
Alliance Contacts*	15 minutes	1 hour	2 hours	2 hours
Preferred	30 minutes	1 hour	2 hours	2 hours
Advantage	1 hour	2 hours	4 hours	4 hours
Standard	1 hour	4 hours	4 hours	4 hours
Lite	2 hours	8 hours	8 hours	12 hours

* Alliance response times are based on a direct call to your Alliance Support Team; if you log your case through Electronic Case Management or via the technical support center, response times will be based on your applicable support plan.

Resolving Your Case

Support engineers read case notes and do preliminary investigations before returning your call to resolve your case. Response times vary according to the priority of the case and the terms of your Sybase support agreement.

Sometimes it is not possible to resolve a case during the initial call back. This happens most frequently when additional information is needed, if the initial discussion indicates that different expertise is required to resolve your case, or if you are reporting a potential product defect, which we need to verify.

If you have additional information about your case, you can update your case electronically using Support*Plus* Online Services or call the main Technical Support Center telephone number. To expedite your phone call and make sure that additional information is recorded accurately, please provide your case number. All information received is immediately passed to the support engineer working on resolving your case.

If a different expertise is required at any time, the support engineer transfers the case to a support engineer with the appropriate expertise and informs you of the change.

If you are reporting a potential product defect, the support engineer attempts to duplicate the problem. To do this, we may need to log onto your system (with your approval), obtain code from you, or use the error message and other information you provide to resolve the problem. We will also check the product defect tracking system to see if another customer has reported a similar problem. Once a problem is duplicated, Technical Support sends the entire information to the appropriate software business unit for final verification that a product defect exists. Your support engineer will notify you when a product defect has been confirmed.

Closing a Case

A case is closed when you and the support engineer agree that a resolution has been reached. Your case may be closed because:

- The information provided by the support engineer has answered your question

- You tell the support engineer that the case is no longer an issue

- You and the support engineer agree that your problem is a result of an application code or design problem that cannot be isolated. In this situation, your support engineer may refer you to the Sybase Professional Services organization.

Answering questions on older releases of Sybase software. Support engineers make every attempt to answer your questions on older releases of Sybase products. However, they only attempt to duplicate product defects for the current software release and just previous release. Product defects are fixed only on these two releases.

Escalation assistance. Sybase recognizes that on occasion customers may encounter critical problems which require a higher level of service. Sybase has established an effective process to support special situations.

If at any point while your case is open, you are not satisfied with the current plan of action, you may request escalation through your technical support engineer. Your request will be routed to the appropriate support manager, who will contact you to discusss your situation and work out a plan for resolution.

Customer satisfaction surveys. From time to time, we send a satisfaction survey to a selected group of customers who have had a case closed during the previous period. Those customers are asked to evaluate how we performed in resolving their case. Your feedback is very important to us. If you receive a survey, please take a few minutes to complete it and return it. Sybase uses this feedback to make certain that its Technical Support meets your needs.

Cooperative Support Agreements

To provide seamless support processes for customers with multi-vendor products, we have established cooperative support agreements with many vendors. These agreements provide designated contacts at the vendor for Sybase support engineers, who will expedite your problem or raise its priority within their support organization.

Software Updates

5

Sybase is continuously improving our software so that you can develop information systems that keep you on the competitive edge of your business. These include: New Enhancement Releases — providing major enhancements to functionality, architecture, and performance, SyBooks — product documentation, and Maintenance Releases — providing quality fixes to Sybase software.

New Enhancement Releases

To keep your information system and applications current and competitive, you can take advantage of new enhancement releases of your Sybase software. New enhancement releases are issued periodically. Enhancement releases, which are fully tested to ensure product quality, may include new features, improved performance, and changes to keep your Sybase software current with changes to your operating system and hardware. They also include quality fixes for software defects identified in earlier versions.

Obtaining new enhancement releases. New enhancement releases are included as part of Sybase Support*Plus* Plans for most Sybase products and are available to customers with active support licenses. Support*Plus* Lite customers must purchase the Update Subscription Program to receive enhancement releases.

SyBooks

With your enhancement releases you also receive updated documentation, which is provided either on SyBooks, CD-based documentation, or in hard copy. Refer to Section 3 for more information on SyBooks.

Maintenance Releases

Sybase periodically releases fully tested, production quality maintenance releases, which include software fixes. Maintenance releases undergo regression testing and compatibility testing with other Sybase products to make sure the release is up to Sybase product quality standards. Regression-tested interim releases with software fixes are issued between maintenance releases.

Obtaining maintenance releases.
Maintenance releases are included as part of
Sybase Support*Plus* Plans or products and can
be requested when they are available.

How to Find Out More

To find out more about a specific software
update or SyBooks, call the telephone number
of the location nearest you listed on the back
cover of this guide. For information about
whether a platform, operating system, or
off-the-shelf software application works with
a particular Sybase release, contact that
hardware, operating system, or application
vendor.

6 Consulting Services

Sybase Professional Services provides a full spectrum of consulting services to assist you. With offerings ranging from business process engineering to detailed architecture design and implementation to hands-on technical consulting, we can tailor a service package to meet your needs. Whatever your level of experience in migrating to client/server technology, Sybase has extensive real-world experience to build a unique solution for your enterprise.

Developing and Implementing Optimal Solutions

Professional Services consultants can help you develop the IT infrastructure to accomplish and exceed your business goals through SAFE™ (Sybase Advanced Framework to Enable) services. The SAFE frameworks include:

- SAFE/PM — Sybase Advanced Framework to Enable Project management. This ISO 9001 TickIT certified framework for managing IT projects to successful and timely completion is used to deliver all services within the other frameworks

- SAFE/BA — Sybase Advanced Framework to Enable Business Architecture. This framework provides a systematic and integrated approach to analyzing, designing and prioritizing opportunities for business operation improvements

- SAFE/ITA — Sybase Advanced Framework to Enable Information Technology Architecture. A practical, step-by-step process, SAFE/ITA transforms business requirements into a usable distributed computing architecture

- SAFE/AD — Sybase Advanced Framework to Enable Application Development. This framework provides a clearly defined structure for developing custom applications that successfully solve specific business problems

- SAFE/OOD — Sybase Advanced Framework to Enable Object-Oriented Development. This framework provides a pragmatic approach to developing client/server applications using PowerBuilder® (or similar tool) against existing relational databases through the utilization of object-oriented analysis and design techniques.

Each framework guides Sybase and partner consultants with proven technical practices and processes. A combination of structure and flexibility ensures that you receive consistently high-quality, end-to-end solutions. Sybase Professional Services experts can work with you to engineer your systems, processes, and organizations to reduce delivery time, improve service response, reduce invoice payment timeframes, increase productivity and customer satisfaction, and more. Consultants can also help pinpoint the business changes that will give you the biggest payback.

Providing Expert Consulting

Our technical consulting services include product deployment, design review, performance tuning, and technology transfer. Additional services include benchmark design/execution and migration from earlier versions or conversion to Sybase products. Sybase consultants can quickly assist you with virtually any aspect of client/server computing.

Developing Open Solutions

At Sybase, open is built-in. Professional Services consultants specialize in developing open interfaces that connect your legacy systems and other vendors' databases to Sybase SQL Server systems.

How to Find Out More

To obtain more information about Sybase Professional Services and our Partners, contact the Professional Services Office nearest you (see listing in Appendix B) or connect to the Sybase web site at www.sybase.com and select the Services and Support section.

Connecting with Other Users

7

Meeting and interacting with other Sybase users provides an important way to share ideas and learn first hand from their experiences. Sybase provides several methods for you to exchange information with other users including: Local Sybase User Groups, International Sybase Users Groups, Sybase OpenLine — a CompuServe forum, and Sybase Magazine.

Sybase User Groups

Sybase user groups, available worldwide, allow you to keep in touch and share information with other Sybase users, vendors, and Sybase employees. You can join Local Sybase User Groups (LUGs) or the International Sybase User Group (ISUG).

Membership in ISUG makes you eligible for numerous benefits, including:

- Free copy of SQL Anywhere™

- Free subscription to Sybase Server Journal, which features technical articles and tips

- $50.00 discount on all Sybase User Conferences and Developer Conferences

- A systematized process for voting on enhancements that help drive Sybase product direction

- A private forum on CompuServe OpenLine

- Training discounts on certification exams, self-study training products, and Sybase education courses

- Discounts on classroom training courses, videos, and the personal use license CBT course

- Access to Special Interest Groups (SIGs)

To join Sybase user groups or to obtain additional information, you can choose one of four contact options:

- Send a fax to ISUG at
  +1 510 922 0882

- Send e-mail to
  isug@sybase.com

- Access "Sybase User Groups" within Sybase OpenLine for membership information and an application. See Section 3 for more information on Sybase OpenLine.

- Access ISUG from the Sybase website at www.sybase.com

Sybase OpenLine

Sybase OpenLine puts you in touch with other Sybase users. You pose technical questions, share ideas, or provide answers. See Section 3 for more details.

Sybase Magazine

Sybase publishes a quarterly magazine that showcases how customers are using Sybase software. If you have not yet received a copy and would like a free subscription, call 800 275 1183 in the U.S. or Canada. For all other locations, call the telephone number nearest you listed on the back cover of this guide. Sybase Magazine is also available as a web-based publication titled Sybase ONLINE. You can access the electronic version from the Sybase website at www.sybase.com.

Additional Services, Products, and Books

Sybase Products

If you want to order additional Sybase products or services, contact your Sybase sales representative or call the number nearest you listed on the back cover for assistance. For information on Sybase Products, connect to the Sybase Web site at www.sybase.com and select the About-Our-Products section.

Third-Party Products

For information about third-party products and services that work with the Sybase product family, consult the Open Solutions Directory. To order a copy of the directory, call the telephone number of the location nearest you on the back cover of this guide or connect to the Sybase Web site at www.sybase.com and select the Partners and Solutions section.

Books on Sybase Products

A resource guide and order service for books on Sybase is available from Sybase Publishing. Sybase Publishing finds the best books on the market about Sybase products, and brings together authors and publishers to encourage the development of additional books. Books from major publishers can supplement Sybase documentation and training with in-depth, timely studies of the products and their use in the real world.

Sybase now has its own official publishing line, Sybase Press, in alliance with International Thomson Computer Press. Sybase Press books and CDs are dedicated to the Sybase professional who seeks information on business problems and industry solutions as well as product features and functions.

Book topics currently available include:

• Client/server

• SQL language

• Sybase SQL Server

• SQL Anywhere

To find a complete listing of available books on Sybase products, or to order a specific book, connect to the Sybase Publishing Web site at www.sybase.com/inc/sypress or send email to sypub@sybase.com.

Sybase Customer Service

Sybase's Customer Service department helps you with questions, suggestions, or problems — when you do not know where to turn. Customer Service can help you with the following:

- Requesting or ordering software updates

- Finding out what platform or operating system a Sybase release is certified on

- Determining what your Site ID (customer number) is

- Changing your technical support contact

- Routing you to the Sybase department that can answer your question

- Sending you customer satisfaction surveys

- Answering questions about your support bill

Call the telephone number of the location nearest you listed on the back cover.

29

Appendix A:
Professional Services Learning Centers

Australia
+61 2 9936 8902

Belgium
+32 2 716 83 11

Canada
800 8 SYBASE (800 879 2273),
press 1, then 2

France
+33 1 4190 4190

Germany
+49 61229 2320

Italy
+39 2 4832 41

Mexico
+52 5 282 8000

Netherlands
+31 3465 82999

Spain
+34 1302 0900

Switzerland
+41 1308 6350

United Kingdom
+44 1628 597089

United States
800 8 SYBASE (800 879 2273),
press 1, then2

Rest of Europe, Middle East, & Africa
+44 1 494 555599

Appendix B:
Professional Services Consulting and OASiS Centers

Professional Services Consulting Centers

Australia
+61 2 9936 8800

Austria
0660 67 14

Belgium
0800 155 62

Canada
905 273 8500

France
05 90 81 35

Germany
0130 81 88 62

Hong Kong
+85 2 2506 6000

Italy
167 87 2036

Japan
+81 3 5210 6000

Mexico
+52 5 282 8000

Netherlands
060 22 2102

Norway
800 11 012

Spain
900 99 44 17

Sweden
020 79 17 05

Switzerland
155 48 81

United Kingdom
0800 44 44 55

United States
617 564 6100

Rest of Europe, Middle East, & Africa
+44 1 494 555599

OASiS Centers

Europe
+44 1628 770600

United States
617 564 6100

Appendix C:
Technical Support Centers

Australia
1 800 252 454
+61 2 9936 8900
Fax: +61 2 9936 8898

Belgium
+32 2 716 83 83
Fax: +32 2 716 83 84

Brazil
+55 11214 4044
Fax: +55 11214 0820

Canada
Central
800 879 2273
Fax: 312 864 7288

Eastern
800 879 2273
Fax: 617 564 6148

Western
800 879 2273
Fax: 510 922 3911

China
+86 10 6856 8488
Fax: +86 10 6856 8489

Czech Republic
+42 22431 0808
Fax: +42 22431 5024

France
+33 1 4190 4242
Fax: +33 1 4190 4245

Germany
+49 211 5976 444
Fax: +49 211 5976 410
Hong Kong

+85 2 2506 6095
Fax: +85 2 2506 6096

Indonesia
+62 21 526 6520
Fax: +62 21 526 6523

Italy
+39 2 4832 4222
Fax: +39 2 4830 0660

Japan
+81 3 5210 6000
Fax: +81 3 5210 5159

Korea
+82 2 3451 5200
Fax: +82 2 3451 5299

Malaysia
+60 3 233 6214
Fax: +60 3 233 6222

Mexico
+52 5 282 8093
Fax: +52 5 282 8025

Netherlands
+31 3465 52666
Fax: +31 3465 52642

New Zealand
+64 4 473 3661
Fax: +64 4 499 9068

Philippines
+63 2 634 5674
Fax: +63 2 631 5569

Singapore
+65 338 0018
Fax: +65 338 8112

Spain
+34 1302 0900
Fax: +34 1302 8937

Sweden
+46 8632 9900
Fax: +46 8750 5420

Switzerland
+41 3780 8620
Fax: +41 3780 8639

Taiwan
+88 62 514 8282
Fax: +88 62 545 6909

United Kingdom
+44 1628 597111
Fax: +44 1628 597112

United States
Central
800 879 2273
Fax: 312 864 7288

Eastern
800 879 2273
Fax: 617 564 6148

Western
800 879 2273
Fax: 510 922 3911

Appendix D:
Technical Support Case Checklist

To expedite the resolution of your question and help you track it, please fill out this checklist before you call your Technical Support Center.

Site ID (customer number): ....

Case number: ....

Priority: ....

Support engineer: ....

Date case opened: ....

Date case closed: ....

Sybase server version: ....

....

Operating system type and version: ....

Front-end (client) product and version: ....

....

Client machine operating system type and version: ....

....

Description of the problem (include error numbers, error messages, circumstances in which problem occurred): ....

....

....

Other useful information (include copy of error logs, reproducible case, number of users on the system, average percent of CPU usage, any other pertinent information): ....

....

....

SYBASE®

Sybase, Inc.
6475 Christie Avenue
Emeryville, California
USA 94608-1006
800 8 SYBASE
+1 510 922 3500
Fax: +1 510 922 3210
World Wide Web:
www.sybase.com

For Asia Pacific Inquiries

Australia
+61 2 9936 8800

China
+86 10 6856 8488

Hong Kong
+85 2 2506 6000

Japan
+81 3 5210 6000

New Zealand
+64 4 473 3661

Korea
+82 2 3451 5200

Countries not listed above
+85 22 506 6000

For Europe Inquiries

Belgium
+32 2 716 83 11

France
Lyon
+33 1 72 33 17 30
Paris
+33 1 4190 4190

Germany
Duesseldorf
+49 211 5976 0
Hamburg
+49 40237 8090
Stuttgart
+49 7119 0050

Italy
+39 2 4832 41

Netherlands
+31 3465 82999

Spain
+34 1302 0900

Sweden
+46 8632 9900

Switzerland
Renens
+41 21637 2131
Zurich
+41 1308 6363

United Kingdom
Leeds, West Yorkshire
+44 11 32 368000
London
+44 1712 034000
Maidenhead, Berkshire
+44 1628 597100

Countries not listed above
+31 3465 82999

For Latin America Inquiries

Mexico
+52 5 282 8000

Countries not listed above
+1 305 267 9344

For North America Inquiries

USA & Canada

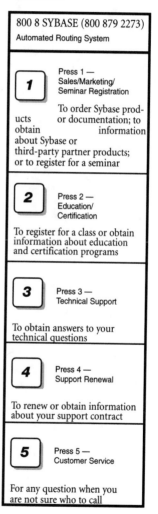

800 8 SYBASE (800 879 2273)
Automated Routing System

1 Press 1 —
Sales/Marketing/
Seminar Registration

To order Sybase products or documentation; to obtain information about Sybase or third-party partner products; or to register for a seminar

2 Press 2 —
Education/
Certification

To register for a class or obtain information about education and certification programs

3 Press 3 —
Technical Support

To obtain answers to your technical questions

4 Press 4 —
Support Renewal

To renew or obtain information about your support contract

5 Press 5 —
Customer Service

For any question when you are not sure who to call

APPENDIX **B**

CALL RESOLUTION OVERVIEW

This section translates the Basic Action Workflow into practical support terms at the level of the specific support call and can be used as a basis for training support engineers on the transaction cycle. It also depicts in broad terms troubleshooting and diagnostic techniques useful for support engineers.

Recall that the Basic Action Workflow has four phases (see Figure B–1):

- *Preparation:* the customer makes a request.
- *Negotiation:* the support engineer and the customer negotiate an agreement.
- *Performance:* the support engineer resolves the issue.
- *Acceptance:* the customer declares whether the issue has been resolved to his satisfaction.

B.1   FRAMING THE CALL

What should the support engineer do during the negotiation phase? She must "frame" the call—that is, define the issue fully. What *exactly* does the customer want? Let's suppose he requested a software fix. Would a workaround be acceptable? Get down to the real concern as opposed to the specific words of his request: what is the customer trying to accomplish? A workaround may be acceptable and even preferable to a fix. Capture exactly what it is that will satisfy the customer in one or two sentences. Record them carefully.

B.2   PROBLEM SOLVING

Once the issue is defined and agreement is reached, we move into the performance phase. The performance phase is an exercise in problem solving. Usually this is very straightforward, but be prepared for tough cases by being systematic and thorough:

- Ensure that you have all the relevant facts. Use a checklist for the product, version, platform, exact symptoms.
- Search available information such as the knowledge base for similar symptoms. Analyze discrepancies.

297

Basic Action Workflow

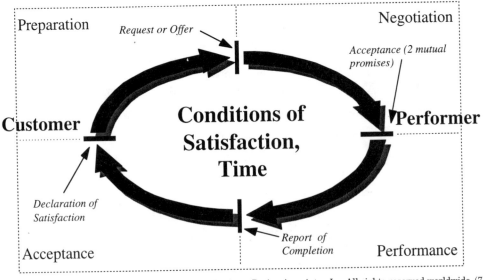

Figure B–1

- If it is truly a new problem, use directed brainstorming techniques as described below to create hypotheses.
- Test each hypothesis and record the results in an organized, systematic way. Make sure you control variables to isolate their effects. If you change a command and an operating system parameter at the same time, you won't know which change did the trick. If you are working with complex systems, organize your search into trees to avoid confusion and duplication.
- Eliminate hypotheses that are easy to check early on, even if they are not the most likely candidates. Conversely, be cautious when you work on hypotheses that require extensive research. Don't invest hours checking something out unless you are confident you're on the right track.
- While you should not waste your time rechecking results you already have (and you should not have to if you proceeded methodically), periodically reassess your progress and question

assumptions if the problem seems untraceable. You might have missed something.

- Once you have a diagnosis, move to a solution, applying the same technique of creating hypotheses and testing them.

B.3 CREATIVE BRAINSTORMING

Many good ideas come from thinking "outside the box." When you are stuck, the following questions may help you find new avenues for solving the problem.

- Have you ever seen a similar situation, even with different parameters?
- Have you ever seen an opposite situation? (For instance, if the problem is with disappearing output, did you ever see double output?)
- Work backward: what would you do to get the desired result?
- What would you do if you wanted to get the faulty behavior you are observing?
- Work forward: can you trace the proper behavior down the process?
- Relax one or several constraints: maybe the operating system, or the programming language.
- Engage with others early; speculating with others is frequently more fruitful than speculating alone. Try talking about the problem with an expert or, conversely, try explaining it to a novice.

B.4 CHECKING SATISFACTION

Finally, what is the role of the support engineer during the acceptance phase? The key here is that the support engineer must make sure that the customer is indeed satisfied. Savvy support engineers will guide customers through the acceptance phase by contrasting the request with the result and asking for an explicit confirmation. Since it may be some time since the request was made, it's essential that the agreement was clear at the beginning. The customer may need some time to test the fix before declaring the issue resolved. Allow a reasonable amount of testing time before closing the issue, or you may get one or more reopened calls on the same problem.

APPENDIX C
DETERMINING STAFFING LEVELS

The following is a step-by-step method for determining staffing levels and matching them to the average wait time for customer calls. The method is based on queuing theory, a mathematical discipline which applies to call centers as well as any other type of queue-based scenario. With a few basic pieces of data, it allows you to predict how many support engineers you need on the phone at any one time, depending on how quickly calls need to be answered. You can also use the method to determine how changes in your staffing levels impact the speed of service you can deliver to your customers.

There are a few technical terms to define before we get going:

- A new unit of work known as an erlang (for the name of the mathematician Erlang who invented this theory). It's, very simply, the amount of work per unit of time. So, for instance, if you get 60 calls an hour and each of them takes 2 minutes of work, your workload is 60 ∗ 2 = 120 minutes or 120 / 60 = 2 erlangs.

- There are several Erlang formulas that relate workload, wait time, and staffing. The one we will use here is the so-called Erlang "C" formula, which describes situations in which a limited number of agents (for us, support engineers) are handling an unlimited number of requests (here, phone calls, which are not really unlimited, but the number of which is great and not bounded), and the requests can be queued if they cannot be handled immediately. There are other Erlang formulas for other situations—in particular, situations where the requests cannot be queued. You don't need to know anything about the formula if you are planning to use a staffing software that will do the computations for you, although understanding the basic steps is useful (plus, you can impress your friends with your esoteric knowledge).

- The average delay of delayed calls, or ADDC, captures the average length of time the calls that cannot be handled right away have to wait (or, if you prefer, the average hold time for calls that go on hold). The formula uses another entity called the ADDC factor, that by definition is the ratio of the delay by the resolution time.

- The average speed of answer, or ASA, is the average length of hold time for all calls—that is, the ADDC spread over all calls.

C.1 DERIVING A STAFFING LEVEL KNOWING THE SERVICE TARGET

You need the following pieces of information:

- Your call volume in calls per hour.
- The average length of your calls, including both the time spent working with the customer on the phone and any wrap-up time needed to complete the transaction. All ACDs record the time spent on calls, many allow the support engineers to also request wrap-up time separately from idle time. If yours does not, you will need to estimate wrap-up time.
- The service level you require—that is, the maximum amount of time you want your customers to wait.

For the sake of this example, let's suppose your call volume is 100 calls per hour, that the average call length is 9 minutes, and that we do not want customers to wait more than 2 minutes in the queue.

- Calculate your workload: 9 $*$ 100 = 900 minutes, 900 / 60 = 15 erlangs.
- Calculate the ADDC factor by dividing the target for the maximum delay by the average call length: 2 / 9 = .22.
- Using the Erlang tables provided, or using a software program, determine the staff required and the percentage of delayed calls (you will need to use the ADDC factor immediately inferior to .22, .20: you need 20 staff, and 16% of your calls will be required to wait; .16 is our actual ADDC factor.
- Now compute the average delay of delayed calls by multiplying the ADDC factor from the table by the call length: .20 $*$ 540 = 108 seconds.
- Finally compute the average delay for all calls: 108 $*$ .16 = 17 seconds. This is your average speed of answer or ASA.

C.2 DERIVING A SERVICE LEVEL FROM THE STAFFING LEVEL

This is the reverse exercise to the one above, and its main advantage is to show how staffing levels influence service levels, and most particularly how you can derive ideal staffing levels. Clearly, the more staff the better, but by using the Erlang formulae you will see that there is a point of diminishing returns, that is, adding more staff does increase the speed of answers, but it does not increase it significantly beyond a certain point. Conversely, if you have too little staff, adding even one person can make a tremendous difference in service levels.

Assume you get 100 calls per hour and that each call takes 9 minutes to handle. Your workload is 15 erlangs (9 $*$ 100 = 900 minutes, 900 / 60 = 15 erlangs). Plotting the average speed of response versus staffing, you can see that the average speed of response does increase as you increase staffing (see Figure C–1), but that the increase is most clear in the left hand side portion of the chart, whereas the increase is almost invisible as you go beyond 21 staff. Specifically, the speed of response increases from 400 seconds to 17 to 9.2 as staff increases from 16 to 20 to 21, but then is lowered only to 4.9 and 2.6 as you add the 22nd and the 23rd staff members, respectively.

Speed of Response Versus Staffing

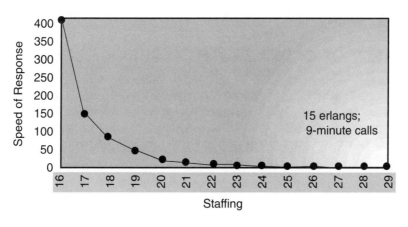

Figure C–1

The situation is the same if you have a small workload. Let's imagine you get only 12 calls per hour and that each call takes 9 minutes to handle. Your workload is 1.8 erlangs (9 $*$ 12 = 108 minutes, 108 / 60 = 1.8 erlangs). With a small workload, the effect of increasing or decreasing staffing are even more spectacular (see Figure C–2). With 2 staff members, the average speed of response is a whopping 33 minutes! With 3 staff, it's a still-sizable 160 seconds, and it drops to 32, then 6.8 seconds with the fourth and fifth staff members.

Speed of Response Versus Staffing

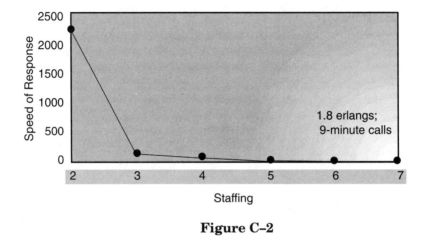

Figure C–2

C.3   EFFECT OF CALL LENGTH ON SERVICE LEVEL

Let's briefly highlight that your average call length has a great deal of influence on the service level. That is, with an equal workload and equal staffing, customers will tend to wait much longer if the average call length is longer. This is fairly intuitive (long transactions block out others for a long time) but is confirmed by the Erlang method.

For instance, let's contrast two situations with a workload of 15 erlangs: the one we just looked at above with 100 calls per hour and an average call length of 9 minutes, and one with just 30 calls per hour but an average call length of 30 minutes. They both work out to 15 erlangs, but here's the graph for the 30-minute scenario (see Figure C–3).

As you can see, the average speed of answer with 21 staff members is 9.2 seconds with the 9-minute calls, and a still acceptable, but much higher, 31 seconds with the 30-minute calls. So delays are longer for longer calls, all other factors being equal.

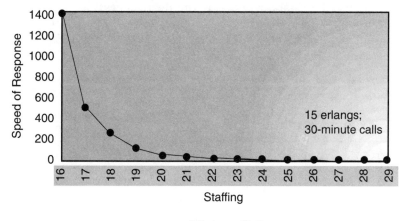

Figure C–3

C.4 THEORETICAL PROOF OF "BIG IS BEAUTIFUL"

As a last application of the Erlang method, let's show that dividing up a group into subgroups requires more staffing for the same level of service.

Imagine that your support center gets 100 calls per hour and that each call takes 9 minutes to handle. As we have already computed, your workload is 15 erlangs (9 ✳ 100 = 900 minutes, 900 / 60 = 15 erlangs). The average speed of response is 9.2 with 21 staff.

Now imagine that you split your one large queue into two queues. One gets 60 calls, generating 9 ✳ 60 / 60 = 9 erlangs. The other gets 40 calls, generating 9 ✳ 40 / 60 = 6 erlangs. Note that the total amount of "work" is unchanged at 15 erlangs.

To approach your service level of 9.2 seconds, you would need 14 staff for the first queue and 10 staff for the second queue, giving you ASA of 9.6 and 13.7 seconds, respectively. So you would need 24 staff, 3 more than under the one large queue scenario, and you would have worse response time.

So is it always a mistake to specialize? No, since the whole reasoning above is based on the assumption that call length is unchanged as you specialize. If you can save processing time by specializing, you can indeed decrease staffing requirements. For instance here, if you decrease call length to 7 minutes for the first queue (a huge saving; it's unlikely to be that easy), then your staffing requirements drop to 11 staff for that queue. (The workload is 7 * 60 / 60 = 7 erlangs, which gives you an ASA of 12.7 with 11 staff.)

In short, specialization makes sense only if you can achieve significant productivity improvements by specializing.

Table C-1.   Erlang C Tables

First Attempt Erlangs	Number Staff	Delayed Portion	Delay Length Call Factor
0.2	1	0.2000	1.2500
0.2	2	0.0182	0.5556
0.2	3	0.0012	0.3571
0.4	1	0.4000	1.6667
0.4	2	0.0667	0.6250
0.4	3	0.0082	0.3846
0.6	1	0.6000	2.5000
0.6	2	0.1385	0.7143
0.6	3	0.0247	0.4167
0.6	4	0.0035	0.2941
0.8	1	0.8000	5.0000
0.8	2	0.2286	0.8333

Table C–1.   Erlang C Tables (Continued)

First Attempt Erlangs	Number Staff	Delayed Portion	Delay Length Call Factor
0.8	3	0.0520	0.4545
0.8	4	0.0096	0.3125
0.8	5	0.0015	0.2381
1.0	2	0.3333	1.0000
1.0	3	0.0909	0.5000
1.0	4	0.0204	0.3333
1.0	5	0.0038	0.2500
1.2	2	0.4500	1.2500
1.2	3	0.1412	0.5556
1.2	4	0.0370	0.3571
1.2	5	0.0082	0.2632
1.2	6	0.0016	0.2083
1.4	2	0.5765	1.6667
1.4	3	0.2024	0.6250
1.4	4	0.0603	0.3846
1.4	5	0.0153	0.2778
1.4	6	0.0034	0.2174
1.6	2	0.7111	2.5000

Table C-1.   Erlang C Tables (Continued)

First Attempt Erlangs	Number Staff	Delayed Portion	Delay Length Call Factor
1.6	3	0.2738	0.7143
1.6	4	0.0907	0.4167
1.6	5	0.0259	0.2941
1.6	6	0.0064	0.2273
1.6	7	0.0014	0.1852
1.8	2	0.8526	5.0000
1.8	3	0.3547	0.8333
1.8	4	0.1285	0.4545
1.8	5	0.0405	0.3125
1.8	6	0.0111	0.2381
1.8	7	0.0027	0.1923
2.0	3	0.4444	1.0000
2.0	4	0.1739	0.5000
2.0	5	0.0597	0.3333
2.0	6	0.0180	0.2500
2.0	7	0.0048	0.2000
2.0	8	0.0011	0.1667
2.2	3	0.5422	1.2500
2.2	4	0.2268	0.5556

Table C–1.   Erlang C Tables (Continued)

First Attempt Erlangs	Number Staff	Delayed Portion	Delay Length Call Factor
2.2	5	0.0839	0.3571
2.2	6	0.0275	0.2632
2.2	7	0.0080	0.2083
2.2	8	0.0021	0.1724
2.4	3	0.6472	1.6667
2.4	4	0.2870	0.6250
2.4	5	0.1135	0.3846
2.4	6	0.0400	0.2778
2.4	7	0.0126	0.2174
2.4	8	0.0035	0.1786
2.4	9	0.0009	0.1515
2.6	3	0.7589	2.5000
2.6	4	0.3544	0.7143
2.6	5	0.1487	0.4167
2.6	6	0.0558	0.2941
2.6	7	0.0188	0.2273
2.6	8	0.0057	0.1852
2.6	9	0.0016	0.1563
2.8	3	0.8767	5.0000

Table C–1. Erlang C Tables (Continued)

First Attempt Erlangs	Number Staff	Delayed Portion	Delay Length Call Factor
2.8	4	0.4287	0.8333
2.8	5	0.1895	0.4545
2.8	6	0.0755	0.3125
2.8	7	0.0271	0.2381
2.8	8	0.0088	0.1923
2.8	9	0.0026	0.1613
3.0	4	0.5094	1.0000
3.0	5	0.2362	0.5000
3.0	6	0.0991	0.3333
3.0	7	0.0376	0.2500
3.0	8	0.0129	0.2000
3.0	9	0.0040	0.1667
3.0	10	0.0012	0.1429
3.2	4	0.5964	1.2500
3.2	5	0.2886	0.5556
3.2	6	0.1271	0.3571
3.2	7	0.0509	0.2632
3.2	8	0.0185	0.2083
3.2	9	0.0061	0.1724
3.2	10	0.0019	0.1471

Table C–1.   Erlang C Tables (Continued)

First Attempt Erlangs	Number Staff	Delayed Portion	Delay Length Call Factor
3.4	4	0.6893	1.6667
3.4	5	0.3467	0.6250
3.4	6	0.1595	0.3846
3.4	7	0.0670	0.2778
3.4	8	0.0256	0.2174
3.4	9	0.0090	0.1786
3.4	10	0.0029	0.1515
3.6	4	0.7878	2.5000
3.6	5	0.4104	0.7143
3.6	6	0.1966	0.4167
3.6	7	0.0862	0.2941
3.6	8	0.0346	0.2273
3.6	9	0.0127	0.1852
3.6	10	0.0043	0.1563
3.6	11	0.0013	0.1351
3.8	4	0.8914	5.0000
3.8	5	0.4796	0.8333
3.8	6	0.2383	0.4545
3.8	7	0.1089	0.3125

Table C-1. Erlang C Tables (Continued)

First Attempt Erlangs	Number Staff	Delayed Portion	Delay Length Call Factor
3.8	8	0.0457	0.2381
3.8	9	0.0176	0.1923
3.8	10	0.0062	0.1613
3.8	11	0.0020	0.1389
4.0	5	0.5541	1.0000
4.0	6	0.2848	0.5000
4.0	7	0.1351	0.3333
4.0	8	0.0590	0.2500
4.0	9	0.0238	0.2000
4.0	10	0.0088	0.1667
4.0	11	0.0030	0.1429
4.0	12	0.0010	0.1250
4.2	5	0.6338	1.2500
4.2	6	0.3360	0.5556
4.2	7	0.1651	0.3571
4.2	8	0.0749	0.2632
4.2	9	0.0314	0.2083
4.2	10	0.0122	0.1724
4.2	11	0.0044	0.1471
4.2	12	0.0015	0.1282

Table C–1.   Erlang C Tables (Continued)

First Attempt Erlangs	Number Staff	Delayed Portion	Delay Length Call Factor
4.4	5	0.7184	1.6667
4.4	6	0.3919	0.6250
4.4	7	0.1988	0.3846
4.4	8	0.0935	0.2778
4.4	9	0.0407	0.2174
4.4	10	0.0164	0.1786
4.4	11	0.0061	0.1515
4.4	12	0.0021	0.1316
4.6	5	0.8070	2.5000
4.6	6	0.4525	0.7143
4.6	7	0.2366	0.4167
4.6	8	0.1150	0.2941
4.6	9	0.0519	0.2273
4.6	10	0.0217	0.1852
4.6	11	0.0084	0.1563
4.6	12	0.0031	0.1351
4.6	13	0.0010	0.1190
4.8	5	0.9017	5.0000
4.8	6	0.5178	0.8333

Table C–1. Erlang C Tables (Continued)

First Attempt Erlangs	Number Staff	Delayed Portion	Delay Length Call Factor
4.8	7	0.2783	0.4545
4.8	8	0.1395	0.3125
4.8	9	0.0651	0.2381
4.8	10	0.0282	0.1923
4.8	11	0.0114	0.1613
4.8	12	0.0043	0.1389
4.8	13	0.0015	0.1220
5.0	6	0.5875	1.0000
5.0	7	0.3241	0.5000
5.0	8	0.1673	0.3333
5.0	9	0.0805	0.2500
5.0	10	0.0361	0.2000
5.0	11	0.0151	0.1667
5.0	12	0.0059	0.1429
5.0	13	0.0021	0.1250
6.0	7	0.6138	1.0000
6.0	8	0.3570	0.5000
6.0	9	0.1960	0.3333
6.0	10	0.1013	0.2500
6.0	11	0.0492	0.2000

Table C–1.   Erlang C Tables (Continued)

First Attempt Erlangs	Number Staff	Delayed Portion	Delay Length Call Factor
6.0	12	0.0225	0.1667
6.0	13	0.0096	0.1429
6.0	14	0.0039	0.1250
6.0	15	0.0015	0.1111
7.0	8	0.6353	1.0000
7.0	9	0.3849	0.5000
7.0	10	0.2217	0.3333
7.0	11	0.1211	0.2500
7.0	12	0.0626	0.2000
7.0	13	0.0306	0.1667
7.0	14	0.0142	0.1429
7.0	15	0.0062	0.1250
7.0	16	0.0026	0.1111
7.0	17	0.0010	0.1000
8.0	9	0.6533	1.0000
8.0	10	0.4092	0.5000
8.0	11	0.2450	0.3333
8.0	12	0.1398	0.2500
8.0	13	0.0760	0.2000
8.0	14	0.0393	0.1667

Table C–1. Erlang C Tables (Continued)

First Attempt Erlangs	Number Staff	Delayed Portion	Delay Length Call Factor
8.0	15	0.0193	0.1429
8.0	16	0.0090	0.1250
8.0	17	0.0040	0.1111
8.0	18	0.0017	0.1000
9.0	10	0.6687	1.0000
9.0	11	0.4305	0.5000
9.0	12	0.2660	0.3333
9.0	13	0.1575	0.2500
9.0	14	0.0892	0.2000
9.0	15	0.0482	0.1667
9.0	16	0.0249	0.1429
9.0	17	0.0123	0.1250
9.0	18	0.0058	0.1111
9.0	19	0.0026	0.1000
9.0	20	0.0011	0.0909
10.0	11	0.6821	1.0000
10.0	12	0.4494	0.5000
10.0	13	0.2853	0.3333
10.0	14	0.1741	0.2500
10.0	15	0.1020	0.2000

Table C–1.   Erlang C Tables (Continued)

First Attempt Erlangs	Number Staff	Delayed Portion	Delay Length Call Factor
10.0	16	0.0573	0.1667
10.0	17	0.0309	0.1429
10.0	18	0.0159	0.1250
10.0	19	0.0079	0.1111
10.0	20	0.0037	0.1000
10.0	21	0.0017	0.0909
11.0	12	0.6939	1.0000
11.0	13	0.4664	0.5000
11.0	14	0.3029	0.3333
11.0	15	0.1898	0.2500
11.0	16	0.1145	0.2000
11.0	17	0.0665	0.1667
11.0	18	0.0371	0.1429
11.0	19	0.0199	0.1250
11.0	20	0.0103	0.1111
11.0	21	0.0051	0.1000
11.0	22	0.0024	0.0909
11.0	23	0.0011	0.0833
12.0	13	0.7044	1.0000
12.0	14	0.4817	0.5000

Table C–1.   Erlang C Tables (Continued)

First Attempt Erlangs	Number Staff	Delayed Portion	Delay Length Call Factor
12.0	15	0.3192	0.3333
12.0	16	0.2046	0.2500
12.0	17	0.1266	0.2000
12.0	18	0.0756	0.1667
12.0	19	0.0435	0.1429
12.0	20	0.0241	0.1250
12.0	21	0.0129	0.1111
12.0	22	0.0066	0.1000
12.0	23	0.0033	0.9090
12.0	24	0.0016	0.0833
13.0	14	0.7138	1.0000
13.0	15	0.4957	0.5000
13.0	16	0.3343	0.3333
13.0	17	0.2182	0.2500
13.0	18	0.1383	0.2000
13.0	19	0.0847	0.1667
13.0	20	0.0501	0.1429
13.0	21	0.0286	0.1250
13.0	22	0.0158	0.1111
13.0	23	0.0084	0.1000
13.0	24	0.0043	0.0909

Table C–1.   Erlang C Tables (Continued)

First Attempt Erlangs	Number Staff	Delayed Portion	Delay Length Call Factor
13.0	25	0.0021	0.0833
13.0	26	0.0010	0.0769
14.0	15	0.7223	1.0000
14.0	16	0.5085	0.5000
14.0	17	0.3483	0.3333
14.0	18	0.2317	0.2500
14.0	19	0.1496	0.2000
14.0	20	0.0936	0.1667
14.0	21	0.0567	0.1429
14.0	22	0.0332	0.1250
14.0	23	0.0188	0.1111
14.0	24	0.0103	0.1000
14.0	25	0.0055	0.0909
14.0	26	0.0028	0.0833
14.0	27	0.0014	0.0769
15.0	16	0.7301	1.0000
15.0	17	0.5203	0.5000
15.0	18	0.3613	0.3333
15.0	19	0.2442	0.2500
15.0	20	0.1604	0.2000

Table C–1. Erlang C Tables (Continued)

First Attempt Erlangs	Number Staff	Delayed Portion	Delay Length Call Factor
15.0	21	0.1023	0.1667
15.0	22	0.0633	0.1429
15.0	23	0.0380	0.1250
15.0	24	0.0221	0.1111
15.0	25	0.0124	0.1000
15.0	26	0.0068	0.0909
15.0	27	0.0036	0.0833
15.0	28	0.0018	0.0769
15.0	29	0.0009	0.0714
16.0	17	0.7372	1.0000
16.0	18	0.5312	0.5000
16.0	19	0.3736	0.3333
16.0	20	0.2561	0.2500
16.0	21	0.1709	0.2000
16.0	22	0.1109	0.1667
16.0	23	0.0699	0.1429
16.0	24	0.0428	0.1250
16.0	25	0.0255	0.1111
16.0	26	0.0147	0.1000
16.0	27	0.0082	0.0909
16.0	28	0.0045	0.0833

Table C–1. Erlang C Tables (Continued)

First Attempt Erlangs	Number Staff	Delayed Portion	Delay Length Call Factor
16.0	29	0.0024	0.0769
16.0	30	0.0012	0.0714
17.0	18	0.7437	1.0000
17.0	19	0.5413	0.5000
17.0	20	0.3851	0.3333
17.0	21	0.2673	0.2500
17.0	22	0.1810	0.2000
17.0	23	0.1193	0.1667
17.0	24	0.0766	0.1429
17.0	25	0.0478	0.1250
17.0	26	0.0290	0.1111
17.0	27	0.0171	0.1000
17.0	28	0.0098	0.0909
17.0	29	0.0055	0.0833
17.0	30	0.0030	0.0769
17.0	31	0.0016	0.0714
18.0	19	0.7498	1.0000
18.0	20	0.5508	0.5000
18.0	21	0.3959	0.3333
18.0	22	0.2781	0.2500

Table C-1. Erlang C Tables (Continued)

First Attempt Erlangs	Number Staff	Delayed Portion	Delay Length Call Factor
18.0	23	0.1907	0.2000
18.0	24	0.1275	0.1667
18.0	25	0.0831	0.1429
18.0	26	0.0528	0.1250
18.0	27	0.0326	0.1111
18.0	28	0.0196	0.1000
18.0	29	0.0115	0.0909
18.0	30	0.0065	0.0833
18.0	31	0.0036	0.0769
18.0	32	0.0020	0.0714
18.0	33	0.0010	0.0667
19.0	20	0.7554	1.0000
19.0	21	0.5596	0.5000
19.0	22	0.4061	0.3333
19.0	23	0.2883	0.2500
19.0	24	0.2001	0.2000
19.0	25	0.1356	0.1667
19.0	26	0.0896	0.1429
19.0	27	0.0578	0.1250
19.0	28	0.0363	0.1111
19.0	29	0.0222	0.1000

Table C–1.   Erlang C Tables (Continued)

First Attempt Erlangs	Number Staff	Delayed Portion	Delay Length Call Factor
19.0	30	0.0133	0.0909
19.0	31	0.0077	0.0833
19.0	32	0.0044	0.0769
19.0	33	0.0024	0.0714
19.0	34	0.0013	0.0667
20.0	21	0.7606	1.0000
20.0	22	0.5679	0.5000
20.0	23	0.4157	0.3333
20.0	24	0.2981	0.2500
20.0	25	0.2091	0.2000
20.0	26	0.1434	0.1997
20.0	27	0.0961	0.1429
20.0	28	0.0628	0.1250
20.0	29	0.0401	0.1111
20.0	30	0.0250	0.1000
20.0	31	0.0151	0.0909
20.0	32	0.0090	0.0833
20.0	33	0.0052	0.0769
20.0	34	0.0029	0.0714
20.0	35	0.0016	0.0677

APPENDIX D

CREATING AND JUSTIFYING A SUPPORT CENTER BUDGET

This section describes how to put together a budget for a support center and, more importantly, how to justify it so that you get the resources you need to run a successful operation. Putting together the numbers is not enough. If you cannot make a case for what you need, you will not be able to accomplish your goals.

Financial information can also be found in other places in this book: for cost of support computation, see the costing section of Chapter 5, "Packaging Support Services"; for compensation information, see Chapter 7, "Managing Support People"; for cost justifications for tools, see Chapter 9, "Tools for Technical Software Support."

We'll discuss how to position and justify your budget before we discuss how to put it together. This is a deliberate choice. We have found that building the budget is not very difficult (and you've probably built others before), whereas the positioning aspect is more art than science, and we encourage you to think about it before you put any numbers down on paper or your favorite worksheet.

D.1 JUSTIFYING A SUPPORT CENTER BUDGET

D.1.1 Select Goals

The key in justifying any budget is to understand the corporate goals and how your group's goals support the overall goals. If your company is trying to increase customer retention, define how the support center can help retain customers. If the goal is to cut costs, can you cut your costs, or operate in such a way that other costs are cut? If the goal is to gain market share, what can you do to help acquire or welcome new customers?

This is not a window-dressing exercise. You should not simply label your goals in the fashion-du-jour in a shameless attempt to get more money. Instead, you need to create a strategy that captures and enhances the corporate goals.

Create a few high-level goals that encapsulate the strategy and can be communicated succinctly and meaningfully upward and downward. Easier said than done. Here are some examples:

- Increase customer satisfaction by 10% (as demonstrated in the customer satisfaction survey).
- Renew 90% of support contracts.
- Upgrade 10% of the existing customer base to the premium support package.
- Improve the raw margin of the support business from 43% to 45%.
- Decrease employee turnover by 20%.
- Decrease per-call cost by 10%.
- Decrease per-customer support cost by 10%.
- Decrease support-related shipping costs by 30%.
- Decrease the average time on hold from 10 to 2 minutes.
- Decrease the average length of a support call from 10 to 9 minutes.
- Increase the percentage of issues resolved on the first call by 15%.
- Improve productivity per support engineer by 10%.

Notice how the goals can easily translate to either dollars on the bottom line or customer satisfaction (which, as you should be evangelizing, also translates to bottom line dollars, since a highly satisfied customer will continue to use the product and will buy more, and since it costs much more to attract a new customer than to retain an existing one).

Also note that the goals sound straightforward and reasonably audacious. This is important. You're going to be pitching to people who don't necessarily know a lot about support. Don't turn them off by using concepts they don't know (they probably think of ASA as film speed, not as the average speed of answer), by picking goals that appear hair-splitting to support outsiders (as in "decrease the average resolution time for DWB version 4.0 from 13.2 to 12.1 days for those calls which do not require a bug fix"), or by choosing wimpy-sounding targets (as in "improve productivity per support engineer by 1.245%").

Remember to pick a few goals, three to five is a good number. You can't get or keep decision makers' attention with too many goals.

D.1.2   Relate your budget to the goals

Everything in the budget should be tied firmly to the goals. Said the other way: anything not firmly tied to a goal will be axed.

So, if you want to increase customer satisfaction by 10%, be sure to explain how your $50,000 increase in training costs relates to it. If you want to decrease call resolution time, get a firm justification on how the new knowledge base system will help you do that, and on how the MIS group will indeed have it up and running in time to affect resolution time next year. Be prepared to defend your approach against other ideas.

We don't mean to imply that you should not accept compromises, but don't let your investment requirements be chipped away by not tying them securely to a goal. If a particular investment has to be forgone, then the goal should be forgotten as well.

This brings us to an important idea for defending support budgets: tie service levels to the budget. Define a correlation between the funding level and the service level. Use your headcount projections to do that. Most of your budget (likely over 70%) is headcount related, so the level of service you can deliver depends very much on how many bodies you can afford to pay for. Fewer bodies, worse service, and you have to be able to quantify it. Prepare a few scenarios that show funding versus service level. All the good work you have done with metrics pays off for this exercise.

An important consequence of the above is that one of your goals should say something about maintaining (or increasing) current service levels.

D.1.3   Pitch your budget

We have two words of advice here: simple and graphic.

Keep the justifications simple. This is actually good discipline, because it forces you to really think about what it takes to accomplish the goals. If you cannot say in one sentence why adding 3 support engineers will increase customer satisfaction by 10%, then how do you know you don't need 4? or 2? Remember that you are talking to people who do not understand the intricacies of support, so make sure you don't use technical or obscure words and concepts. For instance, let's say you want to install an ACD. Don't go off about VRUs and customizable hold times. Take a business approach. Talk about how the customer will be able to self-direct the call through the system to talk to a support engineer on the first call. Talk about how you can reinvest the money you currently spend on Dispatch on more value-added pursuits.

Simple implies reasonably short. You want to give enough details to be understandable, but not so many that you are overwhelming or boring. Starting with just a few goals will help you stay focused. Keep your visuals simple, uncluttered, and few.

Graphics are just one way to make complex information simple. With one graph or picture, you can convey much more information than in many sentences or in a busy spreadsheet. (If you feel you need supporting documents, put them in an appendix, not in the main presentation.) Don't just say you will increase customer satisfaction—show it to them. Show how staffing and service level correlate (see Appendix C for ideas).

D.2 BUILDING A SUPPORT CENTER BUDGET

Building a support budget is relatively straightforward if you have some historical perspective on both financial and operating metrics. If not, you will have to punt, but organize your punting by using this section as your guide.

D.2.1 Revenue

The method here depends on whether you sell service contracts, which need to be recognized over the period of service, or whether you charge per incident, in which case you simply recognize the revenue as the incident is logged.

If you work with per-incident charges, your main worry is to accurately forecast revenue, which in this case is the same as forecasting call volume. Use your metrics to help you. Pay particular attention to any new releases planned, as they will probably cause a significant increase in call volume. The tricky part is to figure out when the increase will hit. We don't only mean to imply that release dates slip—they do—but also that customers could take weeks or months to actually install and use new releases. Past experience is best for this kind of planning: if you can model what happened for the last major release, you will have a good base. Use (product) sales projections to help you, although they are sometimes not detailed enough for your needs. Many times you get either an overall dollar figure, which hides product differences that are crucial for support, or overly optimistic figures, which could tempt you to hire massive numbers of people who will not have customers to talk to.

If you work with per-incident charges but you sell call packs, you may (and we recommend that you do) have them expire after a certain amount of time, say a year. If so, you can recognize any unused revenue at that time. That is, if you sell a 10-pack for $200 and only eight calls were made, you can recognize the remaining $40 at expiration time. Your past experience will tell you whether this is common enough to bother forecasting it.

If you work with support contracts you must recognize the revenue as services are rendered. Typically, you recognize 1/12 of the annual revenue each month. This makes your forecasting much easier, especially with a large established base, since most of the revenue is predictable. Divide and conquer to create your forecast:

- First consider revenue that has already been booked, but has not been recognized yet because of the accounting rule we just described. This is easy (at least if your financial systems are good), since the revenue has already been booked. Just add it up.

- Then, look at revenue for upcoming renewals of support contracts. These are the contracts that exist today but will expire next year. This is trickier, since some of the contracts will simply not be renewed, for whatever reason, and since the renewal price may be different from the current price.

  For the former, devise a drop-off ratio. Use your current one, unless you can anticipate some large problem that would cause it to go down significantly, or you are putting in place some special initiative to increase the renewal rate.

  Anticipate changes in support pricing. If you devised a separate support pricing, as we recommended in Chapter 5, this step is straightforward. If your pricing is a percentage of license price, you will need to determine whether license pricing will change.

- And now for the most difficult part: estimate new support revenue for new customers. Use license sales projections here and hope for the best.

Do a sanity check. Support revenue is very stable and does not fluctuate much even with poor product or a weak economy. If the result of your forecasting is suspiciously different from this year's revenue, something's wrong.

D.2.2   Expenses

Here's a checklist of support costs:

- Staff costs, including salaries and benefits.
- Management and company overhead.
- Training: this is often a significant line item for Support.

- Travel: this is usually not a large expense for Support.
- Facilities: this is sometimes handled as a per-head cost, which includes rent, utilities, security, and other company overhead.
- Phone costs.
- Machines, including hardware, software, documentation, maintenance contracts, staff and facilities necessary to maintain the machines. Include both machines used by individual support engineers and shared machines used to replicate problems. High-end software can sometimes be capitalized. See your controller for advice on what can and should be capitalized and what should be expensed.
- Bulletin boards, on-line forums, Web sites.
- (For ISVs) Marketing and sales costs, including collaterals, mailings, ads, and selling expenses if you sell your support.

Work out your costs based on experience and your specific requirements. As in all budgetary exercises, focus on the big picture and don't worry about the details. This is a plan, not an accounting report. For instance, don't be concerned about what each individual support engineer makes. Use averages throughout. Many line items are in direct proportion with the headcount. For them, use some multiplier figure and drive them from the headcount line for simplicity. For instance, you may budget $2000 per year for training for each support engineer, rather than preparing a detailed list of what classes each support engineer will need next year.

Once you have collected the costs, study the distribution of your expenses. You will find that your personnel expenses are the bulk of your budget, which is why you should always try to increase the efficiency of your operation.

See where you can cut. Although each penny does count, zero in on the big expenses. If you have large or growing costs that you cannot cut, anticipate the objections and prepare a justification for why you must spend that much or that much more. For instance, the training budget has to be tripled because we have to train a small army (give the number) to support the new release, or the travel budget is high because the User's Conference is being held far away from the support center, or the hardware costs are high because we made a corporate decision to support two product lines in parallel for the next five years. You may not want to volunteer the justifications, but have them handy should you be asked for them.

BIBLIOGRAPHY

Blanding, Warren, *Customer Service Operations*. New York, NY: AMACOM, 1991.

Carlson, Jan, *Moments of Truth*. New York, NY: Harper & Row, 1989.

Fisher, Roger, and William Ury, *Getting to Yes*. Boston: Houghton Mifflin, 1981.

Fisher, Roger, and Danny Ertel, *Getting Ready to Negotiate*. New York, NY: Penguin Books, 1995.

Gallagher, Richard, *Effective Software Customer Support*. Boston: International Tompson Computing Press, 1996.

Keen, Peter G.W., *Shaping the Future*. Cambridge, MA: Harvard Business School Press, 1991.

Kepner, Charles, and Tregoe, Benjamin, *The New Rational Manager*. Princeton, NJ: Princeton Research Press, 1981.

Muns, Roger, *The Help Desk Handbook*. Colorado Springs, CO: Help Desk Institute, 1993.

Rose, Bill, *Managing Software Support*. San Diego, CA: Software Support Professionals Association, 1990.

Winograd, Terry and Flores Fernando, *Understanding Computers and Cognition*. Norwood, NJ: Ablex, 1986.

INDEX

—U—

—W—